German History

A Captivating Guide to the History of Germany and Germania

Contents

Part 1: History of Germany

A Captivating Guide to German History, Starting from 1871 through the First World War, Weimar Republic, and World War II to the Present

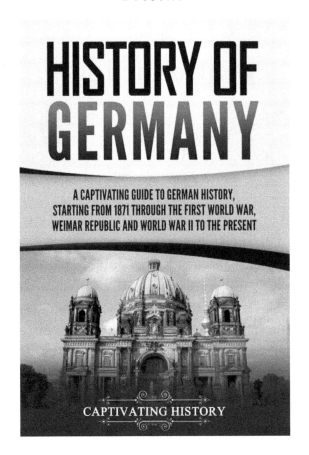

Introduction

The United States is a nation, mostly of people descended from or who are immigrants. Of the over 330 million people who live in the country as of 2021, about 16 percent of them claim some German heritage, which is more than any other ethnic group. This is surprising considering the nation was founded primarily by English colonists and whose Irish-descended population is greater than the population of Ireland itself.

Most of the German immigrants to the United States arrived before World War I, and many arrived before 1871. The year 1871 seems like a sort of arbitrary date until you know that the modern nation state of Germany was founded in that year. Strictly speaking, many of the German immigrants to the US were not really German at all—they were Swiss, Bavarians, Alsatians, Westphalians, or one of the many other German states that existed before the country was united behind its most powerful kingdom, Prussia.

Perhaps the most famous group of German immigrants in the United States are the Amish and Mennonites of Pennsylvania, erroneously called the "Pennsylvania Dutch." They are not "Dutch" (as in from the Netherlands/Holland) but German, with "Deutsch" being the German word for themselves. Americans heard a dialect of German, and to them, it sounded like "Dutch," not "doi-ch" (as one might pronounce the name phonetically).

Illustration 1: Map of German States, 1864-1871

As you may know, the Amish and Mennonites ("Amish" is derived from early leader Jakob Amman of Switzerland and "Mennonite" comes from Menno Simons, the leader of that sect) of the US, whether they live in Pennsylvania or elsewhere, came to the United States fleeing persecution in their home country, like many other people coming to North America. However, while the "Pennsylvania Dutch" were, in a sense, persecuted for their religion, it was one aspect of their religious beliefs that caused their persecution back in Europe—their belief in pacifism. They were opposed to war, and in the Germany of the late 17th to early 19th centuries, war was almost as common as breathing.

The Amish and Mennonites refused to be drafted into the various armies of the states they lived in, sometimes resulting in very harsh sentences, both economic and physical (jail, beatings, etc.). One way they protested and set themselves apart was the growing of beards *without* mustaches; throughout the 17ᵗʰ to 19ᵗʰ centuries, the military men of Europe, particularly in the German states, wore very bushy and elaborate mustaches. The absence of hair under the nose was an obvious "up yours" to the authorities.

As you can see from the map on the previous page, what is now Germany was divided into many principalities, kingdoms, duchies, and bishoprics (governed by a bishop of the Catholic Church). Prior to Napoleon Bonaparte's invasions, there were, at times, nearly three hundred different German entities, but in the time that concerns us, 1864 (when the push for German unity behind Prussia began) to 1871 (when unity was achieved under the Prussian royal house, the Hohenzollerns), there were thirty-nine states.

A quick look at the map above will tell you that there were four more dominant German-speaking entities in the middle of Europe. These were the Austrian Empire, Prussia, Bavaria, and, lastly, Hanover (the present-day British monarchy comes from the House of Hanover, starting with George I in 1714). Of these four, the Prussians and Austrians were the strongest and most influential, and it is with the conflict of these two kingdoms that our story will begin.

Chapter 1 – Prussia

The modern nation of Germany coalesced around the powerful eastern German state of Prussia in 1870/1871. If you could go back in time and visit Prussia in 1617, you might be shocked that this relatively poor and poorly situated kingdom would be the seed around which Germany would grow.

Prussia's soil was not the greatest, and even the great estates of the kingdom sometimes struggled to provide enough crops for food or trade. Rye, sugar beets, and potatoes were the chief crops. As far as the raw materials needed for a modern economy, Prussia itself had virtually none. It gained some coal reserves with the annexation of Silesia in 1741, and it gained access to much larger quantities in the early 1800s with the addition of lands on the Rhine River and to its immediate south when it was given control of them during the Congress of Vienna after the Napoleonic Wars.

The royal family of Prussia had begun as the Margraves (a unique title within the Holy Roman Empire) of Brandenburg in 1417 with Frederick I, Elector of Brandenburg (an "elector" theoretically had a say in the naming of the Holy Roman Emperor). The capital of the Margravate of Brandenburg was a small city (more a large town) called Berlin.

In 1518, the Hohenzollern family ascended to rule Brandenburg, which had slowly been enlarged over the past century by marriage unions and shrewd negotiations with smaller duchies on its borders. In 1618, the electors of Brandenburg became rulers of the larger (but poorer) neighboring state of Prussia. The kings of Prussia were of another branch of the Hohenzollern family, and in 1618, the branches came together with Johannes Sigismund, who died in 1619. He passed the throne to his son, Georg Wilhelm (r. 1619-1640).

Georg Wilhelm was an ineffective king who lived at an unfortunate time. He reigned through most of the incredibly bloody Thirty Years' War, and both he and Prussia only narrowly survived a time in which some part of what is now Germany lost more than half of its population due to war, famine, and disease.

Prussia (officially Brandenburg-Prussia) was fortunate that Georg Wilhelm's heir, Frederick William (r. 1640-1688), was a much more intelligent and accomplished ruler.

(You will note throughout this book that at times, the spelling of names will change from the German spelling, as in the case of "Georg Wilhelm," to English, as in the case of "Frederick William." It's just the convention, depending on the person. The greatest Prussian king was "Frederick the Great," but you never see it as the German "Friedrich der Große" in English language books. On the other hand, you rarely see the name of the last German king, "Kaiser Wilhelm II," written as "Emperor William II." Also, please note that the unique German letter "ß" acts just like a double "s.")

Frederick promoted the growth of a middle trading class in his lands, and the Prussian economy during his reign began to grow beyond what it had been for centuries, the home of large agricultural estates. These estates and the men who owned them (most often military men) were the backbone of support for the king, which continued until the abdication of Kaiser Wilhelm II in

1918. This Prussian ruling class is known by the collective name of "Junkers" (which originally meant "young lord" or "country squire" but which became associated with the strict disciplined military men that ruled the area and which formed the backbone for the Prussian, and later German, officer class).

Among Frederick's many reforms were changes in the army. During his rule, Frederick developed one of the first standing armies in Europe and instituted the method in which German field commanders were given wide latitude in achieving their objectives. This military doctrine truly began in Prussia, and it continued into World Wars I and II and lives on not only in the German Army today but in most of the world's armed forces.

During the reign of Frederick William, the Prussians first came to the fore as a military power to be reckoned with. Fighting in the Second Northern War with Sweden (then a great regional power) against the Poles and Lithuanians (then a great power in decline), Frederick William won the Battle of Warsaw with the Swedes and then turned and defeated the Swedes a short time later when they switched sides against him. At the time (1678), this shocked many in Europe, for the Swedes had a fearsome reputation.

Frederick William's successor, Frederick I, ruled from 1701 to 1713 and was a noted soldier, taking part as a field commander in wars against King Louis XIV of France. During the reign of Frederick I, Prussia officially became a kingdom within the Holy Roman Empire (centered in Vienna, with the Austrian emperor as its head), though it took much political maneuvering to do so, as there were supposed to be no independent kings within the empire. Frederick I settled for the title "King in Prussia." His more famous and accomplished grandson, Frederick II, better known as Frederick the Great, felt strong enough to declare himself "King of Prussia."

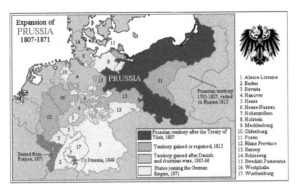

Frederick William I (r. 1713–1740) is often referred to as the "Military King," for it was he who made the Prussian Army into the central institution of Prussian life. Though he is known for the role he played in growing Prussia's army, Frederick William I also did much for the country economically. He began land reclamation projects, which increased the amount of arable land in the country, reformed the tax system, improved roads, and streamlined an already impressive civil service system. He also began building schools and hospitals that were more accessible to the common people than just those at the top.

Unfortunately, many of Frederick William's better accomplishments have been overshadowed by two things, one of them relatively trivial and the other more consequential.

First, the trivial. Frederick William I was fascinated by all things military. This interest ran the gamut from actual battles and weaponry to the pomp of the parade ground. Somewhere in between is Frederick's most noted "accomplishment": he wanted to form a guard unit of the largest men he could find. This unit was Prussian infantry regiment number six, better known to history as the Potsdam Giants, named for the location of Frederick William's palace. Many of the "Giants" were not even Prussian. Most of them were, but a significant number came from other German states, induced by offers of good pay, and a number came from foreign countries, whose leaders sent Frederick William taller than average men for his unit as a goodwill gesture. Not all of these men went willingly, and some deserted. Additionally, quite a few of the Giants were literally dragged off the street or threatened if they didn't join. Making the story even stranger was the king's attempts to pair his Giants off with tall women to create a "race of giants," which he would use as his shock troops. This effort, with its foreshadowing of Nazi attempts at genetic engineering, amounted to virtually nothing.

More consequential in the long run was Frederick William's relationship with his son, Frederick (what else?), who became the famous Frederick the Great. At first, the king loved his son and doted upon him, but as Frederick II grew up, the king and the prince found they had virtually nothing in common.

Frederick II was not interested in military affairs to anything close to the degree his father was, which is strange considering he became one of the greatest military leaders Europe has ever seen. This enraged his father, who denigrated and likely beat his son frequently. Frederick II had a sentimental soul, and while he was forced to learn the military arts, he gravitated toward music, writing, and the theater. At one point in his late teens, Frederick, who would later marry a German princess, had a homosexual relationship with one of the king's pages. This was found out. The page was sent to military duty far away, and Frederick was forced to live in isolation for a time at one of his father's lodges to meditate on his "sin." Another same-sex relationship was found out later, and though this was kept relatively quiet, the prince suffered greatly, including being thrown in prison for a time by order of his father. Frederick and his wife, Elisabeth, spent much time apart and had no children, leading most historians to believe that he was primarily homosexual in his sexual life.

Regardless, Frederick was the sole male heir and became king when his father died in 1740. He reigned for forty-six years, the longest-reigning king of any of the Hohenzollerns of Prussia/Germany.

During his long reign, Frederick continued the tradition of a standing Prussian army and instituted a variety of reforms to make the army more responsive on the battlefield. He kept up with all military matters throughout Europe and kept his troops supplied with the latest weapons. Over the course of his reign, Frederick defeated a number of European countries, sometimes in concert with allies and sometimes alone against great odds. His campaigns were marked by speed, audacity, discipline, and great leadership (both on his part and on the part of the men he placed in command). The man that Napoleon Bonaparte looked up to as his military hero was none other than Frederick the Great.

Frederick was not only known for his military prowess but also for his expansive intellect. Known as one of the most "enlightened" rulers of the Enlightenment, Frederick spoke, wrote, and read French fluently and kept abreast of the thinking of great philosophers such as Voltaire, with whom he formed a personal friendship. He invited painters, architects, musicians, sculptors, and writers to Prussia and commissioned works by many of the great names of the period. He was also an accomplished musician.

However, while Frederick II was not the harsh king his father had been, his enlightened thinking only went so far. He kept firm control of power in his country and suppressed any movements toward a more liberal form of government.

Unfortunately for Prussia, much of the first half of the 19th century saw a decline, both economically and, most importantly, militarily. During the reign of Napoleon, Prussia became a French satellite state until it turned on the French emperor following his disastrous campaign in Russia and then in Waterloo.

It took decades for Prussia to recover from the early part of the 1800s, but in 1862, when a new chancellor was named by King Wilhelm I, the kingdom had regained much of its economic strength, was continuing to develop militarily, and wanted to be able to compete with its stronger European neighbors (primarily France, Austria, and England) on the world stage.

Chapter 2 – The Iron Chancellor

The Prussian monarchy gained a new king in 1861 with the death of Frederick William IV (r. 1840–1861) and the ascension of his brother, Wilhelm I (r. 1861–1888), but in a land where the rule of the king was virtually absolute, it was not Wilhelm that created a united Germany but his chancellor, Otto von Bismarck, known to history as the "Iron Chancellor." That name fits perfectly, for Bismarck was a man who knew what he wanted, knew how to go about getting it, and was only mildly bothered by the human cost it took to get it.

Bismarck was of the land-owning Junker class of Prussia. By the time of his political rise, the Junkers had essentially been ruling Prussia for centuries under the king. Before we go into Bismarck, his history, and his role in the unification of Germany, let's talk just a bit about the Junkers.

When WWI ended, Germany became a democracy with virtually full freedom of expression. Intellectuals and artists of all kinds lampooned the Junker class as outdated examples of tin-pot martinets who obeyed orders on command and who marched on the Kaiser's enemies like wind-up soldiers goose-stepping in one direction until pushed in another. After the bloodshed of WWI, which many in Germany (from the far left to the moderate right) blamed on the Junker class, the Junkers became a sort of laughing stock, set up as examples of mindless automatons, but there was far more to them than just obedience.

The Junker class and the officers of the German military in general (and most of the generals of the pre-WWII army were Junkers) lived by the same sort of ethos that the Japanese samurai were famous for (the Bushido code). The Junker code did emphasize obedience to one's superiors (whether in military rank or by birth) in the same way as its Japanese counterpart did. It also stressed acting in an "honorable" way, though this usually boiled down to obedience, regardless of belief, and keeping one's word. Discipline and stoicism were emphasized, and if there was ever a place where the old saying "Spare the rod and spoil the child" was practiced perhaps more than preached, it was Prussia. Generally speaking, children (especially sons) could expect harsh physical punishments at the slightest infractions—this, among other things, was thought to "toughen them up," for there were only two possible futures for the sons of the Junker class (or at least for the eldest son): landowners or the military, although they usually engaged in both. Other sons might be expected to become pastors, lawyers, or civil servants (or all three).

Duty to the Kaiser and the country was paramount. The individual came a distant second. This was the unspoken creed of the Junker class.

Many if not most of the Junkers governed large estates, sometimes with hundreds of workers on them. These workers were akin to enslaved people in many ways. Until the second half of the 19th century, virtually all the laborers/peasants born on an estate were tied there—they could never leave, at least not without express permission. The discipline meted out to the sons of the Junkers paled in comparison to that meted out to peasants who disobeyed, attempted to flee, or committed any number of infractions (many of which depended on the whim of the landowner). Flogging, being placed in the stocks, and/or exposed to cold weather were just some of the methods used to keep "order" on the estate. Of course, not all Junkers were this harsh, and many of them allowed their workers a modicum of freedom, but still, it was not "freedom" as we think of it today.

At times, even today, political and other cartoons lampoon a politician, policeman, or father who is particularly hard-headed and stupid as a "Junker," and many times, the person being made fun of is wearing the famous Pickelhaube, the "pointed bonnet" worn by the German Army until mid-way through WWI by its General Staff.

Illustration 2: Otto von Bismarck wearing an elaborate "pickelhaube" for this formal portrait taken after 1870.

Though many Junkers could be thick-headed obtuse martinets, many obviously were not. Though the martial arts (and in this case, we are referring to anything to do with combat and war, not karate) were emphasized before all else, many of the Junker class were musically trained and well-read intellectuals. If the Prussian Army had been led solely by dull-witted robots, it would not have become the highly skilled force that it developed into under Frederick the Great.

The power of the Junkers was so profound that, at least in their locality, they could override the decision of judges and easily sway what little representative bodies there might be in towns and cities. If you belonged to a great Junker family or were of a high rank (many times one and the same), your word was essentially law, especially in the area around your estates.

The Prussian Army, and then German Army, was sometimes compared to that of a machine moving in perfect time, each part doing exactly what it was supposed to do, but it should be remembered that from the time of Frederick the Great, independent thinking was encouraged in the Prussian Army. This did not mean that an officer could do whatever he wanted, but generally speaking, once he was given an objective, he was free to come up with his own plan for achieving it. Of course, many times, this plan had to be approved, but on the battlefield, where decisions had to be made on the spot, a Prussian officer was given amazing leeway, likely more than in any army in the world at the time. This leeway did not just apply to generals, as it continued down the chain of command, all the way down to sergeants or corporals.

At the platoon level (about forty men, give or take), sergeants were given a task and many times were asked to devise a plan for carrying it out. This did not happen all the time, and the freedom given to a non-commissioned officer paled to that given to a captain or colonel, for example, but it was a regular feature of the Prussian war machine. Additionally, a corporal was expected to know the requirements and duties of the rank above him (sergeant), the sergeant those of the lieutenant, the lieutenant the captain's, and so on. Thus, should a man fall on the field, his replacement would know what was expected of him.

Today, these two features of the Prussian military don't seem so special or unique because virtually all modern armies have adopted them. It began with the Prussians/Germans, as did the idea of a general staff and much else, including the foundation of modern camouflage theory.

Otto von Bismarck was born on April 1ˢᵗ, 1815, in Schönhausen. In 1865, he was made a count (*Graf*), and in 1871, after his efforts had unified Germany under the Prussian king, he was given the title "prince" (*Fürst*). And, on top of that, in 1890, two years after he had been forced into retirement by the new Kaiser, Wilhelm II, he was made duke (*Herzog*) of Lauenburg, a duchy on the Danish border that had been acquired in one of the wars of German unification.

Bismarck's family had been given lands and nobility five generations before the birth of Otto in 1815. His father, Karl Wilhelm Ferdinand von Bismarck, had been a military officer, and his mother came from well-known families on both sides. Bismarck was the middle child, and he had an older brother and a younger sister. The Bismarcks' ancestral estate is located in Poland today, a result of the border changes that took place after WWII.

Bismarck was highly educated and highly intelligent, and he entered the University of Göttingen (in today's central Germany) and studied law. Throughout his life, Bismarck knew the value of being underestimated. While he was sometimes outspoken and convinced he was right, he also allowed people to form their own image of him by keeping quiet, and in later years, he almost always wore a military uniform, both to show his commitment to the armed forces and to promote the idea that he was simply another dull-witted robotic Junker.

He most definitely was not dull-witted. He spoke five languages and was able to engage almost everyone he met on equal terms on subjects ranging from government to the arts and philosophy. Bismarck's dream in college was to gain a prestigious law degree to become a diplomat, which he saw as a way to both travel and gain influence.

Bismarck, like many of those who recognize they are gifted with abilities far beyond the average person, developed the somewhat "un-Prussian" habit of doing what he wanted when he wanted to do it. He put his apprenticeship in jeopardy by disappearing for a time, chasing after two aristocratic young English women. In his younger years, Bismarck had no use for religion, but after becoming acquainted (in the most platonic sense) with his best friend's wife, he became a devout Lutheran and considered religion as a pillar of the Prussian state.

Like most other young men of his class, Bismarck served for a time in the army and then the reserves. He returned to Schönhausen in 1839 to run the family estate when his mother died. His father had no skill in farming or running a large estate, not to mention little interest. It fell to Otto to govern the estate and set it back on its feet, which he managed to do in very little time.

In 1847, he married Johanna von Puttkamer, who hailed from another Junker family (one of her distant relatives was an admiral under Adolf Hitler and was wounded in the 1944 assassination attempt against him), and she bore Otto three children. By all accounts, his marriage was a happy one from beginning to end.

In the same year, Bismarck was elected to the Prussian parliament (the Landtag). This newly formed body, a reaction to many of the changes that took place in Europe after the French Revolution, held little power, but in 1848, as revolution spread throughout Europe once again, more liberal legislators in the Landtag pushed for a variety of reforms. Bismarck came to the attention of the Kaiser (at that time, Frederick William IV) and those around him for the conservative, reactionary stance he took against the liberals during that tumultuous year.

Within two years, Bismarck was appointed as the ambassador to the German Confederation (a body representing all the German-speaking states, including Austria), then Russia, and finally France. These positions gave him a wide knowledge of events in these countries, a wide circle of friends and acquaintances, and an idea of these nations' foreign policy goals.

During his years as ambassador, Bismarck's reports, insights, and personality made him a noted figure in Prussian politics. Wilhelm I appointed Bismarck as the chancellor in 1862, one year after taking the throne. Bismarck's insight into political matters in Prussia, the other German states, and most of Europe (including Prussia's most likely rivals on the Continent—Russia, France, and Austria) made him the man for the job. While Wilhelm was not a stupid man, he was also not Bismarck, and he preferred to reign rather than rule unless there was a particular item or affair that interested or troubled him. In many cases, Bismarck and the king saw eye to eye, but when they didn't, Bismarck was often able to successfully argue his case to the king. If that did not work, the chancellor was not above manipulation and secrecy. At times, as he became more and more indispensable, he was known to throw a tantrum or two, but he knew exactly when to stop before he crossed a line.

Bismarck realized that for Prussia to really flourish, it would have to expand, and the only realistic way for it to do that was to unify the smaller German states around it. To the east of the country lay Russia, and as powerful as the Prussian Army was and would become, a war with Russia over lands that were not German to begin with was a losing proposition.

In the south lay the other major German-speaking power, Austria. While leaders of both kingdoms had at times bandied about the idea of the unification of Austria and Prussia, there were a number of quite obvious reasons it would not work. The first was who would be the head of the country? Neither sovereign wanted to play second fiddle, and history had shown that the idea of co-rulers was doomed to failure.

Secondly, Austria was a Catholic kingdom, the home of the Holy Roman Empire (the title of Holy Roman emperor, while having some meaning when Charlemagne became the first Holy Roman emperor in 800 CE, was essentially a meaningless title bestowed by the pope just a relatively short time after Charlemagne). Prussia and the lands it controlled in northern Germany were predominantly Protestant. Long and extraordinarily bloody wars had been fought in Germany over religion in the not-too-distant past, and no one was ready to live under a "heretical" monarch.

Thirdly, the other powers of Europe had made it quite clear that no union between Austria and Prussia could or would be tolerated. A huge German-speaking empire in the center of Europe would be too powerful and threaten the interests of nearly all of Europe.

Bismarck was quite aware of all these matters. He wasn't the only Prussian to understand that the German states were the only place for Prussia to expand, but he was essentially the only one with an idea of how it could be accomplished. And he had the power and position to set things in motion.

While Bismarck had a notion of how to achieve his goals, he also knew he was dependent on circumstances and how to take advantage of them. His first opportunity came in 1864 when the Danish king, Fredrick VII, died in 1863.

In 1863, the Danes were a relatively liberal monarchy, but they still hung onto the idea of an empire. At various times throughout history, Danish kings controlled England, Norway, and Denmark, parts of southern Sweden, and/or the German coast. However, in 1863, Denmark was no longer a power to be reckoned with to any great degree, except for the fact that the Danish king personally owned the two duchies (ruled by the king as "duke") of Schleswig and Holstein, which were populated by a German majority and lay between Denmark and the German states.

Denmark itself was governed as a constitutional monarchy, but the two provinces were governed as an absolute monarchy. Even many liberal Danes believed that Schleswig and Holstein both acted as a buffer between Denmark and the Germans and as the last remnants of its former glory. In addition, both states were quite rich in agriculture and shipping. They feared that if the reins of government were loosened on the two states, the population there would vote (either with ballots or swords) to join the German Confederation (the loose union of German states) or, worse, with Austria or Prussia.

Between 1848 and 1852, Denmark had successfully staved off both rebellion and outside interference over the two states in the First Schleswig War, but it was forced to agree that the two duchies were the personal property of the Danish king and his heirs, not the Danish government. When King Fredrick died, he was childless, meaning he had no direct heirs, at least in the minds of the Prussians and Austrians, who also had influence in the area, especially in the southern state of Holstein.

In 1863, the new king, Christian IX, under pressure brought by his parliament and people, unilaterally revised the previous agreement (known as the London Protocol of 1852) and retained personal control of both duchies, angering the German population of the states and giving Bismarck the excuse he needed for war. After all, the Danish king had violated an international agreement, and besides, the German population of the Danish-controlled states wanted to be free of Danish rule.

Both Prussia and Austria declared war on Denmark on January 14th, 1864. Even though the Prussians were the most vocal on the issue, the Austrians had interests in the area and could not afford to allow Prussia to gain the territories for itself. Surprisingly, a number of other smaller German states refused to go along with the war, worried that the seemingly inevitable Prusso-Austrian victory would result in the two larger states becoming even more dominant in German affairs than they already were. In a council of the German Confederation, the issue of war came down to "might makes right"—the Austrians and the Prussians were just too powerful to oppose.

The Second Schleswig War lasted just under nine months. Initially, the Danes voluntarily gave up on the southernmost state, Holstein, and retreated behind their ancient yet somewhat modernized defensive line known as the *Dannewirke* (the "Daneworks"), which had kept out invaders since the time of Charlemagne.

However, this wasn't the 9th century, and the *Dannewirke* was easily outmaneuvered, both by sea and around its flanks, which was exactly how the Prussian-Austrian forces defeated the smaller power. The Peace of Prague, signed in 1866, made official what had been already decided in combat: Denmark would lose Schleswig and Holstein. Schleswig would be given to Prussia, and Holstein would be given to Austria. About 200,000 Danes living in the duchies became citizens of the German Confederation. Within a relatively short time, most of them left for Denmark.

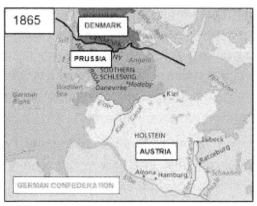

As you can see in the map above, this situation, with Schleswig separated from Prussia by sea and located next to Austrian territory, could prove problematic. Questions of transportation of people and goods (especially now that railroads were making travel and transport easier and faster) would pop up often. Shipping, especially in the famous Kiel Canal, also raised problems. Most diplomats and government officials would consider these questions a nightmare. Not Bismarck. As a matter of fact, the worse relations got between Austria and Prussia, the better it suited him.

This was because Bismarck saw these problems as an opportunity. During the war with Denmark, the Prussians saw exactly how backward the Austrians were compared to them. Many of their weapons were old; their organization was sloppy, outdated, and slow; and their officers (in many but not all instances) were not as good as the Prussians. Now, if only Bismarck could somehow maneuver the Austrians into declaring war on Prussia. If that happened, Prussia would have no choice but to defend itself. And should the Prussians win a victory over the Austrians, that would leave Prussia the dominant power among the German states. And that's exactly what Bismarck spent the next two years trying to do.

For many years, the prevalent belief among historians was that Bismarck engineered this entire plan, from the war with Denmark to the war with Austria and beyond. Starting in the 1990s, Bismarck's role began to be seen in a different light, with people believing that he was simply taking advantage of events as they occurred. Today, most professional historians believe that the truth falls somewhere in between, with Bismarck taking a very active role, knowing what he wanted the final outcome to be, and both riding out and steering events as they happened.

It took a little under two years for Austria and Prussia to go to war. Austria's concern that Prussia was dominating the German-speaking states and becoming too powerful in Europe. In addition to that, there was the issue of the administration of the two duchies of Schleswig and Holstein. However, what ultimately led to war was the Austrian governor of Holstein's decision in late January 1866 to let the major estate holders in *both* duchies hold an assembly. This was a unilateral decision by the Austrian government, which had promised to abide by the principle of joint sovereignty with Prussia when it came to issues concerning both territories. Not only did Prussia see this as an attempt by Austria to extend its influence into Schleswig, which had been given to Prussia in the Second Schleswig War, but also as a direct slap in Prussia' face and a test to see whether Austria could go further in their attempts to weaken Prussian influence among the lesser German states.

Austria believed it was within its rights, while Prussia did not. Throughout the intervening years, indeed since he had become chancellor, Bismarck had promoted and publicized the idea of a *Kleindeutschland* (literally "small Germany") among the many states of Germany united around and under Prussian rule as opposed to *Grossdeutschland* ("Greater Germany"), which had been advocated for decades and was centered on the Austrian Crown. Within Prussia, there was a public outcry against what was seen as Austria's move toward a *Grossdeutschland* or at least the limiting of Prussia's power and rights.

Still, Bismarck waited to see what the Austrians would do in response to Prussia's strongly worded protest. In March, he got his answer. Austria mobilized its armies on the Prussian border—the first step toward war. In late March, Prussia began a partial mobilization itself.

All the while, Bismarck sought to isolate the Austrians diplomatically. First, he secured an agreement with Italy that it would go to war with Austria should war develop between Austria and Prussia. This benefited Italy; for a number of years, the many states of Italy had been fighting a war of unification themselves, centered around the powerful state of Savoy. The largest obstacle left in the Italian struggle was to end Austrian control of several territories that were populated by an Italian majority. In the summer of 1866, Italy went to war with Austria, and though the war was essentially a stalemate, the Austrians were forced by Prussia, Italy's ally, to cede Venetia to Italy (it's a bit more complicated than that, but in the end, Italy got what it wanted).

With Italian troops mobilizing on its southern border and Prussian troops on its northern border, Austria looked to France for an alliance, but Bismarck had beaten them to it. He had approached the French leader, Napoleon III, and they met at the French resort town of Biarritz. No one is exactly sure what the two leaders discussed, but in the end, Bismarck felt that he had been promised French neutrality. He also likely knew that the French leader believed Austria would win the war, in which case France could possibly make territorial demands of a weakened Prussia in the states and cities it controlled in western Germany. If Prussia won, then Napoleon III could try to pry territorial concessions from Bismarck for staying neutral.

So, when the war began, the supposedly powerful Austrian Empire was isolated and on its own. Furthermore, its armies were divided between the north and south (admittedly, more Austrian troops faced the Prussians than the Italians), and the Prussians outnumbered the Austrians and their smaller German allies. Prussia had created the world's first general staff, a permanent body whose job was to plan for future wars in detail, prepare and set in motion mobilization plans, equip and train the standing professional army Prussia had had since the late 1600s, and much more. Austria had no such body. Each general had command of his own army, and when war broke out, a council was convened to discuss what to do. This is akin to a professional football team playing a bunch of neighborhood amateurs.

Making things worse for the Austrians and better for the Prussians was the fact that since the beginning of the century, the Prussians had been laying railroads throughout their territory. The

Austrians had been very lax about railroad development. Leading to the border area between the two kingdoms, Prussia had five major railways. Austria had one. It's quite obvious the advantage in speed, concentration, and maneuvering the Prussians possessed over the Austrians.

The Prussians also put out hundreds of miles of telegraph poles and wires, whereas the Austrians had very few and relied on horse-borne communication from their various headquarters and officers to the field.

As if this weren't enough, the Prussians enjoyed a sizable advantage when it came to personal weaponry. The vast majority of Prussian infantrymen carried the Dreyse needle-gun, one of the first breech-loading bolt-action rifles in history. The name "needle-gun" came from the sharp firing pin inside the weapon, which struck the bullet. In comparison, the Austrians were still using muzzle-loading rifles, which meant that a soldier had to stand or kneel to reload the powder, cartridge, and ball into the barrel of his gun. For every round the Austrians fired, the Prussians fired four or more.

Strangely enough, the Austrians had an advantage in artillery. They possessed breech-loading cannons, whereas the Prussians were mostly equipped with muzzle-loading guns. However, though a corps of Austrian artillerymen and officers were quite proficient with their cannons, most of their men were conscripts who received little training. By contrast, the Prussian system allowed for both a standing army and a sort of national guard (men whose time in the regular army had expired but who were still required to train on a regular basis for a number of years), and these men were quite familiar with their weapons. Additionally, the Prussian advantages in mobility meant that they could bring cannons more quickly to bear than their Austrian enemies.

If it sounds to you like the Austrians were headed for a huge defeat, you would be correct, but at the start of the war, many people around the world expected the Austrians to be victorious or for the war to be protracted. Neither happened. The Austro-Prussian War was essentially over in one battle on July 3rd, 1866: the Battle of Königgrätz (as it was known to the Prussians) or the Battle of Sadowa (as it was known to the Austrians).

Though a number of smaller battles occurred between Prussia's and Austria's allies, including a surprising Prussian defeat at the hands of the Hanoverians (which was soon avenged), the Battle of Königgrätz decided the war. While outnumbered by the Austrians, Prussian mobility and their leadership's quick thinking, along with the much greater fighting spirit of Prussia's well-trained and motivated troops, allowed them to inflict a decisive victory, causing nearly seven times the number of casualties on the Austrians as they themselves sustained. On July 22nd, the Austrians asked for a ceasefire as a preliminary to final peace talks, which resulted in the Peace of Prague, signed on August 23rd, 1866.

The consequences for Austria, Prussia, and the other German states were huge. Prussia would take control of Austria's smaller allies in Germany, Austria would no longer be involved in German affairs, and the German Confederation, a sort of "United Nations" of German-speaking states, where issues were theoretically supposed to be discussed, voted on, and solved, was ended. In its place was the North German Confederation, which was headed by Prussia.

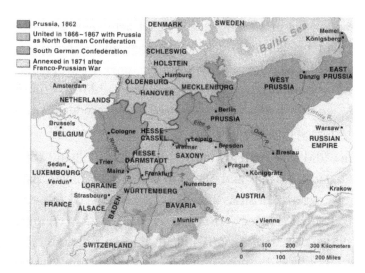

Illustration 3: Prussia after the Austro-Prussian War of 1866 (courtesy of Thompson Wandsworth)

The results of the war were very clear: Prussia was the rising power in central Europe and Austria the declining power. Seemingly overnight, Austria's role in European politics essentially ended. In an attempt to shore up its strength, both internally and externally, the Austrian Crown and the powerful Hungarian minority in the empire agreed on a power-sharing agreement, and a new entity was born: the Austro-Hungarian Empire.

The popularity of both Bismarck and Kaiser Wilhelm I soared after the victory over Austria. They were to reach all-time highs after Bismarck's next move.

Historians may have doubts over Bismarck's role in propelling the events in the war with Denmark and with Austria, but there really is no doubt that Bismarck was almost solely responsible for the instigation of Prussia's war with France, the last power in Europe that could prevent a unified Germany under Prussian leadership from happening.

France's leader in 1870 was the nephew of the great Napoleon Bonaparte, Louis Napoleon Bonaparte, better known as Napoleon III (Napoleon's only son died of complications from pneumonia and tuberculosis in 1832). Napoleon III actually was in power far longer than his famous uncle, and the main reason was that he knew that if he attempted to recreate his uncle's European empire, the entire continent would have turned against him and much more rapidly than they had against his more famous predecessor. No one wanted to see a recreation of the Napoleonic empire.

France did take part in the Crimean War, allying with Great Britain against Russia, and came to the aid of Italian patriots in their war against Austria in 1859. Napoleon III also was the impetus behind France's overseas empire, which conquered or absorbed vast areas of Asia, islands in the Pacific, and a large part of Africa, but he did not attempt to expand France in Europe as his uncle had.

Napoleon III oversaw much during his time in power: the beginnings of the Suez Canal, the reconstruction of much of Paris, and the changes wrought in the economy by developing industries. For much of Napoleon III's "Second Empire," France's economy thrived, but toward the end of the 1860s, France entered an economic downturn marked by large deficits and inflation. Additionally, many people in both the government and the population at large were beginning to tire of rule by royal decree and wanted more representation and say in how their government functioned. The National Assembly, in particular, grew resentful as Napoleon III increasingly only consulted them when he needed more money to spend.

As his popularity dropped in the country, he turned more and more to sycophants and to his wife, Empress Eugénie, who, though once a relatively liberal person, turned more conservative as time went by. The people around Napoleon III began to whisper in his ear, and what they mostly had to say was that Great Britain (having the greater overseas empire) and now the rising power of Prussia were taking all of the glory and that France, which meant Louis-Napoleon as well, was being overshadowed. Louis and his coterie also knew the value of foreign distractions, both in uniting the people and getting them to overlook some of the more glaring problems in the country.

When Bismarck and Napoleon III met at Biarritz before the Austro-Prussian War, Bismarck let Louis-Napoleon believe that if there was a Prussian victory, he would be amenable to giving France land in the western German territory of the Palatinate and in Luxembourg. When the war ended, Louis-Napoleon attempted to "cash in" on his promise to Bismarck, as France had remained neutral in the war. So, Louis-Napoleon put pressure on Bismarck to give those territories to France. Just after the end of the Franco-Prussian War, Bismarck recounted his reaction to the French demands in a speech to the Reichstag (the German parliament). His response to the French ambassador, or at least what he told the Reichstag his response was, was "Good, then it's war!" The story goes that the ambassador rushed home to a sick Napoleon III, who recanted, claiming he had been "tricked" into sending the ambassador while with fever.

Regardless of whether that story is true, between 1866 and 1870, tensions became increasingly high between Prussia and France. The straw that broke the camel's back involved an issue over the succession of a new king in Spain.

In 1868, a rebellion in Spain overthrew Queen Isabella II (r. 1833–1869), whose rule became increasingly autocratic, erratic, and unpopular toward the end of her life. When she was deposed, the authorities in Spain cast about for a successor, one they hoped would rule as a more liberal and perhaps constitutional monarch. With Prussian urging, they eventually settled upon a German prince of the House of Hohenzollern (the house of the Prussian Kaiser), who had a legitimate though distant claim to the Spanish throne.

This prince, Leopold, was acceptable to the Spanish, but he was not at all acceptable to the French. In French eyes, having a

Hohenzollern on the Spanish throne would mean that the rulers of the two major countries on its borders were from the same German family, which was a risk France was not willing to take. And not only did Napoleon III, his wife, and the government felt this way, but so did most of the people of France as well.

Louis-Napoleon vociferously and loudly protested the plan to place Leopold on the throne of Spain to the point of threatening war. The Prussians eventually agreed to remove his name from contention, at least for the time being. This was not enough for the French, and what happened next shows Bismarck at his most brilliant and most devious.

Talks between Kaiser Wilhelm I and the French ambassador to Prussia took place in the resort city of Ems in western Germany. There, the German emperor and the French ambassador diplomatically and politely discussed the issue. At the end of their talks, they agreed to disagree, and while the issue was not settled, it appeared that, at least for a time, war had been averted, which was not what Bismarck wanted.

Bismarck realized that the time was right for a war with France, the last nation in Europe that could stand in the way of a united Germany. As it was, the French felt threatened by Prussian growth in the wars of the 1860s, and if the remaining southern and western German states became part of Prussia, the Prussians would not only become that much stronger but also much of its territory would border France. For both international reasons and reasons of domestic politics, Napoleon III could not allow that to happen.

Bismarck received a dispatch telegram from the Kaiser relating the events of his meeting with the French ambassador. For a moment, it seemed like there was nothing further that Bismarck could do—until he realized that he could "edit" the telegram to make it seem as if the Prussian monarch had deliberately and greatly insulted the French ambassador.

Essentially, the telegram stated that the German Kaiser would not see the French ambassador again and that he was done talking to him. In the language of diplomacy, this is almost a literal slap in the face. Making matters worse, the French agency responsible for translating the telegram confused two very similar looking words, and instead of the German officer, who was an aide to the Kaiser, delivering the message, the translator made it seem as if the message from the Prussians had been delivered by a common, lowly sergeant. This was both an insult and an indication that the Prussians had no respect for the French and their ruler.

Bismarck knew it was just a matter of hours before the Ems Dispatch, as it is known, was published in every newspaper in France. When that happened, he was sure the population would scream for war against the Prussians and that Napoleon III, looking for "glory" as his popularity wanted, would oblige them. Of course, people and officials in Prussia read about the French reaction and called for war themselves, which was exactly what Bismarck hoped would happen.

Illustration 4: Contemporary engraving of Parisians calling for war with Prussia, 1870

France mobilized its army on July 15th, 1870, declared war on the 16th, and sent its declaration to Berlin on the 19th. The states of the North German Confederation, led by Prussia, mobilized their army more rapidly than the French due to their organizational strength and the miles of railway now crisscrossing most of Germany. Additionally, the states of south Germany (the powerful state of Bavaria, along with Baden and Württemberg) declared war on France as well; apparently, the feeling for their brother Germans ran strong despite them having been loyal to Austria only recently. Bismarck, having intentionally whispered in the ears of the south German press about Napoleon's demand for German territory at their 1866 Biarritz meeting, also inflamed the anti-French feeling in the German states.

Though it did not know it, France was beaten almost before the war began. Though French soldiers actually possessed better rifles (the Chassepot) with a longer range than the Prussian Dreyse needle-gun and possessed small numbers of an early machine gun, the French Army had anticipated fighting a defensive war, hoping to break Prussian attacks on trench-works backed by artillery. On the other side, the Prussians constantly drilled for an offensive and fluid war, learning to take advantage of conditions they met on the field and not what they anticipated.

Making matters worse, most of the French artillery were bronze breech-loading cannons, which gave out quicker and were slower to load than the Prussian steel breech-loading cannons they had mass-produced in the years since the Austrian war. Though there were large-caliber Prussian guns with which to shell strong French positions, much of the Prussian artillery was smaller and mobile, allowing the Prussians to use their guns as a kind of tank without the armor. They quickly maneuvered their artillery where it was needed to support Prussian troops' breakthroughs and nullify the longer range of the French rifles.

Under much of Louis-Napoleon's reign, the French Army had been a standing army, with about 425,000 men. The French draft system was fraught with problems, the biggest one being an excessively long time of service (seven years), which both hurt the French economy and sapped soldiers' morale. When the French saw the rapidity with which Prussia defeated Austria and how effective their conscription system had been, they began to implement changes, but these were incomplete by the time of the war in 1870. At the height of the war, the number of French soldiers in the field (combat troops) was far less than the Prussians; there were approximately 950,000 Prussians compared to just over 700,000 French.

Beyond that, the French Army had very few plans and very little coordination between army groups and commanders. They, like the Austrians four years earlier, also had far fewer telegraph lines with which to quickly communicate to their headquarters and capital.

The war was a bloody and savage affair, and it lasted a relatively short time—just over six months. In that time, 45,000 Germans/Prussians and nearly 140,000 Frenchmen lost their lives. Though there were quite a few battles fought, the most important one, and the one that ultimately defeated France and brought down Napoleon III, was the Battle of Sedan.

By September, the important French fortress border town of Metz was under siege, and Napoleon III and his leading generals were determined to relieve it. The French felt that if Metz fell, the bulk of the Prusso-German armies would come pouring into western France. Never mind that German forces had already penetrated France to the north in a maneuver foreshadowing their attack in 1914.

The Germans intercepted French signals, and the two armies engaged in a series of hard-fought battles before the French realized that their attempt to relieve Metz was doomed to failure. In order to save what was left of the French Army in northwestern France, French General Patrice de MacMahon moved the army to the border town of Sedan, about one hundred miles north of Metz. When they got there, the French Army found a town in panic and the people wanting the army to leave lest their city be flattened by the Germans. The situation was so bad that a number of French troops were trampled to death in a panic to get inside the city's fortified walls. It was clear within a day that the situation for the French, many of whom were trapped outside the city in woefully unprepared positions, was hopeless.

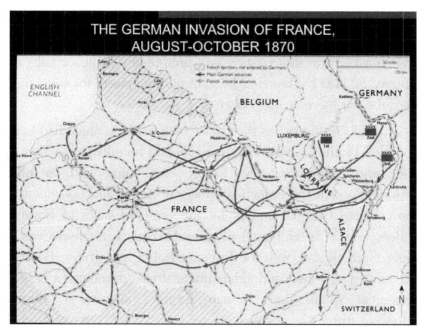

Illustration 5: German armies are marked in dark blue, French in light blue, with the unaffected zone marked in the north.

Among those inside the walls of Sedan was Napoleon III. Both he and his generals realized that the only way out alive, both for them and the city's populace, was surrender, and this is what happened on September 2nd, 1870, when a very sick Napoleon III rode to meet with Kaiser Wilhelm I and gave up.

However, the city and the bulk of the French Army saw this move as cowardly. Napoleon's government fell, and the Third French Republic took its place (you can read more about this in Captivating History's *History of France*). The leaders of the Third Republic ordered the remaining French armies to fight on, which they did, but they were forced back to Paris by September 19th.

For four months, the Prussians and their south German allies besieged Paris, causing mass hunger (the elephants in the zoo were infamously killed for food), panic, and a brief socialist revolution (the Paris Commune, which was put down harshly by French troops when the war ended).

Eventually, with their beautiful city being shelled more and more each day and the Prussian front lines approaching, the French asked for an armistice as a preliminary to peace talks on January 26th, 1871. Though fighting went on in places for some time after, the war was essentially over.

The talks took place at the Palace of Versailles, which had been occupied by the Prussians in an additional humiliation to French pride, and the French agreed to pay an indemnity and, far more importantly, cede the French provinces of Alsace and Lorraine to a newly united German nation, for the southern states of Bavaria, Baden, and Württemberg had agreed to place themselves in a larger German state with the Prussian Kaiser as its ruler. Bavaria, due to its size, power, and independent streak, negotiated a unique agreement within the German Empire, allowing it greater autonomy within Germany.

Alsace and Lorraine had been fought over for centuries, and they contained a roughly equal number of French and German speakers. Naturally, the French residents were unhappy, and many French families left the territories.

The loss of Alsace-Lorraine was the ultimate humiliation for the French, and what's more, it made defending French territory even more difficult in the future. Politically, a whole movement arose within France known as revanchism ("revenge-ism"), which was dedicated to the reconquest of these provinces and a direct contribution to World War I.

But for Germany, a new era had begun. The German states had never been united in one entity before, and a new European power had been born. What's more, this new power had shown to the world the dominance of its armed forces and its harnessing of technology. The changes that came from the Franco-Prussian War were immense. Nations began forming general staffs for the constant upkeep and modernization of their armies. Conscription systems modeled after the Prussians were put in place throughout

Europe. Camouflage as a military science, which was born in Germany, was given priority, as was much else.

For Otto von Bismarck, the unification of Germany was the high-water mark of his career, which would last until the new Kaiser, Wilhelm II, the grandson of Wilhelm I, dismissed him in 1888 to run the state himself.

Illustration 6: This painting by Anton von Werner was done years after the end of the war. The original displeased the Kaiser, who had it destroyed. In this painting, the Kaiser (on the dais) and Bismarck (the central figure in white) are shown as they appeared in 1881, not 1871. The painting is entitled The Proclamation of the German Empire.

Chapter 3 – Wilhelm's Germany

When Wilhelm II became Kaiser in 1888, he inherited a new world power. In many ways, Germany was envied: it was powerful, innovative, and cultured. It was also feared; after all, it had won three major wars in twenty years, and it was suddenly the most populous state in Europe and the most advanced on the Continent (only England surpassed it in economic terms). It was also no secret that the young new Kaiser was determined to raise his country to new heights, which would likely come at the expense of others in Europe.

Before we delve into the complex personality of Kaiser Wilhelm II, let's take a moment to discuss life in Germany under Bismarck and the first years of the Kaiser's rule.

Firstly, despite some truly deep divisions within German society, almost every German citizen was exceedingly proud of their new country. After all, Germany had seemingly done the impossible against a great many enemies, and it was now the leading industrial power in Europe. Most, though not all, Germans were loyal to their emperor, and they worshiped Bismarck almost as a god for what he had accomplished. The army, especially the officers, claimed another place in the hearts and minds of most Germans.

Since the time of Frederick the Great, the Prussian Army had been one of the main pillars of Prussian society. Now, it was one of the main pillars of German society. Without a very effective army, Bismarck's plans would have come to naught. Though the esteem in which soldiers were held varied by region, it is safe to say that in most of Germany, officers (especially generals) were held in a sort of semi-deification. Even in retirement, most men wore the symbols of their regiment on their lapels with pride or stuffed themselves into their once perfectly fitting uniforms for national or local holidays and events. Officers would be called by their title, sometimes even by members of their families, until the day they died. For many young men in the middle and upper classes, being an officer (especially a career officer) was the highest aspiration of their lives, and if it wasn't his hope, then it was the hope of his family.

In small towns and villages throughout Germany (at the turn of the century, most Germans still lived in small towns and villages, though it was rapidly changing), the mayor usually had some military background. Many times, however, it was the highest-ranking officer, who was usually retired, in the area that was approached for the solution to a problem.

At the top of the German political food chain was the new Kaiser, Wilhelm II. His father, Frederick III, had ruled for only ninety-nine days, having known he was dying from cancer of the larynx before he took the throne. When he passed on June 15th, 1888, his son Wilhelm ascended to rule the world's newest power.

There were many in the upper class and even in his own family, the Hohenzollerns, that had trepidations about Wilhelm being Kaiser (now is a good a time as any to explain that the German word "Kaiser" is a translation of the Latin word "Caesar"). Firstly, in a time when people had very little understanding of or tolerance for physical handicaps, Wilhelm was born with a withered left arm, caused by inept obstetricians attempting to save the baby, who was a breech birth. This was made worse by the protocol of the time, which dictated that instead of being nude at least from the waist down, Wilhelm's mother, Victoria (the eldest child of the illustrious Queen Victoria of Britain), had on a long gown, under which the doctors were forced to work for reasons of "modesty." They used forceps to grip the baby's neck and shoulder, forcibly pulling him out of the womb. When the child was delivered in January 1859, he was blue and only revived by vigorous rubbing and handling. Many believe that this relatively prolonged period of oxygen deprivation at birth may have caused personality and mental issues later in life, for the Kaiser became known for being notoriously unstable when it came to his mood.

To have the future king of Prussia be physically challenged (and make no mistake, the word used, even by the emperor, was "crippled") was anathema to the Prussian aristocracy and the royal family. All the modern methods were applied, including vigorous massages on a regular basis, but nothing seemed to work. So, starting from when the future king was about six months old, other methods were used, and so-called experts from around Europe were brought in to attempt to straighten and strengthen Wilhelm's withered arm and hand, which was essentially misshapen into a claw-like appendage.

Cold seawater compresses and sprays were used. At four, the young boy was essentially stretched on a rack, a la the Dark Ages. As he approached puberty, his head and neck began to tilt to the left, but an operation cutting strained tendons stopped that. Other weird methods were also tried. The boy was forced to place his arm in the abdomen of freshly killed deer, the thinking being that somehow the heat and blood might help. Of course, it did not. When told of this, Queen Victoria called it "revolting and idiotic." Other techniques included shock therapy to the arm and tying his good arm to his body to force the prince to use the withered one (he couldn't).

Historians over the years have placed varying levels of importance on the effect of all of this (both the deformity and the treatments) on the Kaiser's personality. While it's a stretch to blame all of the Kaiser's actions on his arm, it also must have had some effect, especially during a time of such intolerance.

What did happen was that the Kaiser developed an extraordinarily strong right hand and arm, which he would use to impress or overawe certain people when shaking hands. He also developed quite a shot and loved hunting, though the game had to be driven in his direction and the weapon primed for him. In his elder years, when he was in exile in Holland, he chopped large amounts of wood with his one arm and could frequently outpace others with two good arms. He also developed into quite an able horseman.

Still, whether it was an effect of the torturous methods he was forced to undergo as a child, the simple fact that he was "deformed," or perhaps just his personality, Kaiser Wilhelm II turned into a mercurial ruler with an inferiority complex. He was determined to outshine his royal relatives in England and Russia (King George V and Tsar Nicholas II of Russia) and other lesser nobility, and he was never hesitant to brag, threaten, or coerce others to get his way. He was a notorious practical joker, but had he not been emperor, he likely would have gotten punched in the mouth, for many of his "jokes" came at the public or physical expense of others, usually those in high places in the army, navy, or government.

Wilhelm and the House of Hohenzollern went to great lengths to hide his arm. In both stills and moving pictures, as well as in person, he would hold a pair of white gloves in his left arm, making it appear longer or of normal length. At times of official business, when he wore a full military uniform, his left hand would clasp the hilt of a sword or he would hold his left hand in his right to attempt to downplay the handicap.

Illustration 7: Kaiser Wilhelm II during WWI

Illustration 8: The ex-Kaiser in Dutch exile

When Wilhelm became Kaiser in 1888, he was determined to rule directly. He chafed under both the counsel of and the legend of Otto von Bismarck, and he knew that as long as the "Iron Chancellor" remained in office, he would be overshadowed. On

March 20ᵗʰ, 1890, a little over a year and a half after taking the throne, Wilhelm felt strong enough politically to fire the man who had created a united Germany.

Bismarck did not go happily, but he had no choice. To his friends and trusted journalists, he told them his worries about Germany's future under Wilhelm, whom he believed was unstable and would drag Germany into a war it could not win.

Bismarck is famous for uniting Germany, and statues of the man are still found throughout Germany, as are street names and schools. However, in domestic politics, Bismarck was not as successful or popular. One of his most infamous policies was called *Der Kulturkampf* ("the culture struggle"). This was aimed at the Catholics, who made up a very sizable minority in the country and a majority in the new states of southern and southwestern Germany. Virtually all Prussians were Lutheran, as was most of the north German population. The Thirty Years' War (1618–1648), a religious war between Catholics and Protestants within Europe, was fought mainly in Germany. Millions died, and old prejudices were still very much alive during the time of Bismarck.

Bismarck and other Protestants in the ruling classes in northern Germany were suspicious of the Catholics in the south, mostly for one main reason: they suspected that the Catholics would be more loyal to the pope in Rome than to the Kaiser in Berlin. To limit that perceived loyalty and to further German unity (at least in Bismarck's eyes), he began to put forward a series of sanctions and regulations on the Catholic Church and its clergy in 1871. This continued until 1875; by then, Bismarck had realized his policies were a miscalculation and had caused further division in the country.

Most of these policies put Catholic clergy, education, and hospitals under government control. For example, the clergy had to be approved by the state, universities and other religious schools were subject to inspection (theoretically, this meant Protestant schools as well, but everyone knew it was the Catholics who were being targeted), and marriage became a civil ceremony. Tensions got so bad that a Catholic zealot came close to assassinating Bismarck in 1874. Liberals in the country decried the discriminatory policies, and the Catholic Centre Party gained a significant number of seats in the German parliament, effectively stymieing Bismarck's policies and forcing the rollback of many.

In the late 19th and early 20th centuries, the winds of change were blowing over Western Europe, mostly brought on by the Industrial Revolution, which was reaching new heights in cities throughout the western part of the Continent but slowly moving eastward as well.

The list of changes that took place is profound. The population was moving in large numbers from the countryside and villages to the cities, changing both the economies and cultures of both. Rapid growth in the city meant housing shortages but also tremendous amounts of building projects (including roads, rails, subways, and bridges). The crowded conditions brought about epidemics, sometimes on a huge scale, forcing politicians, doctors, and city planners to come up with solutions for problems that had never really been faced before.

In the workplace, which meant factories, people who had never been outside of their hometowns or districts except *maybe* more than once or twice in their lives were now living and working with people who might as well have been foreigners. Dialects prevalent all over Europe changed rapidly into new urban ones. Food, dress, and much else were new and changed over time, especially among the middle classes.

Though many people from countries began an immense wave of emigration to the United States (which brought about its own problems, both in America and Europe), millions remained. People speak of America as a "melting pot" of cultures, but the same thing happened in cities in Europe and Germany in the late 19th and early 20th centuries.

For people from Berlin, Bavarians might as well have been from another country (until 1871, they were) and vice versa. The same thing went on all over Europe, as people from rural areas moved into cities. Of course, in larger cities near the borders, there were more than just new arrivals from other provinces. There were also people from other countries. Some of them had been in these cities for years, while others were newcomers. This, of course, brought on new and larger problems of language, religion, and beliefs. For the most part, people managed to get by, and there were few large issues. However, underneath everything, age-old prejudices were brewing. Sometimes they rose to the top and made headlines or rumors, but these were usually temporary or tamped down by the authorities.

Of course, we're speaking here of anti-Semitism. More will follow on the topic, but for now, suffice it to say that Germany's Jewish population, which had existed in the country for centuries, was now being exposed to old hatreds magnified by the concentration of newcomers. These newcomers were oftentimes poor, rural, ill-educated, and brought up with prejudices against people they had never really known, for most of Germany's and Europe's Jews lived in the cities.

In Vienna, Austria, a frustrated young artist from the small city of Linz, whose family doctor was Jewish and who had a Jewish friend help him sell his watercolor postcards, was overawed by the cosmopolitan nature of the Austrian capital, which, in many ways, was experiencing the same changes as in Berlin. Not helping matters was the anti-Semitism of Vienna's mayor, Karl Lueger, who frequently blamed the city's ills on the Jews. Initially, he was put off by the vulgarity of the anti-Semitic press in Vienna, but as he was exposed to it more and more, his outlook began to change. This young man later recorded his experiences in a book:

> Once, as I was strolling through the inner city, I suddenly encountered an apparition in a black caftan and

black hair locks. Is this a Jew? was my first thought...For, to be sure, they had not looked like that in Linz. I observed the man furtively and cautiously, but the longer I stared at this foreign face, scrutinizing feature for feature, the more my first question assumed a new form: is this a German? ...the more I saw, the more sharply they became distinguished in my eyes from the rest of humanity...For me this was the time of the greatest spiritual upheaval I have ever had to go through. I had ceased to be a weak-kneed cosmopolitan and become an anti-Semite.

As I am sure you have guessed, the young man was Adolf Hitler, and he was not alone in his feelings, which drew adherents as more changes and the later economic depression occurred.

Factory work was dangerous. It still is, but at a time when the first truly gigantic factory complexes were being built, health and safety issues were decidedly lower on the list of things factory owners and governments had to deal with. That soon changed. Faced with the immediate danger of the new factories and the mines that fed them, as well as the health issues that followed and with the crowded living conditions created by the new economy, workers began to organize.

As you may know, by the late 1800s, many of these workers were espousing the new theory of communism and its less militant cousin, socialism. Communism, which was put forward by German thinkers Karl Marx and Friedrich Engels (mostly working in England), states that economics functioned in a similar way as the newly popular theory of evolution put forward by Charles Darwin. In communist theory, human economic activity moved from a feudal/medieval stage slowly into one based on profit, localized in small towns and villages while evolving into an economy focused on factories and capitalism. According to Marx and Engels, throughout history, the rich and powerful have exploited the poor, with this only getting worse as time goes by. With the advent of industrial capitalism, they believed conditions would grow so unequal that eventually, the workers would have no choice but to overthrow the upper classes and form a "worker's state" in which all property would be communally held—thus, the name of "communism." Of course, this is a very simple explanation, but even this short explanation, put in a pamphlet with compelling statistics, personal stories, and illustrations, was enough to move many of the workers in European cities toward communism or socialism.

Socialism and communism are not necessarily the same thing, though the words have been and are constantly used interchangeably. In Germany and elsewhere, a less militant socialist movement sprang up in response to the changes brought about by the Industrial Revolution. This was social democracy, and in Germany, the party representing these ideas was the SPD (for *Sozialdemokratische Partei Deutschlands* or "Social Democratic Party of Germany").

An adequate and succinct definition of European social democratic beliefs in the 19th and 20th centuries comes from Washington State University Professor Paul Brians, who in comparing social democratic ideas in 19th-century America with European ones, said, "Social democrats were more successful in Europe, particularly in Scandinavia, following a gradualist approach which involved high taxes to enforce relative economic equality, government regulation of industry, nationalization of large industries, and social welfare."

In the years before Bismarck's forced retirement, the Social Democrats became the largest party in Germany. Though Bismarck believed that socialism (and its more militant corollary, communism) was harmful to both the economy and the existing social structure and spent years enacting oppressive laws against it, he also realized that without some change in the workplace, violent disruption was likely. To that end, Bismarck, working with leading Social Democrats who hated the Iron Chancellor, developed some of the most forward-thinking social welfare laws in the world. Work hours were reduced, the workweek decreased, socialized medicine was put in place, workplace safety standards began, and changes to housing and housing laws were enacted and evolved, though the poorer districts of any German city at the time were unsafe, crowded, and unhealthy places to live. In many ways, Germany, which had an almost completely absolute monarchy after 1890, was the most progressive industrial state in the world, and this was only after just twenty or so years of being a nation.

Germany and the World before WWI

Germans of all stripes could be rightly proud of the accomplishments they had achieved since 1871. Only one thing remained: "a place in the sun." This phrase, attributed to Kaiser Wilhelm II, was actually first uttered by his foreign minister, Bernhard von Bülow, in 1897. Speaking in a debate in the Reichstag about foreign policy, von Bülow said, "We wish to throw no one into the shade, but we also demand our own place in the sun." This statement referred to Germany's wish to participate in the second great age of imperialism, which took place in the latter part of the 19th and early 20th centuries.

For many reasons—economic, political, military, and religious—the great powers of Europe and the United States began to carve up the world between them, conquering many of the territories, kingdoms, and ancient states of Asia, Africa, and the Pacific. The leaders in this "race" were Great Britain and France, although Belgium, Italy, Holland, and Russia all took part. Japan was also a participant in Asia, having developed a modern economy in an amazing amount of time between 1870 and the late 1890s.

As we have seen, Germany had been divided into many states before 1864, and while the Germans were busy fighting for unification and then attempting to build a nation, the other powers of Europe were busy conquering much of the world. This was why von Bülow and the Kaiser wanted "a place in the sun" for Germany, which meant one thing—an empire.

Though there were a great many factors contributing to European and especially German imperialism in the 1890s onward, the desire for "a place in the sun" fit in perfectly with Kaiser Wilhelm's upbringing and personality. Here he was, a "cripple," now in command of one of the world's greatest armies and economies. This was his chance to show that he and Germany were strong, dominant, and second to none.

To do this, the Kaiser, who was an avid sailor and who attended the famed sailing regatta at Cowes in England every year (along with his many royal cousins, who frequently and sometimes openly derided his appearance), was determined to build a navy to compete with and eventually outnumber the greatest navy in the history of the world to that time, the Royal Navy of Great Britain.

Illustration 9: In this turn-of-the-century cartoon, the nations of Europe (Great Britain, Germany, Russia, and France), along with

Japan, contemplate the division of a protesting China. Note the aggressive attitude of the Kaiser toward his grandmother Victoria, the symbol of Great Britain.

Building a navy capable of challenging the Royal Navy was a daunting if not impossible task for Wilhelm's Germany. At the outbreak of WWI, the Royal Navy consisted of 82 battleships, 136 cruisers, 142 destroyers, 80 torpedo boats, 80 submarines, and 15 early versions of aircraft carriers. The navy also included over 300 support and other vessels (riverine patrol boats, oilers, supply ships, etc.), and during the war, the Americans (as it did in WWII) lent or gave the British another nearly 500 ships of varying kinds (excluding major combat ships, such as battleships and cruisers).

At the beginning of the 20th century, when Wilhelm decided to build his navy (*Kriegsmarine* in German), these numbers were a bit smaller, but the strength of the Royal Navy still far exceeded any other nation. Actually, British policy was (and had been for some time) that the Royal Navy would be half again as strong as the next *two* greatest navies in the world. Britain's commercial life depended on the Royal Navy's protection, either in actuality (escort merchant ships) or as a deterrent. More importantly, the Royal Navy (whose "Home Fleet," based in northern Scotland, was its largest) kept the United Kingdom safe from invasions. The survival of their nation and their empire depended on the Royal Navy.

Until this point in time, German foreign policy, for the most part, had been astute and well-thought-out. That was due almost exclusively to Bismarck. The Iron Chancellor also realized that Germany was a "saturated power." By this, he meant that Germany would not actively seek out additional territory in Europe or elsewhere. He knew that the chances of war would greatly increase if Germany attempted to increase the size of its empire, realizing that the great powers of Europe were already wary of his nation, having come so far and so fast. By the time Bismarck was pushed out of office by the Kaiser, the German Army was the strongest in

Europe, and its economy was second to only that of Great Britain—and all of that in roughly thirty years' time.

Bismarck, like most other statesmen of the time, knew that for centuries the British had been guided by their policy of trying to maintain a "balance of power" in Europe. Simply put, with no one country or bloc of countries dominating the others, the chances of war and threats to Britain's economy were lessened.

When Bismarck left, Germany's foreign policy changed radically, as you have read. Surprisingly, while the Germans were eager to construct a fleet that would be a "deterrent fleet" (in the words of the Reich secretary of the navy, Admiral Alfred von Tirpitz, whose last name you might recognize from the famous WWII battleship that was named in his honor), they believed that common sense and the new balance of power in Europe should make England a German ally.

The Germans believed that Britain's economic, imperial, and historic rivalries with France and Russia, the other two great powers of Europe, made it a natural ally of Germany. To an extent, this was true, even down to the German roots of the English royal family, and had this been the only factor the English considered, Germany and Great Britain might have indeed found themselves allies at the beginning of the 20th century. However, a number of German miscalculations made that an impossibility.

The Kaiser's shrill behavior and speeches put the English on alert, offended English sensibilities, and challenged its historic role as the middle-man/peacemaker between the powers of Europe and, to a degree, the world. On the twenty-fifth anniversary of the founding of a united Germany in 1896, Wilhelm, playing to his own vanity and the patriotic feelings of his subjects on that important day, announced that, from that point forward, Germany would demand to be consulted in all European affairs and all important world affairs. As you might imagine, that rubbed British sensibilities quite the wrong way. The other powers of the world were not exactly thrilled either.

However, the German argument did make sense, and many in Britain believed that the balance of power could be kept with German and British interests aligned. The Germans had calculated quite well in that regard, as the balance of power was one of the pillars of British foreign policy and power, but it was not the only one.

The British could be challenged commercially. After all, the economy of the world at that time was based on economic competition and free enterprise. The British could also make room at the diplomatic table for the Germans: after all, they were a great power and had to be taken into consideration. But the one thing the British absolutely could not tolerate was a naval rival, and it was clear from both the Kaiser's public and private utterings that he meant that Germany's "deterrent fleet" would be aimed at only one power: Great Britain. What's more, as time went by and the world entered the 20th century, Wilhelm's words and actions made it clear that he was intent on building a German navy that was not just a deterrent to the Royal Navy but superior to it. This pushed Britain right into the arms of France and Russia, two powers with which it had relatively recently been at war.

Of course, Germany could not hope to build a navy to rival Britain's in a short time. The plan set out by von Tirpitz would take twenty-five years. It was a pipe dream from the beginning. It assumed that the British would not match or out-do Germany's naval growth to maintain her dominance at sea (which she did), presumed smooth economic times were ahead, and, strangely of all, was proposed to not cost any extra money at all, the idea being that taxes and other revenues of Germany's rapidly growing economy would pay for it without the government having to borrow the money or run up a deficit. Of course, this did not happen, and by the time World War One began, Germany had already begun to go into debt to pay for its military.

Germany's "place in the sun" would eventually amount to...well, not much. By the time that Wilhelm sent the navy (along with accompanying expeditionary forces) out to claim that place, there really wasn't that much left unclaimed. By August 1914, the German Empire consisted of the city and bay of Jiaozhou in China (then known as Kiaochow by the Europeans); the Marshall Islands and the newly named Bismarck Archipelago (a group of islands off the coast of Papua New Guinea) in the Pacific and Cameroon; Togo, Namibia (then known as German Southwest Africa), and Tanzania (then called German East Africa) in Africa.

And what did Germany get from these colonies? Nothing for the most part, except some poorly located ports, and it ended up costing Germany more to keep these colonies than any benefit it received. Additionally, the seizure of these areas and Germany's crowing about it for German domestic political consumption did nothing but annoy and alarm the other colonial powers of Europe, along with the United States and, to a lesser degree, Japan, both of which had significant imperial possessions in the Pacific region.

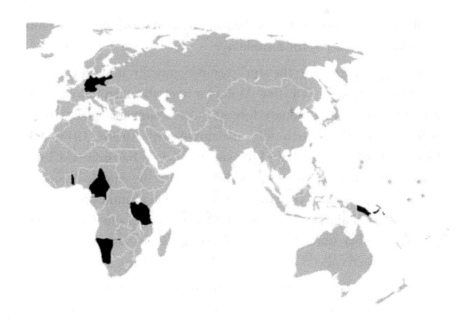

Illustration 10: German Empire before WWI

As you can see from the map above, Germany's colonies were not only few (comparatively) but also separated by considerable distances over land and water. Both France and Great Britain had the location and/or the naval resources to either involve their imperial possessions in their respective economies or connect them by rail (in the case of Britain in Africa). The Germans were not able to use British railways, and their naval resources were stretched thin trying to supply and protect their empire.

One of the "blessings" for the native peoples of the German Empire was that, generally speaking, as long as they did not attack or harass German troops, officials, or citizens, they were left alone. Yes, their resources were exploited, but none of the territories that you see was very rich in the first place, and even before the Germans arrived, they did not have advanced economies and trade to other areas. Namibia was almost 100 percent desert. German East Africa and German Cameroon (Tanzania and Cameroon) were verdant but harsh and not the richest of areas resource-wise.

The same was true for Togo, the German part of Papua New Guinea, and the other German islands in the Pacific.

Papua New Guinea provides an interesting example of the German government. While the British struggled with the tribes of New Guinea in the land under their control, for the most part, the Germans did not. This came down to two related reasons: religion and cannibalism.

Many of the tribes of Papua New Guinea at the time (and until the first decades of the last half of the 20th century) practiced cannibalism. Most of this had to do with religious/spiritual rites and how they related to war or combat. The British, and later the Australians, sent missionaries to both convert the native populations, which consisted of many disparate tribes or clans, to Christianity and end cannibalism. In many of these cases, at least initially, this resulted in bloodshed and repression, and sometimes the missionaries were served for dinner. This provoked another harsh backlash.

The Germans were content to let the natives, who were ostensibly under their control, continue as they had for millennia, as long as the Germans were left alone. This made the German part of Papua New Guinea relatively peaceful during the time Wilhelm II controlled the area. To begin a war with the natives would mean additional costs in lives, manpower, and supplies, which would have to be brought in from the other side of the globe.

In China, however, German behavior was marked for its disregard for life. From 1899 to 1901, the Society of Righteous Harmonious Fists united millions of Chinese peasants together in what is known in the West as the Boxer Rebellion. The Boxer Rebellion cost millions of lives, and it was the result of a conflict with the European powers, which claimed "concessions" in Chinese cities that gave them not only preferential trading rights but also allowed the Europeans (along with the Japanese and, to a lesser extent, the Americans) to apply their own legal systems and much else. Naturally, this caused much resentment among the Chinese, who were treated as second-class citizens in their own countries in the areas under foreign control.

Illustration 11: Troops of the Eight-Nation Alliance in China, 1900. Left to right: Britain, United States, Australia, British India, Germany, France, Austria-Hungary, Italy, and Japan.

In Beijing, the anti-foreign, anti-Christian Boxers surrounded and besieged the Legation Quarter, where the imperial powers had their embassies, most of their residences, and churches, along with much else. The foreigners eventually broke the siege in Beijing as well as the uprisings elsewhere (as a side note, the Chinese government, which was criticized for being weak and "allowing" the foreigners in the country in the first place, tacitly encouraged the Boxers until the tide turned). The Japanese and Germans, in particular, behaved brutally in response to Chinese attacks, which, it must be admitted, sometimes crossed the line into atrocities. It was in China that the Germans picked up one of their WWI/WWII nicknames after Kaiser Wilhelm gave a speech to his departing troops at Bremerhaven in 1900:

> No quarter will be given, no prisoners will be taken. Let all who fall into your hands be at your mercy. Just as the Huns a thousand years ago, under the leadership of Attila,

gained a reputation in virtue of which they still live in historical tradition, so may the name of Germany become known in such a manner in China that no Chinaman will ever again dare to look askance at a German.

Even during a time of war and intense racism, Wilhelm's speech and the behavior of his men in China caught the world's attention. From then on, the Germans were often referred to as "Huns."

On the other side of the world, the Kaiser's brash and off-putting behavior and speeches caused the other great powers of Europe (with the exception of Austria-Hungary) to improve their relationships with each other and, in some cases, form official alliances.

In Morocco, in two crises separated by six years (1905 and 1911), the Kaiser attempted to drive a wedge between France and Great Britain, which had signed the Entente Cordiale in 1904. Part of this agreement between the two nations stipulated that England and France would each control one of the two remaining independent territories of Africa (excluding Liberia, a nation developed by freed American enslaved peoples, which had the support and backing of the US). These two territories were Egypt, which the British coveted, and Morocco, which the French desired.

When the French made their move on Morocco in 1905, Wilhelm visited the region and announced that he believed that Morocco was a free and sovereign nation and that he would only deal with the sultan of Morocco. This was obviously hypocritical given Germany's own colonies, but Wilhelm hoped that the French would be dissuaded in Morocco and perhaps seek territory elsewhere, perhaps at the expense of England.

Wilhelm could not have been more wrong. His interference actually drove the French and English closer together. They, along with Spain, which was directly across the Strait of Gibraltar from Morocco, convened a conference to decide the fate of Morocco without the Kaiser's input. In a short time, the French and Spanish (helped by the English) divided most of Morocco between them. It did not matter if the Kaiser would only deal with the sultan now, as he was just a figurehead.

In 1911, there were several Moroccan uprisings against the sultan, who was and who was seen as a French puppet. In Fez, which was ostensibly governed directly by the sultan, a violent uprising against the ruler began. To retain control, Sultan Abd al-Hafid asked for French troops. The French used this opportunity to take control of the remaining "free" part of Morocco, which the Kaiser saw as a direct affront to him, as he had both friendly relations with the sultan and had recognized him as the legitimate ruler of the country. In response to French action, Wilhelm sent the SMS *Panther* to the Moroccan harbor of Agadir, hoping to encourage the uprising against France.

In accord with the Entente Cordiale, Britain announced its support for France, as did Russia, which had its own agreement with Paris. Germany's ally in Europe, Austria-Hungary, remained silent on the matter, and, isolated, Wilhelm was forced to back down.

This second Moroccan crisis caused a great deal of resentment in Germany, and it again drove Britain and France closer together. The two powers concluded a naval treaty shortly after the crisis, which led to a mutual defense pact that eventually included Russia. Wilhelm had isolated Germany and set the alliances of WWI in ever-hardening cement.

Chapter 4 – The Great War

Very few people were surprised when Europe found itself at war in 1914. Since the French defeat by Prussia/Germany in 1871, international events seemed to be inexorably headed in that direction. The French wanted revenge. The large nations of Europe and a couple of smaller ones competed for an empire around the world. The economies of Great Britain, France, and Germany (and, to a lesser degree, Russia and Italy) were growing almost exponentially as the first years of the 20th century went by, causing another type of competition. There was an arms race at sea between England and Germany, and on land, the powers were developing new and more deadly weapons to equip their growing armies.

In southeastern Europe, the decline of the Ottoman Empire meant that the peoples of the Balkans, most of them under Turkish control for centuries, were both asserting their independence and struggling for influence and/or territory in the area themselves. In addition to the smaller territories of the region, Austria-Hungary sought to expand its power and control. Since it was an essentially land-locked empire, it was shut out of the race for overseas territories that consumed the British, French, Russians,

Italians, and Belgians (who controlled the giant territory of the Congo in southern-central Africa).

Illustration 12: The alliances of Europe, 1914–1915

The rule of the Ottomans had, for the most part, kept a lid on the ethnic and religious hatred that existed in the Balkans for centuries. For much of their rule (from the 16th century onward), their iron-fisted control and power kept the peoples of the Balkan Peninsula from going at each other's throats. There was also the matter of those people hating the Turks and their religion more than they hated each other.

From 1912 to 1913, the Serbs, Bulgarians, and Greeks attacked the weakened Turkish imperial forces in the Balkans and pushed them out of almost all of Europe, except for a small part of Greece and some Greek islands off the Turkish coast (the Turks' empire would be further reduced when it fell apart at the end of the First World War). This was the First Balkan War.

With the Turks out of the way, for the most part, these three countries then turned on each other in the short Second Balkan War, which lasted through much of 1913. In this war, the Bulgarians attacked the Serbs and Greeks, attempting to carve out a small empire of their own. It did not work, and the Serbs and Greeks pushed the Bulgarians back into their own country before the Bulgars sued for peace.

What concerns us here is that at the end of the Second Balkan War, the Kingdom of Serbia doubled in size. The area annexed by the Serbs was populated by a Serb majority, but with the growth of their nation and their armed forces, the Serbs (ruled by King Peter I and the military) were eager to expand their territory into areas populated by a Serb majority or sizable minority. These were the territories of Montenegro and Bosnia-Herzegovina.

The problem was that neither of these territories wanted to be part of Serbia. They knew from the rhetoric coming from Belgrade (the Serbs' capital) that life under Serbian rule was likely not going to be much or any better than what they had experienced under the Ottomans.

Enter the other major player in the region: the Austro-Hungarian Empire. The Austro-Hungarians were essentially locked out of the "second age of imperialism" that occurred in the 19th and early 20th centuries. Though they were not a completely land-locked power, the Austro-Hungarian Imperial Navy was not a force able to sustain and defend overseas colonies, so they looked with keen eyes at the power vacuum in the Balkans in the hope of gaining the prestige and resources that came with adding territory.

Nothing about the Balkans is simple, and its history would have you reading and rereading the same page over and over in order to keep track of the who, what, and where of the diplomatic and military wrangling that took place in the late 19th and early 20th centuries. In 1878, at the end of yet another war between the Russians and Turks, the great powers of Europe met in Berlin to hammer out a new European settlement. For Turkey, this meant, among other things, that it would have to give up Bosnia-Herzegovina to Austria-Hungary in all but name. The Austro-Hungarians were given the right to administer and occupy the area for thirty years (no one at the peace table believed that they would leave at the end of this period).

In 1908, there was an uprising within the Ottoman government, which further weakened the empire. Concerned that this ultra-nationalist movement (known as the Young Turks) might attempt to reestablish the Ottoman Empire in Europe, the Austrian emperor ordered his army to annex Bosnia-Herzegovina directly. With that, the Austro-Hungarian Empire and the Serbians were on a collision course.

All the powers of Europe were concerned with the situation in the Balkans, but none believed that the problems there would lead to anything more than a regional war, if that. The two outside powers most concerned with the situation were Russia and Germany.

Traditionally, the Russians played the role of "big brother" to the Serbs. Both kingdoms were Eastern Orthodox. The vast majority of people within each country were Slavic. The Serbs used the Cyrillic alphabet, as did the Russians. Each nation had a unique outlook on the world but shared more of it with each other than anyone else. Russia could be expected to respond, in some way, to any direct threat to the Kingdom of Serbia. The Serbs knew this and counted on it.

For their part, the Austro-Hungarians were partners with Germany. The ruling Habsburg family were ethnically German, and the history of Germany and the German states was often intertwined with that of Austria and its rulers. However, unlike the relationship between Serbia and Russia, the Austrians and the Germans (and, before them, the Prussians) had warred with each other—more than once, in fact. Still, at a time when the Austrians were facing challenges from Italy, which coveted the eastern coast of the Adriatic Sea, and Serbia (which could and did mean Russia), the closest thing they had to a friend was Kaiser Wilhelm.

The relationship between Austrian Emperor Franz Joseph I and Kaiser Wilhelm II was not as close. Franz Joseph was many years older than Wilhelm, who was the same age as Franz Joseph's eldest son, Rudolf (who was highly popular and who, along with his beloved mistress Mary von Vetsera, committed suicide in 1889). The Austrian emperor (like almost everyone else) thought Wilhelm was unstable, brash, and a braggart, but Germany was the only nation, for reasons of both kinship and location, that Austria-Hungary could really turn to in a crisis, and Wilhelm knew it.

This was the situation in central and southeastern Europe in June 1914 when the Austrian heir to the throne, Franz Ferdinand (Rudolf's cousin and the unloved nephew of the emperor), visited Sarajevo, the capital of Bosnia-Herzegovina to tour and inspect the situation in the province of what would someday be his empire. It was also quite clear to everyone, especially the Serbs, that that archduke's visit was a show of strength and intent aimed directly at the Kingdom of Serbia as a warning not to meddle in the region.

It was already too late for that. Bosnia-Herzegovina was (and is still to a degree) populated by a variety of different ethnic groups. The three most populous were (in no particular order) the Serbs, Croats, and Bosnian Muslims. The Croatians were predominantly Catholic and traditionally looked to western and central Europe for aid, culture, and much else. Genetically, the Bosnian Muslims could've been Serbian, Croatian, or a variety of the different groups living in the area, which also included Albanians, Macedonians, and Slovenes, but during the centuries-long Ottoman occupation, they had converted to Islam. By 1914, the hatred between the groups in the area was based on religion, but by the 20th century, the Muslim Bosnians (or Bosniaks) were essentially a completely different ethnic and cultural group.

Though King Peter I of Serbia and those around him wanted to expand Serbia even at the expense of Bosnia-Herzegovina (and, therefore, Austria-Hungary), they knew that they were in no position militarily to challenge the Austrians, who were still considered a world power.

The Austrians themselves were quite aware of their real position in the world—they were a declining power. Within the Austro-Hungarian Empire, dozens of ethnicities and cultures, from large to local, vied for power, rights, and influence. Over the past forty years or so since the defeat of 1866 at the hands of the Prussians, the Hapsburg dynasty had taken a variety of steps to restore some life into what many around the world saw as a dying empire. The most obvious was the power-sharing agreement with the Hungarians and its ruling aristocracy. There were other attempts to control the situation, from granting more privileges and rights to the different minorities in the country to clamping down on them at times. By 1914, both the Habsburgs and the Hungarians were hoping that a war with the increasingly hostile Serbs would bring the country together, at least for a time.

So, on one side, the Austro-Hungarians were hoping to find an excuse to attack and absorb Serbia, and on the other hand, there were the Serbs, who were themselves eager to expand their influence, if not their borders.

The Austrians knew that unless they had a very good reason to war on Serbia, the world would condemn them as the large empire picking on their "poor, small neighbor." Thus, Emperor Franz Joseph and his hardline chief of staff, General Count Franz Conrad von Hötzendorf, could not be sure they would have the backing of their one and only ally, Germany. However, given a serious Serbian provocation, Germany might make such an exception.

Within Serbia, King Peter I and most of his generals were for expanding Serbia's boundaries but not in a military confrontation with Austria. They knew that if they went to war with Austria-Hungary, they would be defeated quickly. They hoped that a situation might appear in the future (such as serious ethnic strife or the division or fall of the Austrian Empire) of which they could take advantage through political/diplomatic means or intrigue.

Unfortunately, for the Serbs, within its army and its population (especially among the Serb minority population in Bosnia-Herzegovina) was a large and influential group of Serbian ultra-nationalists who were determined to annex Bosnia to Serbia in some way. To do this, they planned and carried out small guerrilla-style attacks and intimidation within Bosnia, but they were mostly just an annoyance to authorities.

However, this group, called "Unification or Death" (*Уједињење или смрт / Ujedinjenje ili smrt* in Serbo-Croatian), more popularly known by its more sinister name of the Black Hand, decided on a more radical course when it was announced that Austrian Crown Prince Archduke Franz Ferdinand would be visiting Bosnia with his pregnant wife, Sophie, in late June 1914.

The commander of the Black Hand, a Serbian colonel named Dragutin Dimitrijević, an intelligence officer in the Serbian Army who had organized an assassination and overthrow of the Serbian government in 1903, decided to take a radical step. He recruited a group of Bosnian Serbs to carry out an assassination attempt of the Austrian crown prince.

As you may know, Archduke Ferdinand and his wife were driving through Sarajevo in an open car when one of the members of the Black Hand, nineteen-year-old Gavrilo Princip, leaped on the running board of the archduke's car and emptied his pistol into the royal couple, who both died, including the unborn child Sophie was carrying. Princip was soon arrested and beaten, and he confessed. He was kept in jail throughout the war, dying of malnutrition and sickness in April 1918.

With the murder of Franz Ferdinand, Austria-Hungary had its excuse for a war, which is quite ironic since Franz Ferdinand was not a popular figure in the higher echelons of the Austrian royal family and government. He had called for more minority rights and autonomy, and he would have likely been much more open to talks with Serbia than anyone else in the ruling dynasty.

Despite his unpopularity in the ruling circles of the Austro-Hungarian leadership, Franz Ferdinand and his wife were given the elaborate send-off their positions required. Once the mourning was over, everyone expected the Austrians to make demands on Serbia.

It actually took until July 23rd for the Austrian terms to be delivered to Belgrade. The end product, a document that listed a number of things the Austrians required of the Serbian government, was actually an ultimatum. In other words, Serbia had to do all of those things or else face Austria-Hungary in a war. There were ten demands on the list, and in actuality, the Serbs were willing to comply with a couple of them. However, complying with the others would mean that Serbia would cease to be an independent state. For instance, the Austrians essentially demanded full power *within* Serbia to investigate the assassination themselves and to choose which officers and administrators would be removed from the Serbian government and army.

While waiting for the ultimatum to arrive, the Serbs consulted Russia, which replied that in the case of Austria-Hungary mobilization, the Russians would mobilize as well. With the Russian announcement, France declared that it would abide by its treaty obligations with Tsar Nicholas II and mobilize its army. On the night of July 23rd, the British offered to mediate the crisis, but in reality, their offer was both too late and was never going to be accepted anyway, for the Austrians knew the Serbians could not agree to all their demands.

Before they issued their ultimatum, though, the Austro-Hungarians had made sure they would not be headed into a crisis alone. They began talks with Kaiser Wilhelm II during the week of July 1st. The Austrians essentially knew that German support was there in case of war, but when they asked the Kaiser for his support, they used the word "punish" in reference to Serbia without explicitly saying that this punishment meant war. It did not matter. Without consulting his chancellor or his generals, the Kaiser issued what is known to history as the "blank check." Wilhelm promised to support Austria in whatever course they took, and he definitely knew that could include war, though when the Austrian invasion of Serbia did take place, it is said to have taken Wilhelm by surprise. By that time, the Serbians had issued a reply to the Austrian ultimatum in which they apologized profusely for the assassination of Franz Ferdinand (the Serbian king and those around him truly did not know what Colonel Dimitrijević had planned) while at the same time rejecting Austria's terms and offering counter-terms.

This was not the first time that Wilhelm had made a rash judgment and been surprised when the outcome didn't go his way, and it wouldn't be the last. However, he had a treaty with Austria that he could not (and would not) abrogate. He also knew that if Austria attacked Serbia, Russia would attack Austria, and a powerful Russia in central Europe was the last thing the Germans wanted. Wilhelm was also keenly aware that German public opinion was overwhelmingly pro-Austrian, and for a number of years, the German government, which was authoritarian and constructed decidedly in favor of the wealthy, especially the wealthy landowners of Prussia, had been facing calls for reform. The Kaiser hoped that this foreign policy crisis and perhaps war would unite the country behind him and the ruling elite once again.

On July 28th, after rejecting Serbia's reply, Austria-Hungary declared war on the small Balkan country. No one believed that the Serbians could hold out long against the Austrians, and Russia was not about to allow a great Austrian presence on its borders and be in control of one of its closest allies and friends. On July 30th, Russian troops on the Austrian border went on full alert. Between July 28th and August 1st, Britain, France, and Germany all tried to prevail upon Austria and Serbia to stand down to no effect, and on

August 1ˢᵗ, the French announced the mobilization of their powerful army.

On the same day, Germany announced the mobilization of its army and declared war, in succession, on Russia, France, and Belgium, which, though aligned with France to a large degree, was a neutral nation, but as the world was about to find out, it was key to German planning.

Great Britain, in keeping with its treaty obligations with France and Russia and in keeping with its desire to maintain a balance of power in Europe, declared war on Germany on August 1ˢᵗ, 1914. Five days later, the Austrians declared war on Russia. With that, most of Europe was at war.

German planning and execution

The German war plans called for the rapid mobilization of both its army and navy. Knowing that the more modern French Army would mobilize more rapidly than the antiquated Russian Army, which had to concentrate its armies from great distances with few railroads, Germany planned to deploy the bulk of its forces in the west, hoping to launch a knockout blow against the French before the Russians could mount an offensive in the east and before Great Britain could get the bulk of its army to the Continent. With the French and British out of the war, the Germans could then move its western armies east to aid the Austrians against the slow-moving Russians.

As you will see on the following page, the German plan was based on early 20ᵗʰ-century plans developed by Field Marshal Alfred *VON* Schlieffen, and it has since become known as the Schlieffen Plan. The Germans hoped to replicate their quick victory of 1870/71 over the French, and the Schlieffen Plan essentially captured the same idea that had been used some forty years before but with the addition of attacking through neutral Belgium in the hope of surprising the French and British, who they felt would be attacking eastward along the Franco-German border.

As they did, the Germans would be wheeling around behind them to cut them off from their homeland, supplies, and base of operations. The war would be over quickly—or so the Germans thought.

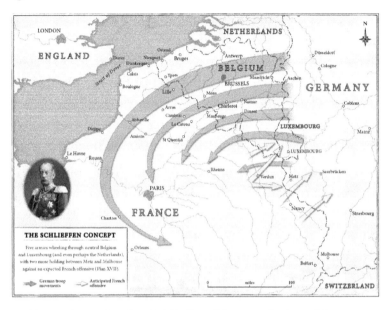

Illustration 13: The Schlieffen Plan, as designed between 1905 and 1914.

There are a number of axioms that seem to always accurately pertain to warfare. Two of them are: 1) the militaries of the world prepare to fight the next war in the same way the last one ended, and 2) "no plan survives contact with the enemy" (or as Mike Tyson put it more recently, "Everyone's gotta plan until they get punched in the mouth.") Both of these pertained not only to Germany but also to all the combatants to one degree or another.

The Germans were able to mobilize two million men in three weeks. These men were organized into eight armies. Seven of these were sent to implement the Schlieffen Plan and invade France and Belgium, the latter of which had been neutral since 1839 and whose neutrality had been recognized by Prussia and then Germany. The 8th German Army was sent eastward to guard the approaches to Berlin should the Russians mobilize more quickly than anticipated.

The Germans did ask the neutral Belgians for the right to pass through their country on their way to France, a request the Belgians rejected. When they did, Germany invaded the small, relatively flat country and conquered it by the end of August. French and a smaller number of British troops had advanced into Belgium to meet the German push, but by the end of the month, they, along with what was left of the Belgian Army, retreated in near-panic back to France. For a short time, it appeared as if the Germans were going to repeat their victory of 1870/71 and march into Paris,

However, as the bulk of the German Army pushed toward Paris, French resistance stiffened along the Marne River, some twenty miles from the capital. The Battle of the Marne was an indication of the fighting to come: massive and ever-increasing artillery barrages and waves of men cut down by the now mass-produced machine gun. Though the men in the front lines certainly did not know this at the time, the Marne River was as far as the Germans were going to advance into France for the rest of the war.

Illustration 14: Battle of the Marne, 1914. Dotted lines are the furthest German advance. Arrows mark the French counterattack. Courtesy Britannica.com

The Germans were forced to send about sixty thousand soldiers to the Eastern Front because the Russians had been able to mobilize their troops much more rapidly than the Germans had anticipated and were moving toward the German border. The loss of these soldiers when it came to the Battle of the Marne may not have made a difference since the French resistance was incredibly stout. The Russians had moved uncharacteristically fast, and the German commander in the east, General Maximilian von Prittwitz, had made some uncharacteristic mistakes, allowing the Russians to advance farther than anyone imagined they could have.

To remedy this situation, a new commander was appointed to command the German armies in the east: General (later Field Marshal) Paul von Hindenburg. Hindenburg then named an obscure general serving as the commander of the Quartermaster Corps (the section of the army responsible for supplies) as his deputy. His name was Erich Ludendorff. These two would eventually direct the entire German war effort.

The Russians' rapid mobilization was partly due to the planning of Russian generals. Another part was that, contrary to the German Army, many of the Russian soldiers were conscripts with little if any training. And while the Russians did have large numbers of cannons, generally speaking, they were on the move without being fully equipped for battle. As was the case in some situations in the Second World War, many Russian soldiers were sent to the front with very few modern weapons or any weapons at all. Unbelievably, they were told to pick up the weapons of their fallen comrades or those of dead Germans.

Still, at the very beginning of the war, before the fighting started, the Russian Army's morale, for the most part, was high. They were going to fight for the motherland and the tsar, whom many still believed was placed on the throne by God and represented the will of God on Earth. That belief would change more rapidly than anyone could have imagined. The Russian Army moved into the frontier of East Prussia, the hub of German nationalism and the home of most of the General Staff of the German Army.

While the Russian Army did mobilize quickly, it was not able to move as fast as the German Army, and that, combined with the leadership of Hindenburg and Ludendorff, doomed them to defeat in what's known as the Battle of Tannenberg. Although the battle is named this, it actually took place over hundreds of square miles, with the Forest of Tannenberg being only one small part of it.

The area south of Königsberg (today's Kaliningrad) and north of Warsaw is dotted with lakes and forests. Using the terrain to mask their movements, the Germans were able to surround a large part of the Russian force and tear it to pieces. The Russian response to many of the German attacks was to charge, and for the first time in their experience, the Russians faced the massed power of machine guns and rapid-firing cannons.

The Russian losses have been estimated to be between 125,000 and nearly 200,000 dead and wounded, 100,000 prisoners of war, and large numbers of guns and other equipment. The Germans lost just under 15,000 dead, wounded, and missing.

The Battle of Tannenberg not only lifted Hindenburg and Ludendorff to glory but also buoyed the German population, who had expected France to be defeated or nearly defeated at this point in the war (after all, that's what had happened in the war of 1870). Kaiser Wilhelm, who had been facing calls for reform at home before the war and into its first days, decided that from that point on, military victories would justify the continued authoritarian rule of his family. He refused to allow any meaningful reform to happen for the duration of the war, a decision that would come back to haunt him in 1918.

With a couple of disastrous exceptions, the Russians stayed on the defensive for the rest of the war. The offensives that did occur, in 1915 and 1917, only allowed the Germans to drive farther into Russia and hastened the revolution that had been brewing in Russia since the turn of the century.

Illustration 15: Kaiser Wilhelm II (r) and Tsar Nicholas II of Russia (l), first cousins, wearing each other's uniforms in the years before the war.

Illustration 16: Location of Tannenberg marked with an "X." Courtesy Britannica.

As you can see from the map on the prior page, the Germans, as well as the Austro-Hungarians, drove deep into Russia, especially Ukraine. Ukraine was a prize the Germans and Austrians sought. Russia's richest agricultural area, complete with large coal deposits, could help the German and Austrian war effort immensely.

By October of 1917, the Russians had suffered nearly nine million dead, wounded, missing, and captured. Over a million of those were civilians. The Germans and Austro-Hungarians had suffered nearly five million dead and wounded.

In that same month, the strength of the Central Powers (Germany, Austria-Hungary, and Turkey, which fought some smaller-scale battles in the Caucasus) stood at nearly 1.3 million, most of those German. If Russia could be removed from the war, those one million or so men could be moved to the Western Front, where the front lines had essentially remained static since the fall of 1914.

Germany was quite aware of the state of the Russian Army from its spies in Russia, the Russian soldiers held in captivity, and the Russian political figures living in exile in Europe. The most prominent of those exiles is a name that is likely familiar to you: Vladimir Ilyich Ulyanov, better known as Lenin, the leader of the radical Bolshevik wing of the Russian Socialist Party.

As reports of various incidents (food riots in Russian cities and towns; soldiers deserting by the hundreds of thousands, sometimes killing the officers who ordered them to attack in another fruitless effort; increasing calls for the tsar to make peace with Germany, which he refused; etc.) reached Germany, the Germans came up with a brilliant plan: they would send Lenin back to Russia to start his revolution. Lenin had openly stated that he felt the war was a conflict between capitalists and aristocrats and that should he come to power, he would immediately take Russia out of the war.

In March 1917, Tsar Nicholas II was forced to abdicate. Alexander Kerensky, the leader of the moderate faction of the Socialist Revolutionary Party, became "Minister-President" of a provisional government. The removal of the tsar was popular, but Kerensky's decision to keep Russia in the war was not.

In April, the Germans allowed Lenin to cross the border from his Swiss exile into Germany. He would go to Sweden, then Finland, and cross the border into Russia to St. Petersburg, the capital of the country. To guard against the chance of Lenin being seen and of his presence stirring up German socialists, the Bolshevik leader was sent to Sweden in a sealed train. In his history of the World War One years, Winston Churchill, who played a major role in both world wars, wrote that the Germans "had turned upon Russia the most grisly of all weapons. They transported Lenin in a sealed truck like a plague bacillus from Switzerland to Russia."

Within a few months, Lenin had rallied his many followers and much of the population of St. Petersburg and staged the Bolshevik Revolution. Among his first accomplishments was taking Russia out of the war.

This was important for Germany for two main reasons. First, they could now shift nearly a million troops from the Eastern Front to the Western Front, where things were bleak, and second, they could impose peace terms on the new Russian government.

The Treaty of Brest-Litovsk, which ended the war on the Eastern Front, was harsh. Its terms called for Russia to give up one million square miles of its territory (mainly in Ukraine but also including parts of western Russia), which held nearly fifty million people. Nearly one-third of Russia's agricultural land was given up, as was a staggering 90 percent of its coal mines. Nearly all her existing oil fields were given to Germany and Austria-Hungary as well.

For his part, Lenin believed it was only a matter of time before either his forces were strong enough to force the Germans from Russia or, more likely, the Germans lost the war in the west and were forced to evacuate anyway. Lenin would prove to be correct with the latter option.

The Western Front and the Home Front in Germany

By the time of Lenin's revolution and the Russian withdrawal from the war, things were beginning to turn against Germany elsewhere. Though the front lines had not shifted much in either direction since the fall of 1914, the cost of the war, both in human and economic terms, was taking a toll on Germany.

The Germans had hoped for a rapid victory in 1914, knowing that any serious prolongation of the conflict played into Allied hands. The Allied Powers, which mainly included France, Great Britain, Russia until 1917, Italy from the spring of 1915, and soon the United States, was too much for Germany to bear alone.

In southeastern Europe, as well as in Russia, the Austro-Hungarian forces were stretched to the limit. The fighting in Russia and Serbia, as well as a grinding campaign of attrition against Italy in the Alps, meant that by 1917, Austria-Hungary was at its breaking point. The many ethnic groups of the Austro-Hungarian Empire were beginning to sense that the empire was teetering on the brink, and many began to form paramilitaries for the time when the empire was no longer strong enough to hold itself together.

The Ottoman Empire, ruled from Constantinople (now Istanbul), was also having a difficult time. The Ottomans, who had already been in decline for more than a century and a half, had fought and won (at great cost) against the British forces at Gallipoli. On top of that, they were not only fighting a losing war in the Middle East and Arabia, where the British were supplying and aiding local forces against the Turks, but were also waging a genocidal campaign against the Armenians in the Caucasus. Both the Austro-Hungarians and Turks were nearly if not completely bankrupt, and the populations of both empires were growing tired of war.

In other words, this meant that Germany was fighting two of the world's greatest powers on its own, and these two powers (Britain and France) would soon be joined by another, the United States.

In Germany itself, the situation was growing worse every day. Despite a controlled press, which essentially told the German public that victory was "just around the corner" for years, people could see and hear for themselves that the situation on the Western Front was not good. They could also feel it in their bodies, for by 1917, the British naval blockade of Germany was beginning to show real results.

The Royal Navy had established the blockade of Germany early in the war. Year by year, the number of ships in the blockade grew. In 1916, Kaiser Wilhelm urged the admirals of the *Kriegsmarine* to challenge the British Grand Fleet (the largest of Britain's many naval formations) in the North Sea and break the blockade. The result was the Battle of Jutland, which ended in a Pyrrhic victory for Germany. The Germans may have sunk more ships and killed more sailors than the British, but the *Kriegsmarine* lost a higher percentage of its total force than the British, who could sustain the losses suffered at Jutland. For the rest of the war, what was left of the German surface fleet stayed in its North Sea ports, where its sailors could see the smoke from the stacks of the British fleet on the horizon, waiting for them to come out.

The British blockade wasn't limited to the area around Germany's access to the sea in the north. All over the world, British ships intercepted, captured, and sometimes sank German merchant ships and others suspected of carrying goods to Germany or German possessions.

The Germans attempted to supply their colonies in the Pacific and Africa by using "surface raiders," armed merchant vessels often flying the colors of a neutral or Allied nation, but after a protracted campaign, virtually all of the "raiders" were captured or sunk. Germany's possessions in the Pacific were lost rather quickly to the Japanese, who had come into the war on the Allied side with the express purpose of seizing German bases in Pacific waters. The British were more than happy with this situation, as it meant they could deploy their fleet elsewhere. (The Americans, who had been anticipating a clash with Japan since the late 1890s, were not so happy.)

By 1917, the blockade and the supply requirements of the army meant that people in Germany were beginning to go hungry, and if there is one thing that rulers know (especially unpopular ones, as the Kaiser was beginning to be), it's that hunger will bring down a government faster than almost anything else.

In response to the British blockade, the Germans set up their own around Great Britain. This was carried out by the new German U-boat (for *Unterseeboot* or "Underseaboat" in English) force. Of course, U-boats were submarines.

The submarine has a much longer history than you may imagine, going all the way back to the mind of Leonardo da Vinci in the 15th and 16th centuries. It saw its first wartime application in the American Civil War, and ever since that time, the prosperous nations of the world had been experimenting with some type of underwater craft. Though most of the great powers of WWI possessed submarines, it was the Germans who made the greatest and most deadly use of them.

Wilhelm's attempt to produce more surface ships was a pipe dream and probably would not have succeeded even in peacetime, but at that time, submarines were relatively easy to build, and what's more, in the First World War, they were virtually undetectable while submerged. To counter the British blockade and hopefully cause some of the ships blockading German ports to redeploy, the Germans mounted a counter-blockade of Great Britain using their U-boat force.

Today, we might chuckle at the naivete of the combatants of WWI in regard to U-boat warfare, but in 1916, submarine warfare was new—the rules "governing" "civilized" behavior at sea were not. The last international conference to meet and revise the rules of naval warfare had taken place in 1856, which was before Germany was even a united nation and before submarines were a practical reality. Those rules required that any vessel attempting to "run" a blockade could not be attacked until it had been stopped or warned by a "shot across the bow" and after an inspection of its cargo and provisions arranged for its crew (whether that was a rescue in lifeboats or being taken aboard the attacking ship).

As you are likely aware by now, there was no way a submarine could abide by those rules and survive. Any ship, merchant or otherwise, armed with a heavy machine gun, not to mention a light naval cannon, could pierce the hull of these early wartime submarines. After some experience in submarine warfare, the British and others found the only reliable defense against submarines to be the "convoy system," in which large numbers of merchantmen would be escorted by naval vessels. Since the U-boats depended on stealth, a formal warning to the crew and an inspection was out, as was taking any survivors aboard. At times, U-boats did radio neutral nations as to the positions of sunken ships (the idea being that these neutral nations would forward them to the British or whomever), but that rarely happened.

Lastly, it must be remembered that the U-boats of WWI had a submerged speed of only about eight knots (nine miles per hour), depending on conditions, and could only stay submerged for about five hours before they had to surface to both charge their batteries and replenish their oxygen supply. For the most part, U-boats, with their very low profile and grayish-black color, would approach convoys or lone merchantmen on the surface, preferably at night, dusk, or dawn, taking full advantage of their construction. Most times, torpedo attacks would be launched from the surface rather than from below the water for greater accuracy. Traveling underwater, while perfect for evasion in survival situations, was really a last resort, which was exactly why the Germans announced they would not abide by the 1856 naval treaty terms, claiming they were outdated and unfair.

Of course, the Allies argued the opposite, exclaiming that submarine warfare was cruel and illegal and making the U-boat crews out to be the worst kind of criminals.

For the first two years of the war, the Germans had attempted to wage "restricted submarine warfare." This meant that they would attempt to avoid attacks on the shipping of neutral nations, especially American shipping. "Accidents" happened, however, most notably the sinking of the British liner *Lusitania* off the coast of Ireland in April 1915, which took nearly 1,200 lives (128 of them American). The Germans argued that they had warned everyone not to board ships bound for the British Isles, which they did. The Americans exclaimed that as neutrals, they had the right to go anywhere. The British accused Germany of sinking a passenger liner that was not carrying war materiel, which was definitely not true, though British propaganda was effective in causing people to believe their message. Not wanting the Americans to enter the war on the side of the Allies (and, in 1915, it was not a foregone conclusion they would), the Germans "apologized" and announced their commitment to restricted submarine warfare.

However, by 1917, with the land war at a standstill and the British blockade taking a toll, the Germans announced unrestricted submarine warfare on all vessels entering British waters. They hoped that by the time the United States entered the war on the side of the Allies, the U-boats would have forced the British, at the very least, to the peace table.

The Germans' U-boat warfare enraged the world, and it was a factor in the United States' entry into the war, though it was not the direct cause, which we will discuss in a moment.

Illustration 17: This British poster (all of Ireland was then a British possession) depicts the sinking of the Lusitania. *At the time, the images were considered "shocking."*

Illustration 18: "Boats out!" German propaganda illustrating the effectiveness and vitality of the U-boat force.

By the beginning of 1917, the war on the Western Front had been in a stalemate for nearly three years. After the Battle of the Marne, both sides began the famous Race to the Sea, which were attempts to outmaneuver each other by outflanking the other's forces by moving northward toward the English Channel. Soon, however, the combat in France and a very small piece of unoccupied Belgium bogged down into the infamous "trench warfare" for which WWI is known.

Until almost the very end of the war, outdated tactics were used to overcome the newest wartime technology, which included machine guns, rapid-firing artillery, and poison gas. The result was a bloodbath that was only imagined by a few forward-thinking people before the war started. For everyone else, WWI shocked them psychologically, emotionally, and physically.

Toward the end of the war, the invention of the tank threatened to change the way the war was fought, but old thinking and poor reliability made the tank more of a weapon of the future than of 1917 and 1918 when it was deployed on the battlefield for the first time. Even then, military men were not sure of its potential.

They were, however, aware of the potential of the airplane, which had been invented just years before the outbreak of the war. Aerial warfare first involved the use of planes (along with hot-air and hydrogen balloons and dirigibles) for reconnaissance, but soon, it evolved into reconnaissance pilots shooting at each other with pistols and dropping grenades or small bombs on the cannons or rifles shooting at them from the ground. The airplane evolved quickly. Machine guns were attached to the rear of two-seater planes; later, forward-firing machine guns were made possible by the invention of the interrupter gear, which made it possible to shoot through propeller blades. Then heavier and heavier bombers were developed to attack munitions depots, troop transports, and, eventually, population centers (though most of this was done very late in the war and mostly by dirigibles or the German Zeppelins).

The most well-known of all the warriors of WWI were the fighter pilots, who seemed to embody the spirit of another age. All sides called them the "Knights of the Air," and the single combat they engaged each other in was reminiscent of a simpler and less brutal time. The most famous of them all was the German ace Manfred von Richthofen, also known as the "Red Baron," who had eighty-one kills. After the Red Baron's death in April 1918, a skilled but arrogant flyer named Hermann Göring, who would rise to command the German Air Force in WWII, took over the Baron's command of the famous "Flying Circus" squadron.

Illustration 19: Colorized portrait of von Richthofen wearing his "Blue Max," the Pour le Mérite, *instituted by the French-speaking king of Prussia, Frederick the Great.*

On April 6th, 1917, US President Woodrow Wilson signed the declaration of war against Germany (and later Austria-Hungary, although not one against the Ottoman Empire, the third of the Central Powers). Wilson had resisted many calls to engage in the war before that time. Though the sinking of the *Lusitania* and other incidents on the high seas were the most emotionally charged reasons for the Americans declaring war, the immediate reason was another German miscalculation and error: the Zimmermann Telegram.

Simply put, in January 1917, German Foreign Secretary Arthur Zimmermann cabled his ambassador in Mexico and told him to propose to the Mexican government that Mexico declare war on the United States. In return, Germany would support Mexico's war effort and ensure that the Mexicans received their former territories of Texas, New Mexico, and Arizona, which they had lost to the United States in the Mexican-American War.

At the time, this was taken as a very serious threat, as the United States and Mexico had essentially been at war with each other immediately before and during the first part of WWI. US forces had been in Mexico chasing Mexican guerrillas and bandits who had been raiding across the border for some time, both for riches and to finance their struggle against the Mexican government, which was no longer friendly with the US. When WWI broke out, the standing Mexican Army was larger than that of the United States.

Not only had Germany sunk American ships and killed American citizens on the high seas and interfered with American commerce, now they were threatening America's borders directly. The Zimmermann Telegram, which was intercepted by British intelligence and decoded, was the last straw. The US declared war, and Germany's fate was sealed. (Foreign Minister Zimmermann himself confirmed the contents of the telegram publicly, which was yet another German error.)

It would take months for the US to get itself on a war footing. In actuality, it took about a year before enough American troops were in Europe to make their presence felt. With the Russians dropping out of the war in late 1917 and the time it would take for the Americans to build, train, equip, and transport an adequate force to Europe, Germany realized it had a very short window to achieve a victorious change in the war.

German Politics

Before we delve into the last German offensive of the war, let's take a moment to discuss what was happening within Germany and its political life in the latter part of the war.

By 1917, especially after the American entry into the war, many of Germany's elite knew the war was lost. The stalemate on the Western Front showed no signs of changing, and the British and French, while sustaining great casualties like the Germans, were able to build more and more munitions as time went by. In contrast, German funds were running out, while the British and French were being subsidized and supplied by the United States. The numerical superiority of the Allies (especially when one considers Italy and both Britain and France's colonial troops, of which there were over a million) combined with the dwindling manpower of Germans painted a bleak picture for Germany. Even after Germany failed to take Paris in 1914, the Kaiser's own son and heir, Crown Prince Wilhelm, had admitted that Germany could not win the war.

Within Germany, people were getting mixed messages. Troops coming home on leave and those in the hospital told tales of horror, supply shortages, and ever-increasing numbers of Allied troops. During the course of the war on the Western Front, a German unit might find itself fighting English, Irish, Scottish, Welsh, French, Canadians, Australians, New Zealanders, Algerians, Congolese, Belgians, Moroccans, and others. This happened to many units, and the Germans began to feel they were fighting against the whole world and growing more weary of it every day.

Both sides felt the uselessness of the attack or "going over the top," which was what cresting the top of the trench was referred to back then. In the Battle of the Somme, British troops lost 30,000 men in *one day*. During the Battle of Verdun, which German generals had hoped would suck in more and more French troops and eventually break the morale of France, cost the Germans nearly 400,000 killed and wounded, with a relatively equal number of Frenchmen. And, in the end, French morale held. By 1917/1918, many within Germany were wishing for an end.

However, the problem was this, and it was felt to some degree by both liberals and conservatives alike: the war couldn't simply end. Too many had sacrificed for that to happen so easily. Germany had to get something for its efforts, whether it be land, reparations, or colonies.

The problem was that no one within Germany could picture the Allies making peace in which Germany gained something. After all, those countries had also sacrificed too. The only alternative, it seemed (and it was met with either resignation or zeal, depending on where you were on the political spectrum), was one last push for all-out victory, which had to take place before the arrival of significant numbers of fresh American troops and their tons of equipment.

1918 Offensive

In the spring of 1918, Germany launched a powerful offensive dubbed the Ludendorff Offensive for the man who had planned it. Both Ludendorff and Hindenburg, who was now in command of Germany's entire effort in the west, believed the casualties for the offensive would reach over half a million men, but they thought that the strength of the drive and its theoretical gains would force the Allies to the negotiating table and give Germany favorable peace terms.

The spearhead of the offensive was a unit dubbed *Sturmtruppen* or "Stormtroopers," and they had been trained in new ways of attacking and exploiting the opponents' trenches. In truth, not only the Germans but also their allies, the Austro-Hungarians, as well as the Allied Powers, had all trained these types of units, but it was the Germans who used them in the greatest quantity and most effectively in the first days of the Spring Offensive of 1918.

As opposed to most of the other major offensives of the war, Ludendorff ordered a short, intense artillery barrage, behind which the Stormtroopers would follow closely. This was not a new tactic, but it proved most effective. Allied troops, who were in a daze from the short barrage (as opposed to the long hours or days-long barrages that would previously have signaled an attack), would emerge from their dugouts to find specially trained, equipped, and highly motivated German troops inside their lines.

Carrying shotguns, small machine guns, dozens of grenades, and carrying hand-to-hand weapons that looked like they came from the Dark Ages, the Stormtroopers would create a breakthrough in the Allied trenches, allowing the rest of their comrades to rush through, then file in behind the Allied lines to the left and right. This went on through the many lines of trenches until the Germans almost reached open country. In many ways, it was the infantry precursor of the blitzkrieg tank attacks that would take place in WWII (in fact, many commanders of the blitzkrieg attacks were WWI combat veterans).

Unfortunately for the Germans, several things happened. One of their aims was to capture Allied supplies, for, after a number of weeks, the Germans' supplies had run out. Another problem that is not spoken of frequently but which you will find in the specialized literature on the subject (two of which are listed in the bibliography) is that many of the first line Stormtroopers were captured after having broken through and raiding French field kitchens and food supplies. In many cases, the French returned to find dozens of drunk and sick German soldiers, who, after being deprived by shortages on their side of the lines, stuffed and drank themselves into a stupor.

Still, the drive was serious, and for a time, it worried the Allied command, but three things happened to the Allies' advantage. French and British resistance stiffened, the Germans exhausted both themselves and their supplies, and the Americans began arriving on the battlefield in consequential numbers.

For the Germans, the arrival of considerable numbers of Americans meant the end was near. Both Hindenburg and Ludendorff, as well as most of their fellow generals, knew the war was over. At first, the Americans made blunder after blunder on the battlefield, fighting as green troops, but they learned quickly, both from their own experience and from the British and French, who were on both sides of the American front lines. More importantly were the over two million Americans waiting on piers and in training grounds in the United States waiting to go "Over There," as the popular American fight song went. Even more significant than the millions of American troops were the seemingly endless supply of ammunition and other supplies that the Americans brought with them and financed for the British and French.

In the early fall of 1918, the British and French, their spirits somewhat renewed by both the holding of the German offensive and the arrival of the Americans, began new offensives all along the Western Front. By late September, Hindenburg and Ludendorff knew it was only a matter of time before complete German collapse. On September 29th, they approached Kaiser Wilhelm II at his retreat near Spa in western Germany and urged him to approach the Allies for an armistice while German troops were still in possession of French and Belgian territories.

That armistice took place on November 11th, 1918.

Chapter 5 – The Treaty of Versailles

There is perhaps no more infamous peace treaty than that of the Treaty of Versailles, which officially ended World War One. While in 1918, the Allied Powers and their citizens cheered the armistice and the treaty that ended the war, within just a few years, many in Britain, France, and the US were beginning to wonder if the Treaty of Versailles had been too hard on the Germans. By the early to mid-1920s, a variety of political groups had risen in Germany, whose main platform was the rejection of the Versailles Treaty and its "onerous" terms. Obviously, the most well-known of these was the National Socialist German Workers' Party (also known as the *Nationalsozialistische Deutsche Arbeiterpartei*, the NSDAP, or the Nazi Party, named from the German pronunciation of the first two words), but many parties and organizations, both large and small, nationwide and local, were vocal opponents of the treaty. During the 1920s, it seemed as if the hatred of the Treaty of Versailles was the one thing that most Germans could agree on.

So, was the Treaty of Versailles "unfair" to Germany? The answer is both yes and no, but before the treaty (which was really several separate agreements bundled together) was even inked, there had to be an armistice. The ceasefire that effectively ended WWI was where the problems began.

In the last months of the war, the Social Democratic Party (SPD), the largest in Germany, had been gaining both strength and influence. Though their platform was multi-faceted, by September 1918, it consisted of one thing: ending the war.

Throughout most of the war, the SPD was divided against itself. A large percentage of its members were completely against the war, seeing it as another war of the ruling classes of one nation or kingdom against another with the "little man" used as cannon fodder. There was a conservative wing of the party that did support the war wholeheartedly, but they were a distinct minority. Most of its members supported the war effort as "good Germans," but as the conflict wore on and victory seemed to elude the German Army, more and more members of the SPD wanted to find a way out.

When peace was discussed in September 1918, it was decided that any peace overture had to come from the leading politicians of the SPD. Members of the military were reluctant for a number of reasons, including the notion that the Allies would be less willing to accept a peace overture coming from the military. Another issue would also rear its ugly head, for while it was the military that urged approaching the Allies, it was the SPD and the politicians who actually made the overture. In the coming months and years, many who had been or were in the German Army (including, hypocritically, Erich Ludendorff) accused the politicians of "selling out" the German soldier. To these men, the politicians had basically stabbed them in the back when victory was around the corner.

But a victory was not around the corner, even though the highly censored German newspapers kept saying so, as did the generals to their troops. They kept mentioning the fact that German soldiers continued to occupy foreign soil while Germany itself stood inviolate. They promoted the idea that the Germans were winning the war, but as you can see from the previous chapter, this was not the case.

The truth was that supplies were running low, the Americans were fully in the war, the Allies were about to crack the German front lines, and, in October 1918, leftist revolutions broke out in Germany, most significantly among sailors at the naval base at Kiel. Germany could not, and most Germans would not, go on. That was the reality.

On the eleventh hour of the eleventh day of the eleventh month, the ceasefire took place, and for all intents and purposes, World War One was over. The Kaiser abdicated on November 9th and went into exile in Holland, where he lived in relative luxury while his country suffered the consequences of a lost war, which was, in part, brought about by his decision to support Austria. He died in 1940, relatively forgotten, during the first years of WWII.

Within a few months, German soldiers, sometimes with orders, sometimes without, began to filter home. Some of them were sent to areas within Germany to help put down the communist uprisings taking place in some of the cities. Many just went home to a country in economic and political shambles.

The Paris Peace Conference and the Treaty of Versailles

One of the largest issues facing the Allies when the Paris Peace Conference began was who was to blame for starting the war. In reality, the Serbian Black Hand movement started it, but since the king of Serbia had repudiated the actions of the Black Hand and since Serbia was an Allied nation, that left the rest of the Central Powers to shoulder the blame for the carnage of World War One.

Unfortunately, for the Germans, they were the "last man standing," as it were. The Austro-Hungarian Empire had come apart at the seams in the last months of the war, and as the Paris

Peace Conference met to not only make peace but also to establish borders in the new post-war Europe, the many ethnic groups of the former Habsburg Empire were either sitting down at the negotiating table themselves or were on the battlefield attempting to form their own nations out of what had been one of the largest empires in Europe.

Almost the same situation existed in the now-former Ottoman Empire. Throughout the war, the British (and, to some degree, the French) had worked to rally the people of the Middle East against their Ottoman masters centered in Turkey. The most famous example of this is the exploits of Lawrence of Arabia in today's Saudi Arabia, but there were similar examples in other Ottoman lands. When the war ended, there was no longer an Ottoman Empire, and it took years for the major powers, which had begun to realize the potential of Middle Eastern oil fields, to draw the lines on the map that we know today, with one exception: Israel. The Turks formed a new country, but it took a nearly genocidal war with the Greeks, which lasted from 1920 to 1922, in order to establish their borders permanently.

That left Germany. Germany had not been invaded. Its borders were intact, as were its factories, coal fields, and farms, which were some of the richest in the world. Add to that the important point that the Kaiser had issued the infamous "blank check" to Austria-Hungary in support of their war against Serbia. Without that, there likely would not have been a war, at least not a global one. Finally, the Germans had inflicted the most damage of any of the Central Powers. Millions were dead, and industries had been picked apart or destroyed in the areas that had been under German control. What's more, Germany had invaded France twice in fifty years. Germany would pay, at least as far as the Allies were concerned.

Politicians and citizens in Germany expected something different. They were willing to accept the idea that their nation might have to pay some reparations, and most were willing to give up Alsace-Lorraine or at least part of it. They were completely deluded. What's more, some of the more conservative members of German society believed that Germany should be allowed to retain the lands it had won from Russia in the Treaty of Brest-Litovsk (a treaty, it should be remembered, that was severe in comparison to what eventually became the Treaty of Versailles).

The way the German delegation was treated during the peace conference should have given some clue as to what the nature of the final peace treaty would be like. When German diplomats attempted to insert themselves into conversations and negotiations, they were shut out almost completely unless it was to answer a question or provide data.

What about the Allies? Simply put, the French wanted revenge and were prepared to resume the war if they didn't get what they wanted, which was an amazingly large amount of money, Alsace-Lorraine, and control over the coal-producing regions of western Germany for a specified period as a guarantee of at least some payment.

The Americans also believed that the Germans should pay reparations for the war, although it was a far lesser number than the French. They believed that Alsace-Lorraine should be French and that the German Army should be limited in size for at least the near future, with which both the French and British agreed.

The British fell somewhere in between the American and French positions, and in the end, they leaned more toward France than America, a position that many in the United Kingdom would come to see as a mistake in the coming years.

It should be noted that when the German politicians approached the Allies, they approached the Americans, believing that they would receive more lenient terms from a nation that had just entered the war and had not suffered the great casualties that the British and French had. They were also mindful of the rhetoric coming from US President Woodrow Wilson, whose speeches contained frequent references to making WWI "the war to end all wars" and constructing a plan for world peace—forever.

When Wilson arrived in France, he was a superstar. Literally millions of people came out to see him. His country had come to the Allies' aid in their time of need, financed the war, and now apparently had a plan to make wars a thing of the past. This last item proved to be the sticking point for Wilson, for to get what eventually became his Fourteen Points passed and to end the conflict in Europe and war forever, he was willing to give France and Britain almost exactly what they wanted.

For about six months, the eyes of the world were on Paris. In May, a finished draft was handed to the Germans for their comments. To say that the Germans, both within and outside the government, were shocked would be putting it mildly. This was made worse by the fact that the Germans' lengthy reply, which was delivered in June, was rejected almost completely. Essentially, the Germans were faced with two choices: sign or the war begins anew.

Though some on the German right exclaimed they were willing to fight to the death rather than see their government sign the treaty, that was both hot air and an impossibility. By the summer of 1919, the German Army no longer existed, at least not in any form that could resist an Allied invasion in any way. Aside from that, there was still revolution in the streets of major cities, hunger, unemployment, and inflation. Germany was spent, and the Allies knew it.

During this period, the dangerous stab-in-the-back myth (*Dolchstoß* in German) began. Like most lies, it began with a kernel of truth. On November 11th, 1918, when, for all intents and purposes, the war ended, no Allied force stood on German soil. Quite the contrary—German troops were still in possession of large parts of northern France and most of Belgium, although they were rapidly being driven back when the ceasefire took place. The

German Army didn't lose the war; rather, it was the politicians who lost it.

As you will recall, it was Generals Hindenburg and Ludendorff, among and others, who approached Kaiser Wilhelm II and recommended that he pursue peace. Now, it seemed, they knew nothing about that. According to them, it had been pressure from the Social Democrats who forced the end of the war (in time, the Jewish heads of some of Germany's banks were seen as the culprits as well). On top of that, the mismanagement of the war economy by the politicians caused a lack of supply. However, it was the German Army and the Kaiser's office that were essentially in command of the war economy from the start, meaning they were the ones that had managed it poorly.

Still, except for the most deluded, most Germans knew they had no choice. They had to sign the treaty. What's worse, the sum of reparations had not even been finalized when the treaty was presented. An unreal figure of 632 billion marks had been announced previously (this would equate to about two trillion in US dollars today), but eventually, that huge sum was whittled down to a still staggering (especially for the time and for an economy in shambles) 132 billion marks (approximately 400 billion US dollars today).

Among the major points of the Treaty of Versailles as they pertained to Germany were the aforementioned reparations, the return of Alsace-Lorraine to France, the demilitarization of the left bank of the Rhine River (meaning no German troops in the area bordering France), giving France the total production of the Saar Basin coal deposits for twenty years, and the stipulation that if Germany defaulted on its payments, both France and Belgium (which had been occupied by Germany for four years and its economy stripped of virtually all industry) had the right to occupy the industrial heart of Germany, the Ruhr Valley in western Germany. Germany's borders in the east were also to be moved about one hundred miles westward, and East Prussia would be separated from the rest of the country by the reemergence of Poland, which had been under German/Prussian, Austrian, and Russian control since the 18th century. Millions of Germans were forced to move from their homes, rich and poor alike. To say this was resented is an understatement.

Germany also forfeited all its overseas colonies, and, possibly the worst of all, the German Army was limited in size to 100,000 men. There was to be no air force, and Germany was allowed only a limited coastal defense navy.

Though the reparations were probably the worst part of the terms of the treaty (by the way, Germany paid the last of its reparations payments in 2010), psychologically, the limits to the armed forces were likely the worst.

As you may remember, the army had been a pillar of German life since the days of the kings of Prussia, and it wasn't just in Prussia that the military was held in high regard or even awe—this held true in many of the German states before 1870. With the unification of Germany in 1871, largely due to the outcome of victorious wars, the army held an almost revered status in Germany. Of course, by the end of the First World War, this feeling had begun to change, especially in the larger cities, where progressive political parties and populations saw the army as a tool of the Kaiser. Arch-conservatives used the army to keep the progressives down. However, for the majority of the people in the country, the army was respected and admired.

The strength of the pre-war German Army was about 750,000 men. This is sort of a deceiving figure since, due to the structure of the draft and length of service required, almost all able-bodied German men served in the army at some point. And when their time in active duty was done, they were put in reserve and were subject to relatively regular training and exercises. Many times, those who became officers made the army a lifelong career. Even in retirement, a captain would not be addressed as *Herr Schmidt* ("Mr. Schmidt"), for example, but as *Herr Kapitän Schmidt* to the day he died. With the stroke of a pen, the Allies ended the future of many German men. To compensate for this loss, among other reasons, many German men joined paramilitary groups. Obviously, the most well known are those of the extreme right wing, such as Hitler's *Sturmabteilung* ("Storm Section" or "Storm Detachment"), better known by its acronym, SA, and its predecessor, the *Freikorps* or "Free Corps." However, a variety of other political groups had their own paramilitaries as well, especially the KPD (*Kommunistiche Partei Deutschlands*, the Communist Party of Germany), with their *Rotfront* ("Red Front") groups.

The German Navy was ordered to sail for Scapa Flow, Britain's largest naval base, in the north of Scotland. Once there, the ships' crews scuttled (destroyed) their ships rather than have them sail under a British flag. The German Navy, which had once been the pride of Kaiser Wilhelm, only existed in a number of coastal patrol vessels. It was not allowed to have any submarines.

The German Air Force was eliminated completely, and no one was able to obtain a pilot's license. The Allies wanted to give the Germans only enough troops to keep order within their own borders and nothing more. Strangely enough, and in relatively rapid fashion, the German General Staff, led by General Hans von Seeckt, organized secret training fields in, of all places, the Soviet Union. Germans who wanted to become pilots soon learned a "workaround"; they learned to fly gliders, which were not restricted by the Versailles Treaty. Many of the *Luftwaffe* aces of WWII learned to fly gliders in the 1920s.

And on top of all of this was the infamous (for the Germans, at any rate) Article 231 of the peace treaty. This clause laid the blame for World War One entirely on Germany. To the Allies, this, of course, justified all of the restrictions listed above and more, but Article 231 had a psychological effect on the German nation as well. The article was named the War Guilt Clause, but the idea that the Allies, who mobilized their armies at the same time as Germany and who came to the aid of Serbian assassins, would blame the Germans for the entire war caused resentment in Germany, which would simmer and boil until well after Hitler was elected chancellor in 1933.

Illustration 20: "Germany's children are hungry!" Sketch/poster by famed German artist Kathe Kollwitz, 1923 (courtesy https://www.kollwitz.de/en/germany-s-children-are-starving-kn-202).

Chapter 6 – The Weimar Republic

Between February and June 1919, a new national assembly of Germany met in the central-eastern German city of Weimar to put together a new constitution. The Kaiser had fled to Holland, and the army, while still an organized entity, was in shambles after the war. Some on the right wanted the new government to be run by the generals, but neither the vast majority of Germans nor (more importantly) the Allies would have tolerated that.

The Weimar Assembly was dominated by the SPD (the Social Democratic Party), though other parties, both large and small, were represented. The most significant of these was the Centre Party, which represented the Catholics of Germany. The Communist Party was not involved or wanted; at the time, various, somewhat autonomous branches of the Communist Party were busy trying to establish a "dictatorship of the Proletariat" (the working class) in cities around Germany. This happened in Hamburg, parts of Bavaria (which was becoming a right-wing haven), and cities and towns in Saxony in the east and the Rhineland and Ruhr area in the western part of the country.

The most serious of these uprisings happened in Berlin. It began on January 5th, 1919, and was led by the most militant wing of the German Communist Party, the Spartacist League, named after the famed Roman slave who led a rebellion from 71 to 73 BCE. Its leaders were Rosa Luxemburg and Karl Liebknecht. Both had been members of the Social Democratic Party and its more leftist offshoot, the Independent Social Democratic Party (known in German as the *Unabhängige Sozialdemokratische Partei Deutschlands* or the USPD). However, they both broke from them when the SPD voted to support the war. Both became quite radical as the war went on, to the point of criticizing Leninism in Russia and the socialists around Europe. Luxemburg, Liebknecht, and the SPD had taken part in the sporadic fighting that broke out at the end of the war, which helped result in the end of the war, the abdication of the Kaiser, and the armistice.

During that time, they turned their considerable talents to organizing the Spartacist League and its newspaper, *Die Rote Fahne* or "The Red Flag," and attempted to put together a paramilitary group that could resist the numerous right-wing paramilitaries beginning to sprout up all over Germany.

The Spartacist uprising in Berlin developed rather spontaneously out of a march against the police, which grew from a few thousand to hundreds of thousands of people. Some people in the crowd were armed with firearms, knives, or tools. During the march on January 5th, differing groups occupied offices of the ruling SPD, as well as various newspapers run by the SPD and more conservative parties, which had been calling for the violent suppression of the communists in Berlin.

Amid the chaos, fifty-three leading members of the Communist Party and the Spartacist League met to form a provisional government of Berlin, but they were divided in both purpose and goals. Karl Liebknecht called for the armed overthrow of the country's government. Rosa Luxemburg considered the entire enterprise an unorganized fiasco and made a speech against it, but she did join in the call for a general strike on January 7th.

When this strike of nearly 500,000 people or more began, elements began to both attack government buildings (and take over many) and call on the army and police to join them. Talks went on between Prime Minister Friedrich Ebert, his defense minister, and the representatives of the strikers throughout most of the day, but they ended in a stalemate. At that point, the Spartacists announced they would take up arms against the government.

The entire episode would likely have played itself out much more peacefully had cooler heads prevailed. After all, the Spartacists had no real support outside Berlin, at least none that could get to them, and even within Berlin, people were tired of the violence and suffering. Had the government made a few concessions about working conditions, the armed uprising likely would not have taken place.

However, with the call for violence and similar events occurring in other cities, along with concerns that the army might move in and take power should the SPD government not move against the communists, Ebert called in both the military and various branches of right-wing paramilitaries calling themselves the *Freikorps*. The *Freikorps* was composed mostly of combat veterans, with almost all of them still armed with weapons from the war. These groups had sprouted up all over Germany and were secretly funded by the government, at times with the urging of the Western Allies, who were not keen on seeing a communist takeover of Germany.

The suppression of the Spartacists in Berlin took about a week, at times with pitched battles (including field mortars) going on in the streets. Both Luxemburg and Liebknecht were found in an apartment building and arrested. Liebknecht was beaten bloody and shot three times, his body later being sent to the morgue naked and unidentified until later. Shortly thereafter, Rosa Luxemburg was brought through the lobby of a building, where she was hit twice in the head with a rifle butt and then beaten further by a gang of *Freikorps* men. She was taken to the back of a truck and shot in the back of the head, her body dumped in the nearby Landwehr Canal. It was not found until later that summer.

The Spartacist uprising was a disaster from the start, but it has taken a larger place in history than what it actually effected. Like the hyperinflation that was to follow, the uprising terrified both the government and many citizens of Germany, most of whom, especially outside the poorer areas of the bigger cities, were conservative or moderate in outlook. They remembered a time before the war when Germany was the most prosperous country in Europe, and they believed the communists threatened a rebuilding of that economy, especially under the terms of the Treaty of Versailles.

They also saw the uprising and communism in general as being inspired by Russia and "foreign forces," which literally meant foreigners but also very pointedly meant Jews. Karl Marx, though an atheist, was born a German Jew, and many of the Russian revolutionaries who took over Russia in 1917 were Jewish, which is no surprise. In a nation that had known virulent anti-Semitic pogroms for centuries, communism, with its call for universal brotherhood, would have been highly appealing. Lastly, Rosa Luxemburg, though a naturalized German citizen, was a Polish Jew by origin. In right-wing newspapers and flyers before the uprising, she was often referred to not simply as Rosa Luxemburg but as "The Jew, Rosa Luxemburg" or "The Polish Jew." In years to come, even before the rise of the Nazis, the impact of the violence not only in Berlin but also throughout Germany caused an uptick in anti-Semitic language and violence.

Throughout Germany, the *Freikorps* violently and sometimes atrociously put down communist uprisings, killed leaders, and intimidated the population. In the border areas between Germany and Poland, a vicious low-level war took place, with atrocities being committed on both sides, which, of course, fueled greater hatreds yet to come.

Illustration 21: Freikorps' recruiting poster: "Comrade! Help me against Bolshevism, the Polish danger and starvation." Dated from the time of the Spartacist uprising.

The *Freikorps* were eventually suppressed by the army at the order of the government and with the urging of the Allies. They had become too numerous and were showing a willingness to defy the government when it suited them. The level of violence committed by many of the *Freikorps* units also frightened many in Germany. As the years went by, a great number of the *Freikorps* went on to join the Nazi SA, where their violent tendencies were encouraged. Similarly, the communists also formed their own paramilitary, consisting of workers and a considerable number of war veterans. These two forces would wage war in the streets of German cities with increasing regularity and violence in the later years of the 1920s and early 1930s.

Not long after the uprisings, Germany was faced with another threat, this one more serious: France.

In November of 1922, Germany was unable to pay the second installment of the reparations required by the Treaty of Versailles. Talks produced no solutions, and as stipulated in the treaty, on December 27th, 1922, the French and Belgians moved troops into the industrial Ruhr area of Germany. Troops took over the region's coal mines, factories, and railways. Naturally, there were incidents between French and Belgian troops and Germans, a couple of which you can view on YouTube.

In response to the Franco-Belgian occupation, the German government told workers to use tactics of "passive resistance" against the occupiers. They refused to show up to work, and if they did show up, they immediately went home or sabotaged the machinery. At the massive Krupp steelworks, tensions between workers and French troops escalated to the point of bloodshed, with French soldiers firing on German protesters. At this point, the German government, now run by Prime Minister Gustav Stresemann, promised to pay the wages of the workers in the area.

Hindsight is 20/20, as they say, and had the French and Belgians been a bit more flexible in their demands, the entire situation might have been avoided. However, in June 1922, the very able and popular German foreign minister, Walther Rathenau, a Jewish German, had been assassinated by right-wing extremists linked to the *Freikorps* (another reason for their disbandment) for having engaged in talks with the Soviet Union (which were actually beneficial to Germany). Rathenau was an able minister, and he was respected not only in Germany but also by the Allies. His death was a huge blow.

Let's take a moment to consider the impact of the reparations payments on Germany and German businesses. Governments receive money in a variety of ways, but two of the prime ways are through taxation and bonds (think of these as long-term loans). When the reparations repayment period began, the German government was broke and had been for some time. In fact, almost the entire war effort had been conducted on credit. Of course, when the government fell apart and defaulted, many banks went with it, as did people's life savings. Businesses could no longer get loans, and they could neither pay taxes nor people's salaries. This hit businesses both large and small. Some of the world's largest industrial companies either went broke or were nearly broke by the early 1920s.

Unfortunately, to make matters worse, the government had to raise taxes, for instance, placing taxes on foodstuffs that individual consumers bought but could no longer afford. Businesses, to make up for the shortfall they were paying in taxes, had to raise their prices. When prices go up and the value of currency goes down, you have inflation. Eventually, the German government was trying to get blood from a stone, and when they did get paid, that money had lost its value. However, they still passed what they could on to the Allies in their first installment under the Versailles Treaty.

Now, throw into the mix a fateful decision made by the German government to fulfill their promise to pay the workers of the Ruhr and other regions affected by the occupation and passive resistance—they printed more money. Today, we know the effects of this precisely because of this time period. The policy-makers of the German government did, too, to an extent, but the 1920s was a time when many governments were changing from currencies based on gold to a fiat system, which was essentially currency based on demand and the market. As a result, these policy-makers were not completely aware of the nightmare they were creating. This nightmare was the German Hyperinflation of 1922/23.

Many doctors of economics have written their doctoral theses on the German Hyperinflation, and thousands of books have been written about this very brief but nightmarish situation. Suffice it to say here that if you have one of an object, especially if it's the only one, it's very valuable. By printing more money, the German government was reducing the value people put on money every time the printing presses rolled on—and they rolled on, and on, and on. Soon, inflation was so out of control that people were literally being paid to show up to work and again at lunch, for between the hours of 8 and 12, money had lost its value hundreds of times over. At the height of the hyperinflation, the German government was issuing bills in the amount of *one hundred trillion* mark notes.

Say, for example, you had ten thousand marks in the bank. Before the war, this would've been worth roughly two or three thousand US dollars. During hyperinflation, you couldn't buy a loaf of bread for ten thousand marks. People's savings went up in smoke. People got paid millions of marks, which means landlords then suffered since rents stayed the same. If you had a long-term lease that called for twenty marks a month, well, that was easy to pay, but the landlord was then left with a twenty mark note, which was worth less than a modern-day penny. He had to pay his mortgage with money he did not have, and thus, the chain went on and on.

People went hungry and lost their jobs; no one knows exactly how many people starved to death. Soup kitchens were opened all over Germany, usually run by churches or the International Red Cross. People's pride went out the window, and the country's pride went out the window. As a result of all this, people began to flock toward the communists and the parties of the extreme right.

Illustration 22: Hyperinflation bill from July 1923

Eventually, the government issued a new currency, the Rentenmark, which was actually based on the American dollar. This, as well as other steps taken over the course of 1923, finally ended the economic turmoil, but the damage had been done. The hyperinflation left a huge scar on the collective German psyche. When the Great Depression struck in 1929, the nightmare of 1923 came rushing back into the German consciousness, and people began to make choices based on fear.

Illustration 23: German making a withdrawal from a bank in 1923. A popular rumor was that a man had taken a wagon to the bank to get his money. He was held up, and the thieves took the wagon but left the pile of money. Women would go into a store to buy a sack of potatoes carrying bags of money. Thieves would watch them go in with the money and take the potatoes, which were worth far more, for food or trade.

The hyperinflation was a wake-up call, not only for Germany but also for the Western Allies. They knew that if Germany went through too many economic earthquakes, she might turn to communism, for with every jolt to the economy, more people joined the far-left (and the far-right, but we will get to that shortly). In the Soviet Union (the USSR), throughout the 1920s, Stalin and the Soviet propaganda ministry successfully sold a bill of goods to many of their own people and the people in Europe and America, stating that communism was the way of the future. They issued reports, data, pictures, posters, and sponsored yet carefully escorted tours, which all showed that the USSR was making economic leaps and bounds. Much of it was false, but people wanted to fall for it, and so they did.

To prevent the fall of the German economy and nation and also to secure their reparations payments, the Allies began to slowly engage successive German governments with new, deferred, and milder ways to pay the war reparations. What follows is simple in the extreme, but it will help readers understand both how Germany slowly got on its feet in the later 1920s and one cause of the Great Depression of 1929.

The United States, which, while losing over 100,000 men in its short time in WWI, was not invaded, did not go through shortages, did not suffer economically (quite the contrary), and did not have the same hard feelings toward Germany that existed in Britain and France. From about 1916 onward, both Britain and France financed their war efforts and then turned around and bought weapons and supplies from the US. When WWI ended, the United States had become the strongest economy in the world, which sparked many cries of "war profiteering" and investigations in Congress.

Of all the combatants in the Great War, the US was the only nation not essentially flat broke, but people worried that the ripple effects of a European economic breakdown after the war would reach the shores of the United States. Therefore, over the course of a number of years and many discussions involving the Allies, most importantly, Germany and the United States (sometimes with the knowledge of the others and sometimes not), a system was put in place that would allow Germany to both pay back its debts and be able to invest in businesses to revive its economy. The United States would loan it the money to pay Britain and France at new interest rates. (After all, loaning money without interest just means you're out that particular sum of money, which you can't use for a period of time. Thus, interest is charged to make the loan worthwhile.) In turn, the British and French would use this money to pay back the United States for the loans they received during the war, which would then go back to Germany... Do you see how that works? It was an illusion, but it worked, at least for a while.

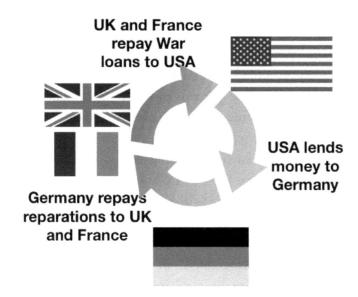

UK and France repay War loans to USA

USA lends money to Germany

Germany repays reparations to UK and France

Now, obviously, there were many other contributions to the Great Depression, but one of the least recognized was the cycle of payments pictured above. Hundreds of billions of dollars were taken out of circulation (therefore, they were not being used for investment, erosion control, public works, or for many of the other reasons for the Depression). This system worked until it didn't.

Still, from late 1923 onward, with fits and starts, the German economy began to improve. However, there is still one event of 1923 that we need to discuss, and it took place in Munich on November 9th, 1923. (Pay attention to the amazing recurrence of November 9th in German history as we go on. We have encountered one already—Kaiser Wilhelm II abdicated on November 9th.)

On November 9th, 1923, Adolf Hitler, accompanied by the famous General Erich Ludendorff; future German Air Force chief and first head of the Gestapo, Hermann Göring; and Ernst Röhm, future head of the SA, along with hundreds of followers, attempted to overthrow the government of Bavaria in the first step on a planned "March on Berlin" to overthrow the national government, similar to how Benito Mussolini had overthrown the Italian government in his famous "March on Rome" in October 1922.

Hitler's plan crumbled for various reasons, including cold feet on the part of some army officers and Bavarian politicians, poor planning, and an overestimation of his party's support. The famous Beer Hall Putsch (*putsch* is German for "coup") amounted to nothing, but Hitler's trial by right-wing judges (there was no jury system in Germany) gave the natural-born speaker a platform for announcing his resentment over the end of WWI, the Versailles Treaty, and the state of Germany. It was failure that propelled Hitler to success. His trial, the writing of his book *Mein Kampf* (*My Struggle*) while "incarcerated" in Landsberg Prison, and his decision to achieve power by legal means all stemmed from the failure of November 9th, 1923.

As a side note, Hitler's cell was essentially an apartment from which people and packages could go. It is well known that Hitler had a sweet tooth, so the people who visited him often brought chocolate or other sweets.

Illustration 24: Hitler in his "cell" at Landsberg with visitors for tea. His chauffeur, Emil Maurice, stands behind him.

Today, the days of the Weimar Republic are known almost as much for their artistic and cultural achievements and happenings as they are for the rise of Hitler and the Nazis. The years of relative stability (1924 to 1929) saw Germany, especially Berlin, become one of the cultural capitals of the Western world.

Why did this happen? In the years before the unification of Germany, when the country was a conglomeration of states and principalities, the laws and unspoken rules of censorship differed from area to area, but generally speaking, German artists, writers, and musicians were able to express themselves relatively freely. If they were not able to do so where they lived, they very often relocated, sometimes where laws governing expression were laxer, where the money was better, or both.

When Germany united in the latter part of the 19th century, things began to change, and several laws restricting expression were passed. With Wilhelm II's coming of age, the censorship of the government grew more profound, especially in regard to the written word, as it was much easier to censor than artistic works such as sculpture and painting. Remember that Wilhelm II was an absolute monarch at heart and a believer in the "divine right of kings" deep in his soul.

As a comparison, two periods of American history may further illustrate what happened in Germany under the Kaiser. Though both the 1920s and 1950s are famous for their rebellious groups (the flappers and bootleggers of the 1920s and the beatniks and motorcycle gangs of the 1950s), much of American society was a self-regulated, flat-top haircut culture of picket fences, cut lawns, cocktails parties, anti-communist witch hunts, and conformity. The famous American novel *Babbitt* by Sinclair Lewis (1922) portrays this life and culture perfectly. Though there were obvious differences (the worship of the military being one of them), German society during the Wilhelmine era was much the same.

As you have read, the end of WWI and the way it ended tore German society apart, and while artists of all kinds create even in the worst of times, the news and the events of the day drew people's attention far more than the latest painting or dance craze. Survival and political strife were the order of the day.

Once the occupation of the Ruhr and the hyperinflation had gotten under control, things began to settle down in Germany, at least on the surface. And as they did, life could get back to "normal"; only "normal," at least in Berlin and a couple of the other major cities, was a totally different thing than it had been.

One of the big changes that took place in the 1920s was the importation of American culture, especially jazz culture. This was truly the first time that American culture had invaded the shores of Europe, and making things even more foreign was the fact that many of the jazz artists coming to Europe (especially Paris and Berlin) were African American. They were leaving the United States for money and for a place to live and perform that was, for the most part, less discriminatory.

Berliners, as well as those in Hamburg (and yes, they are called "Hamburgers") and other cities, went crazy for American jazz, as well as the dance and fashion that went along with it. Naturally, many jazz fans were young city dwellers, but jazz made its way, in the form of radio and records, into smaller cities and larger towns as well. Not to be overlooked was the massive amount of drinking that went on at clubs and parties throughout Germany—again, Berlin was the most notorious. There was also a rise in drug use. Cocaine was legal, as it was in the United States as well, and heroin- and opium-based narcotics were easily available. The hundreds of thousands of wounded veterans were a ready customer base. Adding to that, pharmacists sold their drugs under the table for much more than they purchased them. Marijuana was relatively rare, but hashish from North Africa made its way to Berlin. This was "popular culture" for the masses, and it is well portrayed in the German TV program *Babylon Berlin*, which you can find on Netflix.

What a lot of people don't realize is that during the stable years of the Weimar Republic, the government funded the arts a great deal—far more than had ever been done throughout the Wilhelmine era. Though this funding was considerably lower on the budgetary totem pole, the thought behind it was sound: fund the arts and help return society to "normal."

Before we talk about the movies, paintings, plays, musicals, and novels of the Weimar era, we should also remember that, like other periods in other countries throughout history, the "golden age" of Weimar arts and culture came between two abysmally stagnant periods culturally. We've already spoken about the censorship and uniformity of Wilhelmine Germany, and obviously, what came after the Weimar era was far, far worse, so it should be no surprise that many people looked (and look) back at this period with fondness and nostalgia. And, of course, as people age, nostalgia grows.

Still, however, there is no question that what happened in Germany in the middle and late 1920s was a phenomenon, and while there were other centers of artistic achievement in Germany, Berlin became a magnet for people wanting to express themselves freely and to make money off those who did.

There are several reasons for the flowering of the arts in Germany during this time. Some have already been mentioned. Others include a terrific originality that took place in Berlin and spread outward to the rest of the Western world, and within this originality was the kind of eclectic mix of mediums, styles, and personalities that usually happen only once in a lifetime.

Berlin, being Germany's capital, had always drawn a variety of people despite being the center of an authoritarian regime. What's more, it was looked at as a "border city" between Western and Eastern Europe, kind of like a frontier, and like most frontier cities, it drew a wild and creative crowd after the destruction of WWI.

In a sense, Berlin was the home of modern performance art. Warehouses, empty buildings, and vacant lots were all transformed into theaters of one sort or another. One of the many themes, not only of the performance art and street theater of the time but also in movies and books, was technology. Remember, WWI was the first mass-produced war and brought not only machine guns but also submarines, airplanes, tanks, and the radio to the fore. Many of Berlin's performances during this time were about how technology was changing life and how small and inconsequential human beings were becoming in the face of these new technologies. Perhaps the most famous and long lasting of these examples is the film *Metropolis* (1927) by Fritz Lang.

Berlin also became the center of European filmmaking during this period, and the studio at Babelsberg outside Berlin was one of the largest in the world. It still produces movies (Quentin Tarantino insisted his *Inglorious Basterds*, with its WWII theme, be filmed there). While movies such as *Blue Angel*, *The Cabinet of Dr. Caligari*, and *M* were controversial and worldwide phenomena (and launched the international careers of Marlene Dietrich and Peter Lorre, to name just two), just as many bad films were made, with many of them trying to make money off youth culture and the Jazz Age.

Jazz wasn't the only music being made in the Weimar years. Most famously, the musical *The Threepenny Opera* became the first German musical, and it was a hit overseas as well, especially with its depiction of street life in Germany.

Classical music moved away from the works of the 1800s and into new territory as well. The most famous German composer of the time was Arnold Strindberg, whose works exploring atonality were a unique investigation into the construction of music. However, all but the most serious of musicians found it remote, dreary, and uninspiring. Music, too, seemed to reflect a new age of technology.

Architecture did as well, and perhaps the most famous school of architectural design during this time was Bauhaus (literally "House for the Building Arts"). Bauhaus not only considered architecture in the design of its buildings but also function and, to a degree, useful style. Walter Gropius, Ludwig Mies van der Rohe, and other architects consulted with artists in other mediums, such as Paul Klee and Wassily Kandinsky, to create a new style that walked a line between function and form. Many of their buildings also reflect the effect technology had on the thinking of the time.

Of course, not everyone in Berlin was an artist, writer, musician, or sculptor. Most people in Berlin were housewives, workers, fathers, or wounded vets begging for pennies—in other words, they were regular people. Some of them embraced the changes, while some did not. Still, others were spectators of a sort, as there always are in situations like that—for example, most of the "hippies" that lived in San Francisco in the late 1960s and early 1970s arrived long after the "hey-day" of the "Summer of Love" of 1967.

Still, being in Berlin in the mid-1920s must have been something to behold, especially for the young. One of the things the period is most famous for is the experimentation with sexuality and gender, which went on in public at the clubs and behind closed doors (sometimes at those same clubs!) Though there was much experimentation going on, especially in Berlin, it was never as widespread as the media and politicians (then and now) made it out to be, but it made great headlines and salacious secret reading.

For reasons that sociologists are still trying to explain, Berlin (along with Paris) became a hub for sexual experimentation in the 1920s. Some of it was likely due to the idea of still being alive after the war, hyperinflation, and civil unrest, among other things. Much of it was likely due to the liberal atmosphere generated in the theaters, clubs, and dance halls. Whatever the cause, Berlin became infamous as a place where "anything went." The movie *Cabaret* (1972), based on the book *Goodbye to Berlin* (1939), portrays the time and the feeling extremely well.

In 1968, US presidential candidate Richard Nixon proclaimed that Americans of the "silent majority" would vote for him and stand up for "traditional American values," as opposed to the "free love" and drugs the hippies practiced and used (which were never as widespread as the media and Nixon made them out to be). Way before Nixon's call for the "silent majority" to rise up and take America back from the hippies, a wide spectrum of political parties (mostly on the right but some on the left as well) were condemning Weimar culture and the changes seemingly taking over German life.

Though the nightclubs and cabarets of the 1920s went on into the 1930s, the onset of the Great Depression in October 1929 put a serious damper on the celebratory lifestyle of Weimar Germany and especially that of Berlin. What was to come was more hunger, unemployment, political strife, and violence, resulting in a regime that would put an end to almost every aspect of Weimar culture within six months of it taking power.

Illustration 25: Cabaret poster of the 1920s: "Berlin, the city of beautiful women," a comic opera. The bear is the symbol of the city of Berlin, as are the flags.

Illustration 26: "Our last hope."

Chapter 7 – Hitler, Anti-Semitism, and the Rise of the Nazis

This e-book is an introduction to the history of Germany from 1870 to the present day. Perhaps you purchased it for yourself because you felt there were some gaps in your knowledge or as a gift to a young person who is tackling the subject at school. If you're one of the people who are familiar with Hitler and the rise of the Nazis and WWII, you're likely to be familiar with much or all that follows in this chapter. However, since these books are written as introductory guides and since learning about this time period is of the utmost importance, we are going to start at the beginning and cover the entire horrible period in as much detail as possible.

Hitler was born in Austria in 1889 in the small town of Braunau am Inn. His father, Alois, was twenty-three years older than his third wife and Hitler's mother, Klara, who was also Alois's first cousin once-removed on his mother's side. It is not known who Alois's father was, which haunted the anti-Semitic Adolf in later life with thoughts that he might possibly be of partial Jewish heritage. Hitler had five brothers and one sister. Only his sister Paula lived into adulthood, dying in 1960. Hitler did have a stepsister, Angela, the daughter of his father's second wife. Angela's daughter, Geli, Hitler's niece, was Adolf's first and perhaps only true love other than his mother. She died by her own hand in 1931, most likely due to the oppressive nature of her relationship with Hitler, who, by that time, was a national figure.

By all accounts, Alois Hitler was the typical Austrian/German father of his age, perhaps even more so. He was an authoritarian father who beat his wife and children, and Adolf seems to have seen his mother as both protector and someone to protect as he got older. Volumes of psychological studies have been written to determine if Hitler's childhood was the main factor in what he later became.

What we do know is that Hitler was utterly devoted to his mother, and following the death of his father in 1903, Klara moved to the small provincial city of Linz with her two children. By 1907, Hitler had moved to Vienna to study art, but he was recalled to Linz because his mother had been diagnosed with breast cancer. After a long battle, a mastectomy, and a primitive and painful form of chemotherapy, she died at home with her family. An interesting facet to this story is that the family doctor, Eduard Bloch, was Jewish. By all accounts, Hitler liked and respected Bloch. Later in life, Bloch reported that he had never seen someone so devastated by a death as Hitler was by his mother's. Later on, Hitler allowed Bloch and his wife to flee Austria without trouble during the Nazis' persecution of the Jews after Germany's union with Austria in 1938.

With the death of his mother, Hitler returned to Vienna, living off his portion of his father's civil servant pension and the watercolor postcards he sold on the streets of the Austro-Hungarian capital. For many years, it was believed that Hitler lived in abject poverty in Vienna (this largely came from his own account of that time), but while he surely did not live a life of luxury or even a lower-middle-class existence, he was not destitute as he portrayed. Nonetheless, it was not an easy existence, and for much of his time in Vienna, he lived in what used to be called a dosshouse but now would be referred to as a cheap men-only motel for the relatively down-and-out.

What most residents of the places where Hitler lived remembered were his sudden rantings. He was normally a quiet man who kept to himself or kept company with his friend from Linz, August Kubizek, who shared a similar history, having lost both parents. Suddenly, though, Hitler would stand up and begin ranting about art or the lack of cultural awareness among his fellows. And after having spent some time in Vienna, he began ranting about politics and the Jews.

Hitler was not without artistic talent. He likely could have pursued a career as an illustrator for an architectural or real estate company or perhaps illustrated books or magazines. That was not for Hitler, though. Around this point in his life, he seemed to develop the megalomania that would both raise him to world power and lower him into madness. Hitler fancied himself a "fine artist" in the vein of Michelangelo, Titian, Rembrandt, and others. Even the most inexperienced eye could tell he did not have that type of talent, but few do.

Hitler twice submitted his work for admission to the highly esteemed Vienna Academy of Art and was rejected both times. The rejections noted Hitler's ability to render buildings and scenery adequately, but his attempts at recreating the human form were elemental and without feeling. At this time, Hitler was also rejected from the Vienna School of Architecture for the bureaucratic reason of not being able to provide a secondary school diploma from Linz.

These failed attempts to achieve what he had long dreamed seems to have been one of the foundational points for Hitler's transformation from a relatively quiet, apolitical street artist into a man fixated on both politics and one of the cultural trends of the time, at least in Germany and Austria: the "science" of race.

However, in actuality, race was not an issue limited to Germany and Austria. In much of Western Europe and the United States, segments of the dominant population and the upper classes began to ask themselves why it seemed that the white European nationalities had come to dominate much of the world by that time. They were also on their way toward dominating what was left, including China.

The idea of superiority was not limited to Europeans. The Chinese had called themselves the Middle Kingdom for millennia, as it was the kingdom around which the rest of the world revolved and which was due respect and tribute. There were segments, rather large segments, of people in Muslim/Ottoman lands that had felt the same way, and though much of that belief was centered around religion, the subject peoples of the Arabic Mohammedan Empire in the late 8th century until the 12th century would tell you that it was clear that the Arabs felt themselves superior to many of the people they had conquered, including those in parts of Spain. There are other examples throughout history outside of Europe, and it continues to happen today.

What makes the European notion of supremacy, which began in earnest in the late 1800s onward, different and notable is that it was coupled with both military might and "science." By the start of World War One, much of the globe was either overlorded or heavily influenced by Western countries. This was due to the rich natural resources; high population density, with its accompanying rapid exchange of ideas; the rise of the centrally governed nation state throughout Europe and its high level of organization; and its weapons. Vast distances, climate, topography, and tribal warfare contributed to the comparative weakness of much of the rest of the world in the late 19th century.

One exception was Japan, which had united in the early 1600s. The Japanese refused to let Westerners into all but one or two cities for centuries, and it was also relatively small and isolated. With the arrival of the Americans under Matthew Perry in the early 1850s, Japan was forced to open to the world for trade, but they did so wisely, limiting Western contact and setting the Westerners against each other. In the early 1870s, Japan rejected its feudal system and set about developing a modern economy with an emperor at the head of a parliamentary government led by aristocrats and industrialists. In the late 1890s and in 1905, Japan shockingly and convincing defeated China and Russia in two wars and set itself upon a course of imperial expansion that would lead to WWII in the Pacific. Not far under the surface of Japan's expansion was the notion of the superiority and "purity" of the Japanese race. Late 19th-century/early 20th-century Japan is the most convincing example outside of Europe of both the tendency of humans to set themselves above others and the desire to conquer them.

However, while the Japanese could point to the ancient and supposedly divine nature of their imperial family, the Europeans used the evidence of their military might and Darwin's theory of evolution and its accompanying notion of the "survival of the fittest."

Simply and concisely, among much of the literate population of Europe, the idea that human beings were both part of and the apex of the natural world began to spread, and within that belief, the idea caught on that, similar to what happens in nature, those who were stronger and adaptable survived and thrived. Those who did not died out or were killed. That was the rationale behind white supremacy of the time.

What historians, anthropologists, sociologists, and psychologists have found since the time of Hitler is that, generally speaking, the ideas of racial supremacy start or reignite among segments at the top of society and from the lower middle class downward. The reasoning behind the first is relatively obvious. Among the latter is the idea of being part of something more powerful than just oneself and one's "poorer and less powerful" situation. As Hitler's popularity grew, many in the middle class, especially in the countryside and villages, became attracted to the philosophy of German (or white) supremacy.

Another group to which these beliefs often appeal are younger males, who frequently feel controlled by and/or are at the whim of others, and you can easily create a hostile young man (and, in more recent times, women) who believes the world is against him.

Hitler was not the first to spell out these beliefs, though he wrote about them considerably in his book. The French aristocratic theorist Comte ("Count") de Gobineau (1816–1882) began writing extensively on the ideas of white supremacy combined with evolutionary theory in the latter part of the 19th century. It was Gobineau that incorrectly applied the word "Aryan" to the Germanic peoples of northern Europe.

Alongside Gobineau in influence was Houston Stewart Chamberlain (1855–1927), an upper-class Englishman who later settled in Germany and wrote in German. Chamberlain was the epitome of the rebellious loner, just as Hitler became, and for that reason, among others, he was a favorite of Hitler's. In 1899, Chamberlain's German-language book *Die Grundlagen des neunzehnten Jahrhunderts* (*The Foundations of the 19th Century*) became one of the foundational stones of "scientific" white supremacy that became popular at the time, especially in German and Austria. The science of Chamberlain's book was really opinion dressed up in scientific and philosophical language without any scientific evidence or fieldwork of any kind.

Both Gobineau and Chamberlain used the term "Aryan" to describe the Germanic "races" of Europe. (Today, science only recognizes three or four "races" of human beings, and even that is done hesitantly. "Ethnicity" is more often used today.) According to Gobineau and Chamberlain, Aryans were groups of very ancient peoples (some white supremacists of the time had them occupying the mythical island of Atlantis) who had supplied the foundational stones of the great civilizations of the past, such as Greece, Rome, and Persia. In fact, it is from the latter that we get the actual term "Aryan"; the word was used as a descriptor for groups of people who lived in the area of Persia (modern-day Iran) to northern India.

Gobineau and those who followed him believed that the ancient Aryans were tall, athletic, blond, and blue-eyed and that the original "bloodline" of the ancient Aryans had survived in northern Europe but had faded out in the Middle East and India due to interbreeding with "lower" races, specifically the Semitic peoples, which include Arabs but primarily refers to the Jews. Again, all of this was based not only on wishful thinking but also on appearances—none of this was based on any kind of scientific study or data.

Hitler latched onto the ideas of Gobineau and especially Chamberlain. He also took their ideas and combined them with others, which were espoused by two figures who influenced him more directly and emotionally—Vienna's mayor at the time of Hitler's residency there, Karl Lueger, a vicious anti-Semite, and the famed composer Richard Wagner, whose operas elevated Germanic heroes above the lower "races" of German and Nordic mythology and who was a notorious anti-Semite. (Interestingly, Houston Stewart Chamberlain's life and outlook were said to also have been changed by Wagner's music and operas, and later in life, he married Wagner's daughter, Eva).

Lueger's anti-Semitism was loud, crude, and political. He railed against Jews as a "foreign element." In Vienna and Austria of the time, most Austrian Jews were highly assimilated into society, as they were in Germany. They generally kept to themselves but obviously practiced their religious beliefs, though an increasing number of German and Austrian Jews were becoming less observant. However, to Lueger and others, the Jews in Austria were symbolized by those who had come to Vienna from the eastern parts of the Austro-Hungarian Empire. This population was more observant and much more visible, wearing traditional clothing and hairstyles, especially among the men. This helped to set them apart. Hitler appears to have begun developing truly virulent anti-Semitic opinions after being in Vienna for some time and consuming Lueger's speeches and writings, along with those of the mayor's political allies.

Before we continue with the story of Hitler's life before his rise to power, we should make an attempt to explain why anti-Semitism exists in the first place. To begin with, please remember that this e-book is an introduction to German history and that, unfortunately, anti-Semitism in that country led to the Holocaust. In simplifying the roots of anti-Semitism, please know that we understand the topic is both deep and emotional, but for our purposes here, we are going to limit our discussion of the topic to a very basic explanation, with which you may or may not fully agree with but which summarizes the knowledge of many historians who are experts on the topic.

Anti-Semitism has six basic historical foundations that go back to the time of the Roman Empire. Rome has two distinct periods: the Roman Republic (509 BCE–27 BCE) and the Roman Empire (27 BCE–c. 410 CE). What's confusing is that Rome began its conquests, the building of its *empire*, under the Roman Republic.

First, when the Romans expanded into the area that today encompasses Israel, they encountered something they had never experienced before: a monotheistic culture—one that worships a single deity. Virtually all of the other cultures conquered by or assimilated into the Roman Empire were polytheistic like the

Romans, meaning they worshiped many gods that resembled the Romans pantheon in all but name.

Three problems arose from this. Firstly, the Romans and Jews fundamentally did not understand each other's views of the world and the universe. The Jews insisted that the Roman gods were false and vice versa. When Rome was eventually ruled by an emperor, beginning with Augustus, the state insisted that the people it dominated essentially had to worship the emperor as a god, whether this emperor was dead and alive. This was something the Jews would categorically not do.

During Jesus Christ's lifetime, tensions between the Jews and Romans were high, with occasional uprisings and frequent riots against Roman rule occurring. The Romans had traditionally adopted a "divide and conquer" strategy in the formation of their far-flung empire, and, to a degree, the clash of ideas between Christ and his followers and the Jewish establishment suited the Romans very well until it threatened to get out of hand.

You likely know the story. Jesus was accused by the Jewish authorities of claiming he was the Messiah, the savior of the world, and the Son of God. This both went against contemporary Jewish teaching and threatened the "powers that be" among both the Romans and the Jews. At his "trial," Jesus was offered up to the Jewish crowd by the Roman governor of Judea, Pontius Pilate. Pilate offered the crowd two men, one of whom would go free and the other who would be crucified: Jesus and the accused murderer Barabbas. Threatened by Jesus's supposed heresy, the crowd demanded that he be crucified and that Barabbas go free. You know the rest of the story.

However, as Christianity became the dominant religion of the later Roman Empire and the Early Middle Ages after the Western Roman Empire's fall, the Jews came to be blamed for the death of Christ. This idea was combined with new myths surrounding the Jews, becoming a deadly fallacy. In an age of great faith in religious leaders and illiteracy, these ideas became almost a required belief, especially as Jews believed that the Messiah was still to come, which enraged Christians, who saw this as denial of Christ's divinity.

This Jewish "blood guilt," as it came to be called, makes as much sense as blaming a white farmer in 21st-century Iowa for the genocidal wars against the Native Americans in the 18th and 19th centuries. Still, ignorance, combined with beliefs backed by authority figures, can be powerful.

The bubonic plague (known as the Black Plague or the Black Death) struck Europe with a vengeance in the mid-1340s to the 1350s. Some estimates have the death toll at nearly 25 percent of Europe's population, but the plague (along with other deadly diseases, the most prevalent of which was smallpox) struck with alarming frequency until relatively modern times.

The idea that the plague was spread by rodents, or rather the germs in the fleas, which then fed on the blood of infected rodents, was relatively unknown, though some did have the notion that somehow fleas and rodents were responsible. What people did not know with certainty until the mid-1800s was that disease was spread by germs. They believed it was spread by bad air, bad water, perhaps bad blood, and pus, but they did not realize it was something one could not see, like germs.

In the Middle Ages, due to the reasons explained above and others, Jews were frequently required to live separately from the rest of the population. When they weren't required to do so, they often did so voluntarily for safety. As a result, it seemed to many that the Jews did not get the plague, or at least not as often. Again, you must remember, this was a time of profound ignorance and illiteracy. So, when people asked themselves, "Why don't the Jews get the plague or suffer from it as bad as everyone else?" they came to the conclusion that the Jews had started it. Simple as that. They started it, were immune from it, and were spreading it to the rest of the population as revenge or at Satan's command.

The Jews, of course, got the plague as well. They simply may have died at a lesser rate simply because the people who blamed them for it forced them to live apart, therefore making them more protected from the spread of germs.

In addition to the "blood libel" of Jesus's death and the plague, other myths around the Jews arose. When something is separate and alien, and especially when the observer is uneducated, gaps in knowledge are replaced by supposition, superstition, and fear. Along with the above, Jews were frequently accused of witchcraft and holding human sacrifices. A popular myth talked of Jews kidnapping Christian virgins, cutting their throats, and using their blood in their unleavened matzoh bread.

And as if this wasn't bad enough, other edicts from the Catholic Church indirectly made life worse for European Jews. The most notable for our purposes here were the laws against usury, the loaning of money for interest.

Usury was seen as "un-Christian," as people believed it took advantage of those who were in a worse economic position. Since interest rates were not set, they were essentially whatever the lender decided he could get, and the more desperate a person or business was, the higher the interest rate. It was also seen as slothful since one made money but did nothing to earn it.

Now, if someone came to you and asked you for a 100,000-dollar loan and you didn't charge interest, what would happen? First, you would not be able to use that money yourself for investments or whatever for however long it took for the person to pay you back. Second, inflation makes money worth less over time, so the 100,000 dollars that you lent (without interest) might be worth only 80,000 when you got it back, so in the end, you lose money if interest isn't charged. Interest makes a modern economy function.

Since Christians were forbidden to lend money at interest and since everyone in Europe, except the Jews, was subject to these laws (though, of course, many Christians violated these edicts), who would one go to for money when no one else would lend it to you because it was a losing proposition? The Jews. And we know what frequently happens to relationships between people who loan money—resentment.

Making this worse, many people would take loans from Jewish lenders and skip the agreed payments or simply not pay at all. When this happened, the Jewish lender would often be powerless to collect. As a result, interest rates rose (as did resentment), and Jews complained to the authorities, who oftentimes saw the Jews as "money-grubbers" whose sole concern was profit. Jews also went into the pawnbroker business, which is essentially another form of loans at interest. By doing so, it caused them to be viewed as taking advantage of poor Christians.

As time went by, several Jewish families in Europe became large banking interests, the most famous of which were the Rothschilds, who are still a favorite target of white supremacists and conspiracy theorists today. Of course, many non-Jewish families became bankers too, but they were often viewed in a different light.

Outside of their own settlements, in much of Europe, Jews were forbidden to engage in certain trades. For much of the Middle Ages, guilds, organizations of specific trades, such as woodworkers, saddlers, bakers, or painters, to name a few, dominated small businesses in Europe. It was in the interest of these guilds to limit competition, and one way this was done was by passing laws that restricted what professions Jews could participate in.

This forced many Jews, especially in the cities, to go into areas that were not forbidden to them. We've already mentioned banking. Law, administration, the arts, writing, and acting as middlemen between the guilds and the general public were not forbidden. In Germany, in 1933, when Hitler came to power, the Jews represented about 1 percent of the population: seven hundred thousand out of seventy million. In most other parts of Europe, the ratio was about the same, with Eastern Europe, especially Poland and Russia, being on the higher end (and both countries endured far more vicious anti-Semitism for most of European history until WWII, something of which the Nazis took full advantage).

Of course, most Jews were poor and were persecuted frequently. However, in the cities where there were more opportunities, Jews were seen as having massive influence compared to their proportion of the population, and the ironic thing was that much of this perceived influence was caused by laws or customs created by the Europeans themselves.

In the early 20th century, anti-Semites added communism to the long list of things for which to blame Jews, as Karl Marx was a Jew, as well as a number of leading communists in the Soviet Union (though they were still a minority). Oddly enough, the Nazis also blamed the Jews for "greedy capitalism," which is the exact opposite of communism.

It was thought that the Jews, as they supported the ultra-capitalists and communists, were trying to rule the world from the shadows. This was "proven" with the publication of the so-called *Protocols of the Elders of Zion* in the early 20th century, which claimed to be the transcripts and ideas of leading Jews planning to take over the world. The work is a piece of fiction, and it was called out as such by most at the time. It clearly lifts sentiments and literal paragraphs from a number of earlier published works published. Still, in nations and areas that had historically experienced anti-Semitism, including the United States, where half a million copies were paid for by Henry Ford, a notorious anti-Semite, the *Protocols* seemed real enough and seemed to confirm their already long-held beliefs.

With the advent of what came to be known as social Darwinism, the idea that certain "races" were superior to others and that "only the strong survived" caused the persecution of the Jews to go beyond religious persecution. This pseudo-science declared that

Judaism was not just a religion but a "part of the blood." German families with Jewish last names, even if they had converted to Christianity decades, perhaps even a century or so before the rise of Hitler, were not safe. To Hitler and others at the time, "Jewishness," as well as "German-ness," was biological, not something you could discard by converting.

Like any prejudice, most anti-Semites could not even begin to tell you the historical causes behind their anti-Semitism. It was simply passed down from generation to generation, friend to friend, neighbor to neighbor, and it was made worse by both the occasional mention of certain ideas (like the idea that their Jewish neighbor in Poland might somehow be responsible for the death of Christ) and events (like the Great Depression). That's the thing about hate, though; it doesn't have to be logical. It just has to make you feel better than someone else. And since hate does not require logic, reason, or facts to exist, it is difficult to counter and easy to spread.

Illustration 27: Nazi poster for their film The Eternal Jew, *which compared disease-carrying hordes of rats to Germany's Jewish population. The poster depicts the infamous caricature of an Eastern European Jew holding out money with one hand and a whip in the other while holding a map of Germany stamped with the symbol of communism.*

World War I for Hitler

By 1914, Hitler, an Austrian, was a confirmed anti-Semite and began to adhere to the popular ideas of German/Nordic superiority. Because the Austro-Hungarian Empire consisted of a mélange of different ethnic groups, and because he perceived Germany as being stronger, Hitler evaded the Austrian draft and crossed the border into Bavaria when war threatened to erupt. He joined the German Army when war was declared. A famous picture of Hitler in Munich cheering the war news is most likely a fake (it was later serendipitously "discovered" to be taken by the man who later became Hitler's official photographer, Heinrich Hoffmann), but we can assume, both by Hitler's own writings and speeches and the general mood of the country in August 1914, that he did indeed cheer the outbreak of the war.

Hitler served in the 16th Bavarian Reserve Infantry Regiment throughout the war. He served on or near the front lines on the Western Front. His primary job throughout the conflict was that of messenger, running information from the rear trenches to the front. By all accounts, he served dutifully and bravely, earning the Iron Cross Second Class in 1914 and the Iron Cross First Class in 1918. Ironically, the officer who recommended the latter was Lieutenant Hugo Gutmann, who was Jewish. Hitler had also been wounded by shellfire in 1916, but he returned to the front before he was due to.

Illustration 28: Corporal Hitler (left), the day he was awarded the Iron Cross First Class.

In October 1918, Hitler was a victim of a British gas attack, which left his eyes highly irritated. In the years since the war, studies of contemporary accounts of his and other cases from the time attribute Hitler's end-of-the-war blindness to hysteria; in other words, he had reached his breaking point. Still, for all intents and purposes, he was blind. When the news of the armistice and Germany's seeming surrender reached him at the convalescent hospital in northeastern Germany, Hitler reported that upon hearing the news, his sight came back, and he felt "destined" to lead Germany from the hard times he was sure would come. The event was longer and more drawn-out than what Hitler portrayed, but the crux is that Hitler seemingly went from rejected artist to a man who had convinced himself that somehow "providence" had singled him out for a great destiny.

After returning to Munich once the war ended, Hitler was one of the few Germans who remained in the army. In 1919, he was tasked with keeping an eye on several far-right political parties emerging in the violent aftermath of WWI in Bavaria. One of these groups was the DAP (*Deutsche Arbeiterpartei* or "German Workers' Party"). After attending a number of their meetings and frequenting the beer hall where they gathered, Hitler realized that the DAP espoused many of the same beliefs that he had developed, such as his hatred of the Versailles Treaty and its many restrictions, German superiority, the need for Germany to gain "living space" (*Lebensraum*) in Eastern Europe and Russia for its densely populated country, and the notion that the German Army, especially its *Frontsoldaten* or "front line soldiers," had been "stabbed in the back" by the SPD and the Jews.

As 1919 rolled into 1920, Hitler began to make speeches to party members and those curious about the party in various right-wing hangouts in Munich. Almost immediately, Hitler and his comrades within the party realized that he possessed an extraordinary talent for speaking. On February 24th, 1920, Hitler and the DAP held a meeting that two thousand people attended. Hitler's speech, which described the twenty-five-point platform of the party that he and two others had written, and its reception solidified his place as one of the DAP's leaders. In March 1920, he was discharged from the army and then worked full-time for the party.

By 1920, Hitler had become one of the leaders of the DAP. In 1921, by virtue of his speaking ability, which was beginning to draw large crowds in Munich, Hitler became the leader of the party, which changed its name from *Deutsche Arbeiterpartei* to *Nationalsozialistische Deutsche Arbeiterpartei* (also known as the National Socialist German Workers' Party, the NSDAP, or the Nazi Party).

The name change reflected a desire by its leadership to set it apart from other right-wing parties and the political left, which frequently used the word "workers" to highlight their adherence to socialism or communism. In the case of the NSDAP, aspects of socialism were mixed with intense nationalism, as opposed to the communists' ideas of the universal brotherhood of the workers.

By late 1921, Hitler, recognizing his own speaking (and therefore recruiting) capability, as well facing down a mutiny within the party, had become the absolute undisputed leader of the NSDAP. Alongside Hitler, as he moved his way toward becoming the unquestioned leader of the Nazis, was Ernst Röhm, an army captain who became the commander of the party's paramilitary, the *Sturmabteilung* or SA. Hermann Göring, the successor to Manfred von Richthofen's squadron in WWI, also became attracted to the movement and Hitler. Göring was a nationally recognized figure due to his role in WWI. By the 1920s, Munich had become a magnet for extreme right-wing politicians and believers. Among them was Rudolf Hess, a WWI veteran who had spent much of his youth in Egypt and developed a profound dislike for anyone who was not white, as well as Heinrich Himmler, a young man who had just missed action in WWI to his utter regret. Hess was to become Hitler's deputy and transcriber of *Mein Kampf*, while Heinrich Himmler became the head of Hitler's protection detachment or *Schutzstaffel*, a section of the SA better known as the SS.

One of Hitler's more important early supporters was General Erich Ludendorff of WWI fame, who was a central figure in right-wing politics in Munich after the war. It was Ludendorff that supposedly lent "legitimacy" to the Nazis' Beer Hall Putsch of 1923. This coup attempt ended in utter failure, but Hitler's testimony in court, which was really speeches permitted by the presiding judges, made him a national figure, as his "speeches" were reported in the national papers. However, while Hitler did garner national attention, most Germans regarded him as more of a political oddity, as a person who would soon pass from the political scene than any kind of real politician.

When Hitler was released from Landsberg Prison in late 1924, the NSDAP was in disarray. For much of 1925 and 1926, Hitler worked to rebuild the party and make it a national presence. The experience of 1923 had taught him that a small local revolt would hardly succeed in propelling the Nazis to national power. He determined that the Nazis' road to national power was going to be determined at the ballot box, so, along with his followers, he set about creating a national organization that would be represented in every German state, city, town, and village. It was at this point that Hitler became the unquestioned leader of the party and began to be addressed as *Führer* ("leader").

In 1924, a small man with decidedly dark "un-Aryan" features, a club foot, and a noticeable limp joined the party, and within a short time, he became the leader of the NSDAP in Berlin, a notoriously leftist city. This was Dr. Josef Goebbels, who had studied language and language history in Heidelberg and who was rapidly becoming a master of propaganda. Nazi propaganda depicted Hitler and the NSDAP as vigorous, powerful, and dedicated to Germany and its people (especially the "forgotten man" at the bottom of society). Conversely, the Nazis' opponents were portrayed as out of touch, old, corrupt, uncaring, and arrogant. Of course, much of the NSDAP's propaganda was aimed at the Jews and communists, who were often considered one and the same, and "helping" the German population understand that they were the main source of the nation's woes.

From 1924 to 1929, the Nazis built a highly efficient organization. However, as things began to become more stable within the Weimar Republic, party membership grew relatively slowly, though the Nazis did have a national presence and did elect its members to both state legislatures and the Reichstag, the national parliament, though in relatively small numbers.

It took the Great Depression to propel Hitler and the Nazis to national power.

Chapter 8 – The Nazis Take Power

Throughout the 1920s, the Nazis grew in membership. In 1925, there were just under 30,000 members. In 1929, there were nearly 110,000. This does not account for the number of people who worked for or supported the Nazis and were not official party members, which was probably underestimated at the time, both from the nature of early scientific polling and the reluctance of many "respectable" Germans to be openly identified with the NSDAP.

Despite the growth in their members and despite considerable work in organization, the NSDAP, while somewhat strong in conservative German states like Bavaria, was not able to pull more than 3 percent of the vote for the Reichstag. They did particularly poorly in the cities, and while they had already made their presence known in the countryside, villages, and towns, they made a bigger push in these areas for future elections. Though the population of Germany had changed considerably from the time of Bismarck and industrialization, most Germans still lived in rural areas or in small towns and villages.

Within both the cities and without, the Nazis increased their support by forming wings that were designed to appeal to specific demographic groups. You likely know of the Hitler Youth (*Hitlerjugend* in German), which appealed to young and teenage boys as a vital and strong alternative to the Boy Scouts and other youth groups that existed throughout Germany. Of course, the constant indoctrination and propaganda aimed at the youth helped their movement. These young men or boys, especially when their families were going through tough times or when their parents just didn't understand them, appreciated someone telling them not only that they were worthy people but that they were worthy of conquering the world.

Alongside the Hitler Youth, which was male-only, was the BDM or *Bund Deutsche Mädel* (the "League of German Maidens" or the "Band of German Maidens"). (As a side note, many times you'll see this translated as the "League of German Girls," which is incorrect. "Maidens" was used purposely to convey both purity and hearken back to another time, a supposed "German Golden Age."). The BDM did encourage girls to take up athletics, as you will see in many propaganda films, but it also stressed domestic life and child-rearing. In the Nazi worldview (or *Weltanschauung*, a word you can frequently see in Nazi speeches, as well as modern history books about the period), a woman's place was in the home, raising large numbers of children to help the Germans conquer and colonize the world. Before the Nazis took power, and more quietly afterward, many non-Nazis, especially more "proper" young women, came up with a nickname for the BDM: *Bund Deutsche Matratze* or "League of German Mattresses," as it was well known, and has since been proven with data from the period, that the number of pregnancies among girls and young women increased after Nazi Party and youth rallies.

Illustration 29: A German student propaganda poster. "The German student fights for Führer and People." The flag and uniform are that of the Hitler Youth.

Illustration 30: Poster for the League of German Maidens.

As you can plainly see, the Nazis' obsession with blond-haired, blue-eyed "perfection" is very evident.

The Nazis penetrated many segments of German society, from lawyers to farmers to teachers. As times got worse in 1929, these groups and the German public at large kept beating the same drum. "See what the November criminals, the Versailles Treaty, the Allies, the communists, and the Jews have done to Germany?" "Germans have lost everything." "The people are begging in the streets. The people have no dignity. No honor." "Hitler will restore Germany's strength, honor, and dignity!" Just right there, you essentially have a synopsis of every speech made by Hitler and his minions from 1929 until they came to power in 1933.

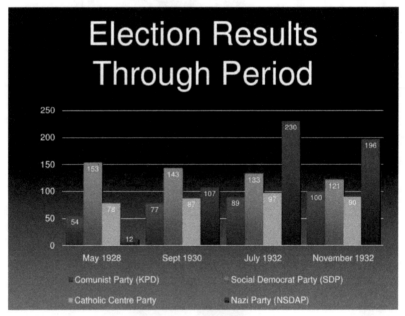

As you can see from the chart above, the Nazis gained ninety-five seats in the Reichstag after the crash of 1929. The Communists also gained seats, but while their gains came almost exclusively from the cities, the Nazis' base after 1929 was broader. Add to that the notion that the other major and some of the minor parties would gather against the Communists when needed.

In 1925, Field Marshal Paul von Hindenburg was elected president. He was seen as a strong figure, and the conservative parties and interests in Germany believed they could count on him to keep the extremists in line. This primarily meant the Communist Party, but before 1929, it also meant the Nazis.

However, after 1929, the nature of German politics changed. Many people believe that things changed toward dictatorship only after Hitler took power. This is incorrect. From 1929 onward, conservatives in both the Centre Party and those allied with the military became the chancellor. Each of them—Heinrich Brüning, Franz von Papen, and Kurt von Schleicher—ruled for short periods of time: two years and two months 169 days, and 56 days, respectively).

What these men all had in common was a hatred of liberal democracy, communists, the Social Democrats, and disorder. To varying degrees, they each wanted a return to the monarchy or perhaps a dictatorship with Hindenburg as its figurehead. None of them was willing to nor had the support to take direct action to make this happen, but from 1929 to 1932, each of them made important changes to the German political landscape, which helped Hitler establish his dictatorship when he came to power.

As you can see from the chart above, the Nazis gained the most votes in the election of July 1932. In addition to taking advantage of the bad times that had beset Germany and the world, Hitler and the Nazis also employed modern techniques in their election efforts. They made a point to seem decisive, a party of action and movement. At the top was Hitler, who seemed to appear all over Germany, almost at the same time. Hitler was the first politician to make use of the plane as a campaign tool, flying thousands of miles during election cycles and appearing in cities from north to south, sometimes on the same day. By the time Hitler took power, he and Josef Goebbels had become masters of political propaganda.

Throughout the 1920s, the SA had fought street battles with paramilitary groups of other parties, primarily that of the Communists. It was not just political opposition that the SA went after; of course, Jews and those who dressed in more modern Jazz Age type clothes and wore their hair longer were also targets of increasing levels of street violence during the Depression. For a time, the SA was banned, but as times got worse and as the Nazis gained more power, the traditional conservatives believed they could use the Nazis and their thugs against their own political opponents. However, the SA, whose leader, Ernst Röhm, made no secret of his wish of replacing the army with his SA, which, by the mid-1920s, numbered 400,000 men (after Hitler became chancellor, this number increased to over *two million*). This last notion, combined with Röhm's not-so-secret homosexuality and his leaning toward a more radical socialism than Hitler, made the army uneasy, but they were still hesitant to throw their support behind Hitler. This would change in 1934.

In July 1932, the Nazis became the largest party in the Reichstag, but another election was called that November. In this election, Hitler and the Nazis lost votes, and many historians believe that they might have continued on a downward spiral if events had played out a bit differently. The NSDAP was practically broke from the repeated state and national elections that took place at the time, which was due to both scheduling and no-confidence/coalition voting. The economy had begun to show small signs of improvement, and the people were tired of the street violence taking place every day, especially in the cities.

Hitler had asked or put out feelers for President Hindenburg to name him chancellor: once in July, when his popularity was greatest, and again in November, when the Nazis still held a considerable number of seats despite losing support. Hindenburg disliked Hitler. A lot, in fact. Both times, he categorically refused to consider it.

However, between November 1932 and January 1933, the plotting of several politicians resulted in Hitler being named chancellor of Germany by Hindenburg. The chancellor in November, Kurt von Schleicher, had developed an economic plan to alleviate the pains of the Depression, but he could not find enough political support to make it a reality. He had gone to Hitler, but Hitler refused to throw in with Schleicher. When Schleicher had come to power, Schleicher had approached the left-wing of the Nazi Party behind Hitler's back. Worse still for Schleicher, he had essentially pushed the former chancellor, Franz von Papen, out of office in a sort of non-violent coup. That drove Hitler and von Papen into each other's political arms.

It was clear to everyone that Schleicher's plan was as unpopular as the man himself (it should be noted that his plan actually might have helped). Between November and January, von Papen and Hitler negotiated in fits and starts over a power-sharing agreement. In January 1933, the Reichstag took a month-long recess. Schleicher was a very unpopular man and had made many political enemies over the course of his career, especially during his short time as chancellor. Schleicher knew that when the Reichstag reconvened, there would be a no-confidence vote against him, so he went to Hindenburg, who, as president, had the power to name a chancellor or call elections. Hindenburg refused, and Schleicher had no choice but to resign.

That was when Hindenburg was approached by von Papen, who told Hindenburg, who by this time was clearly showing signs of senility, that he had worked out a power-sharing agreement with Hitler that allowed von Papen to both rein in Hitler and his party and stabilize political life in Germany. This time, reluctantly, Hindenburg agreed. Hitler became the chancellor of Germany on January 30th, 1933.

The former chancellor, Schleicher, for a number of reasons, was gunned down by a Nazi assassin on the Night of the Long Knives in June 1934.

Illustration 31: "The Field Marshal and the Corporal struggle with us for freedom and equality." Despite mutual enmity, the relationship between the two men was portrayed as friendly to the public.

Chapter 9 – The Nazis in Power

When Hitler came to power in 1933, he immediately set the state on two courses, with a third, the main one, yet to come. He was aided in his first two efforts by the fact that in the years from 1929 to 1932, Germany, under the last three chancellors and President Hindenburg, had moved decidedly to the right. They had increased the power of the federal government over the various *Länder* (states) and had used constitutional tricks to increase the office of chancellor.

They had also used the threat of street violence to get their way, but not in a way that seems obvious. With many Germans tired of the fighting between political parties, the chancellors promised that if they were given increased power, they would rein in organizations like the SA and the *Rotfront* ("Red Front"). They did this for a time, but they were not above using Hitler's men or the thought of them to intimidate opponents.

Secondly, they had slowly begun a patchwork program that was to undermine the power of the Reichstag. Many of these conservatives were monarchists, and another large group was hoping for a military dictatorship under Hindenburg, but he consistently refused. He was no friend of democracy, but he had taken an oath to uphold the Weimar Constitution, and a German officer's oath was everything.

When Hitler took power, he was somewhat limited in what he could do, "somewhat" being the keyword here. Under the power-sharing agreement he had made to become chancellor, the Nazis were only to hold three cabinet positions. Two were of relatively minor consequence. The third was the Ministry of the Interior, which gave Hitler power over the police.

The first thing Hitler did with his power as chancellor, along with the conservative, communist-hating members of his cabinet, was to go after the communists. Violence against the communists was already on the rise from the moment Hitler was sworn in, but about a month later, on February 28th, 1933, he was helped in that course by the actions of one man.

That man was Marinus van der Lubbe, a Dutch communist who was likely either emotionally disturbed or mentally challenged or both. For years, many historians, journalists, and the general public believed that the Nazis carried out the arson of the Reichstag, but in more recent times, more evidence has come to light showing that van der Lubbe carried out his plan without the Nazis' knowledge. Whether he acted at the urging of fellow communists in Germany or the Comintern (the international organization of communists run from and commanded by Moscow) is still being debated.

The Reichstag fire was a gift to Hitler and the Nazis. They were already bumping up against some opposition within the government, which was going to make implementing their program more difficult. The Reichstag fire provided the Nazis and all anti-communists (most importantly, the military and the police) with an excuse to crack down on communism in Germany. As a result, the Nazis, with the support of the conservative parties that still existed, declared a state of emergency, loudly declaring that "the country was under assault from communism." The Nazis, due to their widespread conservative support, suspended all civil liberties in

Germany for an unspecified amount of time. On March 23ʳᵈ, 1933, the Reichstag, with Hindenburg's approval, passed the Enabling Act, which allowed Hitler to rule by decree for the next four years. And with that, freedom in Germany was dead.

Immediately, the Communist Party was outlawed. Soon after that, the Social Democratic Party, Germany's oldest political party, was outlawed as well. In each case, Hitler set the SA, the police, and his secret police on his enemies. (Germany had always had a secret police, but their powers had been somewhat limited in scope. That was no longer the case.)

The secret police, known to history as the "Gestapo," an amalgamating acronym of the German "GEheime STAatsPOlizei" (the acronym is capitalized only for illustration), was run and founded by Hermann Göring, the WWI *Luftwaffe* ace and early ally of Hitler. In 1934, Göring became the Minister of the Interior for the State of Prussia, as well as chief of the German Air Force (the *Luftwaffe*). Taking over the Gestapo in 1934 was Heinrich Himmler, the head of the SS.

With the Enabling Act, tens of thousands of Nazi opponents, both real and imagined, were rounded up and put in the concentration camps that were sprouting up all over Germany (some of them were actually built by the inmates, who were forced to sleep in the elements until construction was finished). The first major camp was at Dachau, just outside Munich, in Bavaria. This camp was run by Theodor Eicke, a sadist who laid the foundations for life in the camps. The guards of the camps were members of the SS, specifically the Death's Head Formations or *Totenkopfverbände*, which would later expand to include hundreds of thousands of men and an SS infantry division.

On May 1ˢᵗ, 1933, Germany celebrated May Day, which was recognized around the world for some time as the "Day of the Workers." The next day, Hitler outlawed all labor unions except the Nazis' own *Arbeitsfront* ("Work Front" or "Labor Front").

Thousands of the leading men and women of unions around the country were rounded up and thrown into the camps.

For the most part, most of the low-level communists and labor union members were released after some months in the camps. Their time spent there included hard labor, beatings, a starvation diet, and other torture. They were released on two conditions: they take an oath never to oppose Hitler or the Nazi Party (specifically meaning they could not join any secret reorganization of a union or party, but "opposition" could mean anything, including mouthing off to a policeman at the wrong time and place), and they never speak of the camps to anyone. On returning home with missing teeth, unset broken bones, and undernourishment, no one needed to talk of the camps, for it was obvious what went on there (though people, including camp staff, did talk, albeit in whispers).

Throughout Germany, the Nazis began what Hitler called *Gleichschaltung* or "coordination." This meant the "coordination" of German public life with the goals of the Nazi Party. This included implementing the Four-Year Plan to revitalize German economic life and bringing production under government supervision, "reforming" the courts and the legal system, and increasing the control and censorship of the press and all media under the Propaganda Ministry. The Nazis also changed the German education system to reflect Nazi beliefs and organized local committees to instruct the people on the proper way to behave (listening to the "proper" music, reading the "right" books, etc.) and to report on those that did not.

The most infamous symbol of the Nazis' efforts to reshape Germany in their image is the book burnings, which began in Berlin on May 10th, 1933, and spread around the country over the next few days. Libraries and bookstores were emptied of their proscribed ("forbidden") books and burned at the Berlin Opernplatz, a popular gathering spot and square. Books by some of Germany's leading authors of both past and present were burned, as well as foreign books, including books by Jack London (who was extremely popular in Germany but portrayed freedom-loving and anti-social characters), Helen Keller (as a deaf, mute, and blind person, she was considered "inferior" by the Nazis), and others.

Another author whose books were burned was famed German poet Heinrich Heine, whose political opinions and poems about freedom the Nazis found objectionable. Heine wrote in one of his books about the Christian crusades, "That was but a prelude: where they burn books, they will ultimately burn people as well." Today, Heine's quote is engraved at the memorial to the victims of Nazism at the spot of the Berlin book burning, which was led and encouraged by Josef Goebbels, the German propaganda minister.

Illustration 32: Book burning at the Opernplatz, May 10th, 1933.

Within about six months, the Nazis had "coordinated" most aspects of German public life. However, two groups remained in Hitler's crosshairs: the SA and the Jewish population of Germany.

As the Nazi Party grew, the SA and its head, Ernst Röhm, began to have dreams of their own. Among their aspirations were to be let loose to "deal" with the enemies of the Nazi Party and their own foes, specifically the Communist *Rotfront*. With the Reichstag fire and the Enabling Act, the SA was indeed set loose on those groups and many more. That left the SA with its main goal of supplanting the German Army itself.

There were several problems with this. Primarily, the army did not want to be supplanted, and it was the strongest armed force in the country. What's more, Hitler might need them to keep order or, more likely, to implement the military plans he laid out in *Mein Kampf*: the invasion and conquest of Eastern Europe and Russia.

Hitler could not afford to alienate the army in 1933. At this point in time, the army was still powerful enough to overthrow him should it decide to do so. So far, Hitler's actions had jibed with the army's interests, and while many in the army, especially at the top levels, were disgusted by the crude propaganda and street violence of the Nazis and the SA, they looked the other way as the Communist Party and the SPD were attacked and outlawed.

However, not only did they not approve of the men of the SA, whom they saw as crude, ill-disciplined thugs, which they were, they were also increasingly nervous about Röhm's and other SA leaders' calls for both supplanting the army and its political stance, which was more leftist than that of Hitler. For example, Hitler called for "coordination" between big business and the government. Röhm espoused ideas about the government takeover of big business.

The army also saw itself, and had for many years, as the most stable pillar of German society, and it was looked upon that way by most Germans. Army leaders also believed that they could act, either overtly or covertly, to limit Hitler's actions if it became necessary.

In the spring of 1934, the rhetoric of the SA leaders was getting more strident. They wanted to be more than just Hitler's "enforcers." They wanted a place of respect in the new Germany. Everyone knew that meant as the army, even if the SA did not come out and say it. All this reached Hitler's ears via informers within the SA, some of whom acted on their own and some of whom were in the SS.

The SS was, at least in name, part of the SA, and its commander, Heinrich Himmler, was subordinate to Röhm. Himmler had risen to command the SS in 1929, taking the title *Reichsführer-SS*. The SS had begun as Hitler's bodyguard unit and was also used in the dissemination of party propaganda, but by the time of the Reichstag fire, Himmler had both increased membership (about sixty thousand men in 1933) and maneuvered his way into the overall command of the German police. The *Sicherheitsdienst*, also known as the SD or "Security Office," was part of the SS, and it was tasked with monitoring the party and other organizations for disloyalty. The Gestapo also fell under SD control.

While the SA was made up mainly of WWI combat veterans, street thugs, and men from the working classes, a significant portion of the SS was made up of college graduates, intellectuals, and former army and police officers. The SS was viewed, both within and without the Nazi Party, as being more disciplined and trustworthy than the SA.

Things with the SA came to a head at the end of June 1934. By this time, Hitler had heard enough rumors about Röhm's aspirations (including perhaps the replacement of Hitler) to be concerned with a "second revolution" led by the SA. On June 30th, he acted. Röhm and the SA party leadership were on holiday at a lakefront resort in northern Bavaria. Elements of the SS led by Himmler, along with the SD (led by Himmler's soon-to-be notorious right-hand man, Reinhard Heydrich) and Hermann Göring's personal police echelon, converged on the resort and arrested Röhm and the SA leadership. Making things worse for Röhm and many of the others was the fact that they were caught in bed with other men. This event, known to history as the Night of the Long Knives, resulted in Röhm's death—he committed suicide in his jail cell—and the deaths of eighty-five other SA leaders. This was the official death toll. The unofficial death toll likely approached one thousand as Himmler, Heydrich, and Göring, as well as their commanders, took the opportunity to strike at their own political and personal opponents.

Germany was shocked, but, in a way, it was also relieved. The SA had been an unpredictable and violent force on Germany's streets for a decade. Citizens were shocked that Hitler would act against one of his oldest allies, but in a speech shortly afterward, the Führer explained that his "love for Germany" and "law and order" compelled him to act, despite his personal history with those in the SA.

Most importantly, the army was relieved. Its place in Germany was secure. However, it had sold its soul to Hitler. In return for acting against the SA, Hitler demanded that every man, from private to field marshal, take a public oath of loyalty to him, personally, which they did. As was mentioned earlier when discussing Hindenburg's role as president, German officers and the army in general considered an oath absolutely binding, and Hitler was well aware of this. By the summer of 1934, Germany was Hitler's, especially after the death of Hindenburg in July, which allowed Hitler to combine the office of chancellor with that of the president.

Illustration 33: Himmler, Hitler, and Röhm.

The SA continued to exist, but it had been brought to heel by the Night of the Long Knives; from then on, it was used more for Nazi Party activities and the spread of propaganda rather than street violence. After decapitating the SA and bringing the army under his control, Hitler was free to engage in his two primary aims: bring the German armed forces back to full strength and remove the Jews from Germany.

To do the first and to solidify his position among the people, Hitler needed to make good on the main promise he had made throughout his campaigning years: restore the German economy. He would not be able to do anything without Germans working and producing again, and, of course, his popular support would wane if he didn't deliver.

For years after the end of WWII, many historians believed the Nazi propaganda about the revival of the German economy. Josef Goebbels, if he was alive today, would tell you that all propaganda contains a kernel of truth, no matter how small, and the truth is that Hitler did indeed revitalize certain elements of the German economy.

Since about the middle 1980s and especially after the fall of East Germany (which allowed scholars to view its many records that had previously been unobtainable), historians generally have revised their opinion of Hitler's "economic miracle." Those who were helped the most were those at the top and in the industries he needed in order to proceed with his main goals of re-militarization and military conquest. With the unions under control, the industrialists, who were the recipients of massive spending contracts, were firmly in Hitler's pocket. Some specialized workers, such as chemists and engineers, saw their incomes rise significantly under Hitler, but the bulk of German workers did not.

The industrial workers of Germany, the men who Hitler had made so many promises, got no significant increases in pay and now had no union protections. Though you will see documentaries detailing Hitler's recreation programs for the workers (known as the "Strength through Joy" program), with its cruises, day trips, and picnics, this was more for show. The bulk of the workers never went on any kind of joy cruise. And complaining did no good. Those who complained often ended up with a beating, a trip to the camps, or both. By this time, the Nazis had informants in virtually every large workplace in Germany.

The one statistic that everyone could point to was unemployment. Without a doubt, Hitler put the Germans back to work. Much of this was done through large public works projects, most prominently, the Autobahn highway system.

The Autobahn's purpose was to make it easier for Germany's coming mechanized army to move throughout the country, but it was labeled as "a road to the future." Hitler promised that most of the Germans would soon own cars and be able to take vacations throughout the country with ease, thanks to the Autobahn. If you ever travel to Germany on the original miles of the Autobahn, you will be amazed—the roads still go through some of the most beautiful countrysides in Europe. Hitler himself planned much of it with his artist's eye; in some cases, he had roads redirected and rest stops and vista points built so that the people traveling could enjoy some particularly gorgeous views, especially in the south of the country. However, most Germans didn't own cars and wouldn't own them throughout the Nazi period.

Still, unemployment was reduced by over two million in the first year and a half of the Hitler regime, and that alone gained the Führer increased support among many in the working, lower, and middle classes. Additionally, these numbers included women, who, despite the Nazi belief that women should remain at home and have children, entered the workforce in larger numbers as the Nazi years went on. There were 4.2 million women in the workforce in 1933 and 5.2 million in 1939. This number would increase again in the middle of the war when the Nazis realized they had better let women work in the factories.

How was Hitler's program financed, though? It was done through deficit spending, which was something many of the governments of the West did when they began to turn the corner on the Depression. The Germans were concerned that this deficit spending might mean a return to hyperinflation, which had scarred Germany so deeply. This was avoided by creating a phantom corporation called the Metallurgical Research Corporation or "Mefo" (its German acronym), which issued bonds and credits alongside currency. When the bond was due, it could be collected in regular currency.

In 1936, Hitler ordered the formation of a Four-Year Plan, which was how long he expected it would take for Germany to be ready for war. The aim of the Four-Year Plan was to increase Germany's exports while reducing its imports (imports largely meant raw materials and food). However, both because of the economic reality and Hitler's increasing unpopularity in the world, the Four-Year Plan never came close to its goals. By that point, no one really paid any attention, though, as WWII had begun in 1939, one year sooner than Hitler originally planned.

The increases in credits to large industries were all part of one goal. And this goal was not the betterment of life for the average German citizen but rather for re-militarization and war.

Throughout the late 1920s and into the 1930s, small numbers of men had been training to fly in Russia alongside the thousands of Germans who subverted the restrictions on flying lessons by flying gliders. As was mentioned in a previous chapter, this plan was concocted at the highest levels of the German General Staff. In addition to work being done in Russia, which included developing ideas for new fighter planes, the German Navy, which had been forbidden submarines, was working in Finnish waters with Finnish submarines in the hopes of having a German submarine fleet sometime in the near future. Politics and international relations make strange bedfellows, for Finland and the Soviet Union were enemies. The Finns wanted strong ties with Germany, which had aided them in their war of independence against Tsarist Russia during WWI, in case of a clash with the Soviet Union. For the Soviets' part, they received hard Western currency in exchange for letting the Germans use bases in Russia and Ukraine, even though Germany was known for its anti-communist rhetoric, both before and after Hitler's rise.

In 1933, Hitler had canceled all required reparations payments due under the Treaty of Versailles. Simply put, by this point in time, the nations of the West (meaning primarily Great Britain, France, and the United States) were in the midst of the Great Depression themselves and had turned inward. Additionally, in both English-speaking countries but especially in the UK, the feeling had arisen that the reparations imposed on Germany were both unfair and contributed to the Depression itself. Without the support of the English, the French were not willing to confront Hitler. Germany also withdrew from the League of Nations at this time.

In March 1935, Hitler announced that Germany was no longer going to abide by the military restrictions imposed by the Versailles Treaty, and he reintroduced conscription and the rearming of Germany. These moves alone, combined with the refusal to pay reparations, further increased Hitler's popularity in Germany. From 1935 onward, an ever-increasing percentage of the German national budget went toward rearmament, and an ever-increasing number of German workers were involved in it in some way to the point that Germany could point to near zero unemployment by 1938. However, this statistic disregards the fact that the "chronically unemployed" or *arbeitsscheu* ("work-shy") were forced into jobs for which they were not qualified or sent to the camps.

*Illustration 34: Prisoners being driven into Dachau, a drawing by
Michal Porulski, a Polish priest who was interned
there during the war.*

The War against the Jews Begins

Even before Hitler took power, the SA made life for Germany's Jews miserable. Most people, both Jewish and Gentile opponents of Nazism, knew what areas of the big cities were heavily populated by Nazis and tried to avoid them if possible. Germany's Jewish population, in contrast to other European nations (especially in the east), was highly assimilated and did not particularly stand out. However, those Jews who were Orthodox did, with their black clothing, hats, and hairstyles that gave them away. This was particularly the case for men, who knew that being caught alone in certain areas was asking for a beating.

You must remember that Germany before and after WWI was a highly regulated state; every family was required to register their address with the police. Jews and other minority groups (for example, Poles) often lived in certain neighborhoods, which was (and still is) something minorities and immigrants did in other countries, including the United States. Blond-haired German Jews might be identified simply by giving someone their street address. Before the Nazis, this was done when conversing with others or conducting business. After the Nazis came to power, this information was kept close to the vest.

When Hitler became chancellor, the SA went on an orgy of violence against the Jews, especially in the bigger cities and especially in Berlin. At the time, this shocked much of Germany, even those who were "mildly" anti-Semitic, as street violence and coarse behavior were considered "un-German." Many conservative allies of the Nazis were put off by the violence, and at the beginning, Hitler put a stop to much of it, knowing he had to solidify his power before taking any radical steps. The Nazis were even deterred, for a time, when they established a boycott of Jewish businesses. The international response forced Hitler to relent, but as his position got stronger within Germany, he was less and less responsive to pressure, both internally and externally.

By 1935, Hitler's hold on power was virtually complete, and with that, he ordered functionaries within the Nazi Party to draft what became known as the Nuremberg Laws. Every year in September, the Nazis would hold a rally in the southern city of Nuremberg, about one hundred miles north of Munich. In 1935, Hitler decided that the party rally would be a good time to announce his intention of formulating new laws governing race and the "Jewish question" in Germany. This initial set of laws was passed against the Jews, but soon after, other minorities, including the Roma (once derogatorily known as "Gypsies") and the small number of black people in the country, were targeted as well.

The Nuremberg Laws were actually two documents: The Law for the Protection of German Blood and German Honor and the Reich Citizenship Law.

The Law for the Protection of German Blood and Honor read as follows:

SECTION 1

1. Marriages between Jews and nationals of German or kindred blood are forbidden. Marriages concluded in defiance of this law are void, even if, for the purpose of evading this law, they are concluded abroad.

2. Proceedings for annulment may be initiated only by the Public Prosecutor.

SECTION 2

Relation outside marriage between Jews and nationals for German or kindred blood are forbidden.

SECTION 3

Jews will not be permitted to employ female nationals of German or kindred blood in their households.

SECTION 4

1. Jews are forbidden to hoist the Reich and national flag and to present the colors of the Reich.

2. On the other hand they are permitted to present the Jewish colors. The exercise of this authority is protected by the State.

SECTION 5

1. A person who acts contrary to the prohibition of section 1 will be punished with hard labor.

2. A person who acts contrary to the prohibition of section 2 will be punished with imprisonment or with hard labor.

3. A person who acts contrary to the provisions of section 3 or 4 will be punished with imprisonment up to a year and with a fine or with one of these penalties.

SECTION 6

The Reich Minister of the Interior in agreement with the Deputy of the Fuehrer will issue the legal and *administrative regulations which are required for the implementation and supplementation of this law.*

SECTION 7

The law will become effective on the day after the promulgation, section 3, however, only on 1 January 1936.

The Reich Citizenship Law read:

The Reichstag has unanimously enacted the following law, which is promulgated herewith:

Article 1

1. A subject of the state is a person who enjoys the protection of the German Reich and who in consequence has specific obligations toward it.

2. The status of subject of the state is acquired in accordance with the provisions of the Reich and the Reich Citizenship Law.

Article 2

1. A Reich citizen is a subject of the state who is of German or related blood, and proves by his conduct that he is willing and fit to faithfully serve the German people and Reich.

2. Reich citizenship is acquired through the granting of a Reich citizenship certificate.

3. The Reich citizen is the sole bearer of full political rights in accordance with the law.

Article 3

The Reich Minister of the Interior, in co-ordination with the Deputy of the Führer, will issue the legal and administrative orders required to implement and complete this law.

When these laws were published, whether in newspapers, magazines, or posters, they were frequently accompanied by the chart below to illustrate what constituted a "German," a *Mischling* (a person of mixed German-Jewish heritage), and a "Jew."

Illustration 35: The Nuremberg Laws illustrated. Original Nazi chart showing ancestry of (from l to r) Germans, "Mischlings 2nd Grade", "Mischlings 1st Grade" and Jewish people

Addenda to these laws forbade Jewish doctors from treating Germans, Jews from serving in the armed forces, or Jewish lawyers defending Germans; these examples are just the tip of the iceberg. However, exceptions could be made by Hitler himself. For instance, there was *Luftwaffe* General Helmuth Wilberg and *Luftwaffe* Field Marshal Erhard Milch, who had a bizarre family tree made up at the insistence of Göring.

With the passage of the Nuremberg Laws, street violence against Jews and the increased incarceration of Jews supposedly breaking the laws increased. Germans who were found having relations with Jews were publicly shamed, and those married to Jewish Germans were "encouraged" to divorce them (most did not).

Illustration 35: Infamous picture of SA men with a German woman and Jewish man caught together. Her sign reads, "I am the biggest pig in the neighborhood and only lay with Jews." His sign reads, "I am a Jewish boy and only take German girls to my room." In German, their insults rhyme.

In about three years, Hitler had gone from losing votes in the last free German election to gaining absolute power over Germany. He had decreased unemployment and repudiated the Treaty of Versailles. In March 1936, he had ordered German troops into the demilitarized Rhineland against the terms of the treaty and gotten away with it, and he was even rebuilding the German armed forces. The capstone to all of this was the Berlin Olympics of 1936.

During the Olympic Games, the SA and other branches of the government and party, as well as the citizens, were overtly instructed and covertly told to "ease off" on the persecution of Jews. The most famous examples were the removal of signs in parks and on park benches that said "No Jews! Germans only!"

German Jews interviewed during this time said they were afraid that once the world had left, having been fooled that the situation wasn't that bad in Germany, things would be worse for them. They were right to be fearful.

One more thing about the Berlin Olympics. In the United States, a big deal was made (and still is) over the fact that Jesse Owens, an African American, was the star of the games. It's no secret that this angered Hitler, but generally speaking, both the Führer and the German people considered the games a German victory. After all, Germany won the most gold medals at the games by far. However, not many people in the US were and are aware of this fact.

When the Olympics were over, things didn't return to "normal" for the Jews of Germany. They got worse. And making things far, far worse for not only the Jewish population of Germany but also Europe and the world were two international crises: the annexation of Austria to Germany in March 1938 and the Sudeten (or Czech) crisis in September. Both events were victories for Hitler. His popularity soared, and he saw that the British and French were incredibly reluctant to chance another war. By November 1938, Hitler felt unassailable.

On November 9th, 1938, Hitler ordered a new round of persecution of the Jewish population. The "excuse" for the order was the assassination of German diplomat Ernst vom Rath in Paris, who was killed by a young Polish Jew named Herschel Grynszpan. Grynszpan was angry about the prospect of being deported back to Germany and his family's inability to flee that country. Sadly, vom Rath was not an anti-Semite, and he was already under investigation by the Gestapo at the time of his death.

Hitler ordered the persecution that followed for revenge, and he apparently "encouraged" the Jews to leave the country. However, by that time, the laws on emigration and the money it cost to leave

Germany made it virtually impossible for any but the wealthiest or most famous Jewish people to flee.

This persecution is infamously known to history as The Night of Broken Glass or *Kristallnacht* in German. Throughout Germany and Austria, Jewish businesses, synagogues, and homes were ransacked, with their windows smashed in (hence the name); oftentimes, these buildings were set alight. The fire departments were ordered to stand down. All across the country, those Jews brave enough to take to the streets in an attempt to save their businesses or places of worship were beaten, and they were often taken to camps or prisons. Even those who tried to remain out of sight in their homes were oftentimes dragged out into the street, beaten, mocked, and forced to do the most menial of tasks. In Vienna, crowds of Austrian Jews were forced to clean the streets for hours on their knees with toothbrushes while crowds gathered to jeer and spit on them.

Thousands of buildings were either totally or partially destroyed. Many of the synagogues of Germany and Austria, which had been standing for centuries, were gutted by fire, their holy books and much else tossed into the gutter. In the 1990s, former Hitler Youth member Alfons Heck appeared in a documentary about that group and growing up in Nazi Germany. He stated that it was his belief that "after Kristallnacht, none of us could pretend not to know what was going to happen to Germany's Jews." Everything was out in the open, and Hitler saw that the vast majority of Germans would not lift a finger to help their Jewish neighbors. They were either indifferent, anti-Semitic, or afraid of what might happen to them if they interfered. It is the assertion of many historians that *Kristallnacht* did indeed encourage Hitler, Himmler, and the Nazis to go further in their plan to "rid" Germany of its Jews.

Illustration 36: The Night of Broken Glass, November 9ᵗʰ, 1938.

International Affairs

When he heard the muted international response to his repudiation of the Versailles Treaty and rearmament, Hitler realized that Britain and France were both afraid of another European war and were too focused on the effects of the Depression within their own countries to interfere with his plans in any significant way.

When Hitler ordered his troops into the Rhineland on March 7ᵗʰ, 1936, he told his troops to return across the Rhine should the French open fire on them. He knew that his country was not ready to fight a war, at least not yet. When the French did not open fire, instead choosing to bring their troops home, Hitler sensed he could get away with more.

In March 1938, after years of agitation by Austrian Nazis (including the assassination of Austrian chancellor Engelbert Dollfuss in 1934), riots and anti-government actions were launched throughout the country, especially in the capital of Vienna. They were close to launching a long-planned coup d'état when the Austrian chancellor, Kurt von Schuschnigg, offered, albeit under pressure, to install a number of Nazis in his cabinet. A few months later, Schuschnigg called a special election for the Austrian people to vote on the question that Hitler had been screaming about for years: the union of Germany and Austria.

On March 11th, days before the election was to be held, Hitler sent an ultimatum to the Austrian chancellor, threatening a full-scale invasion and mass destruction should he not resign and name an Austrian Nazi as his successor. After much maneuvering, miscommunication, further threats, and an order to begin the invasion on March 12th, Schuschnigg resigned. On the morning of March 12th, the new Austrian chancellor, Arthur Seyss-Inquart, who was later hanged for crimes against humanity for his role in the Holocaust in Holland, "invited" Hitler across the border.

When Hitler crossed the border and entered Vienna, he was given a hero's welcome. Many Austrians supported the move, as it restored them to a powerful position, one they had not held since before the fall of the Habsburg Empire in 1918. It also brought order after years of infighting. The Nazi takeover of Austria, which became known as the state of Ostmark under Hitler, also brought out the worst in many Austrians, especially in the capital, where Hitler had first been exposed to anti-Semitism. Though it might seem strange to hear today, many German Nazis were shocked at the level of viciousness toward the Jewish population that took place in Austria. Remember, though, this was before the extermination of the Jews had begun, so many Nazis were not completely inured to the violence directed against the Jews.

Though the Treaty of Versailles had expressly forbidden the union of Germany and Austria, the British and French sat on the sidelines, as did the leader of the Soviet Union, Joseph Stalin, who was eager for the powers of Europe to fight each other. Excuses were made in the British Parliament and the French National Assembly, as well as in the press of both countries. "It's a German affair." "The Austrians wanted it." "Do you want to fight another bloody war over Austria?"

One voice stood out above the crowd, however. This voice was a member of Parliament, and he had been the First Lord of the Admiralty during WWI. This man was Winston Churchill, and he decried and attempted to shame his government's inaction in response to Hitler's aggression but to no avail.

Throughout Hitler's book *Mein Kampf,* as well as hundreds, if not thousands of times in his speeches, he had proclaimed his desire to bring together all the Germans of Europe into one nation. Throughout history, groups of Germans had moved to other parts of Europe in search of a better life or had been on the "wrong" side of border changes following a war, such as WWI.

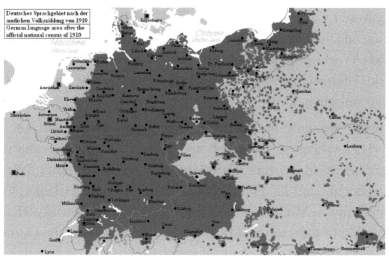

Illustration 37: Ethnic German populations, c. 1910. There was also a sizable number of Germans in the Volga Basin in Russia. (Courtesy Rex Germanus, Wikicommons).

As you can see on the map above, the area that today is the Czech Republic (in 1938, it was Czechoslovakia) bulges into the area between Germany and Austria. In the border areas between the three countries but within Czechoslovakia were the Sudeten Germans, who took their name from a local river. Soon after the annexation of Austria, Hitler began demanding that the Sudetenland be incorporated into Germany. He accused the Czech government of encouraging anti-German laws and persecution and ignoring the plight of the German minority within their country.

The truth is that there were some laws, especially regarding language, that were anti-German, and some anti-German incidents did occur. However, these were blown out of proportion by the Nazis in their propaganda, and they completely ignored the Sudeten Nazis' acts of violence against the Czechs in German-majority areas.

The Czechs categorically refused Hitler's demands, and they could have held out for some time against Hitler's armies if they had been given guarantees from France, Britain, and the USSR that they would come to the Czechs' aid. The Czechoslovak Army was strong and had strong border defenses in defensible terrain. The Skoda Works produced some of the best cannons and tanks in the world. Ultimately, however, the Czechs would not be able to defeat Hitler without help.

Stalin announced that he would come to the aid of the Czechoslovakians if the British and French did. But they did not. Eager to avoid another European war, Prime Minister Neville Chamberlain and his French counterpart, Édouard Daladier, took several trips to Munich to meet with Hitler and his new ally, Benito Mussolini of Italy, to see if there was a way to appease the German dictator and avoid war. And, of course, there was: give Hitler the Sudetenland. So, that is what they did—and not one Czechoslovakian official was invited to the talks that would decide the fate of their nation. Without the mountains and forests of the Sudetenland, Czechoslovakia was indefensible.

Abandoned by its "friends," the Czechs agreed to Hitler's terms and evacuated the Sudetenland. Hitler had won again, without firing a shot. In England, Neville Chamberlain got off his plane and waved his agreement with Hitler in the air. "I believe this is peace in our time," he said. In Parliament, a short time afterward, Chamberlain was given a rousing round of applause for keeping the peace, but Churchill, now with a larger number of followers, stood up and said, in part, "You were given the choice between war and dishonour. You chose dishonour, and you will have war." One year later, Hitler marched his troops into the rest of Czechoslovakia unopposed.

Shortly after Chamberlain and Daladier left Munich, Hitler commented to those around him, "We have met our enemies, and they are worms." Seeing how easily the British and French abandoned their "ally" in Czechoslovakia, Joseph Stalin was determined to come to terms, at least temporarily, with Hitler.

Illustration 38: The Munich Conference, September 1938. Left to right are Chamberlain, Daladier, Hitler, Mussolini, and Ciano (Mussolini's son-in-law and aide).

For two decades, Hitler had made it plain that he had three main goals: *Lebensraum* ("living space") in the USSR, the removal of the Jews from Germany, and the destruction of world communism, which he and other Nazis believed was being run by a Jewish cabal from Moscow.

Similarly, Russia had always been on the alert for Prussian or German power. For many years, the Prussians and Russians shared a long border in occupied Poland. Under the communists, and especially since the rise of Stalin, Hitler was seen as the archenemy, both of the Soviet Union as a nation and of communism as a political ideology.

However, after the disaster of the Munich Conference (at least for the Western Allies and the USSR), Stalin realized that he would be on his own as well if Hitler attacked the Soviet Union, especially since the USSR was their ideological enemy. Stalin knew that, for a variety of reasons (mostly of his own making), the Soviet Union would not be able to resist Hitler effectively in 1938. He would need to buy some time.

While Stalin was pondering his next move, Hitler was planning his: the conquest of Poland. He began his plan in the same way he had begun the operations against Austria and Czechoslovakia, with the need to bring all ethnic Germans into the Reich and under his protection. As you can see in Illustration 37, there were many ethnic Germans living in Poland. Many had lived there for centuries, along the ever-changing borders between empires and countries. Others had found themselves in Poland after the end of WWI when the Allied Powers carved out the Polish nation from what had been the Russian, Austrian, and German Empires. The biggest point of contention was the so-called "Polish Corridor," which separated much of East Prussia from Germany proper. It was as if much of Prussia, the home of German unification, was now an island surrounded by the Poles. Within the Polish Corridor was the Free City of Danzig (today's Gdansk, Poland), which was under the protection of the League of Nations and was neither Polish nor German, though, by 1936, most of the city's governing senate was made up of local Nazis.

Hitler and his propaganda minister, Josef Goebbels, stepped up the anti-Polish propaganda, which stated in a variety of ways that the Germans in Danzig and in the Polish borderlands were being mistreated. In Danzig, this was not the case, as the city had a German majority. In the Polish/German border area, there were some anti-German incidents, but these paled in comparison to the anti-Polish activities that went on in Germany after WWI. When Hitler came to power, many Poles, whose families had lived in Germany for decades or more, emigrated to Poland for their own safety.

Throughout the summer of 1939, Hitler became shriller in his demands for what he called a "settlement of the Polish question." This was simply a euphemism for his intended invasion of Poland, which virtually everyone on the planet knew was coming. Between the annexation of the Sudetenland and the summer of 1939, both France and especially Britain had begun massive rearmament programs to discourage Hitler from any further moves in Europe, but it was "too little, too late." They each gave the Poles a guarantee that they would declare war on Germany should Hitler invade their nation.

The Poles hoped that this guarantee would deter Hitler, but Stalin and many others realized that it was likely Hitler would "finish off" Poland before the British and French could do anything substantial. They could not directly come to the aid of Poland, and while mounting an invasion of western Germany was not likely, it would take time to prepare even if there was the will for it, which there was not.

Both Hitler and Stalin knew this, and both were worried about what the other would do. Hitler worried that the Russians might come to the aid of their fellow Slavs in Poland, while Stalin worried that a successful German invasion of Poland would put Hitler right on his border.

On August 23rd, 1939, the governments of Germany and the Soviet Union announced a nonaggression pact. They pledged not to attack one another for ten years, along with massive trade deals and a secret agreement that involved dividing Poland between them. To say the world was shocked, after all the violent rhetoric between the two nations over the years, would be putting it mildly.

WONDER HOW LONG THE HONEYMOON WILL LAST?

The Soviet Union and Germany were not only ideological enemies; they had also supported opposite sides in the brutal Spanish Civil War, which lasted from 1936 to 1939. Both sides sent tanks, pilots, planes, and arms to their allies in Spain (the Germans supported nationalist/fascist General Francisco Franco, while the Soviets supported the communists and socialists). The war in Spain gave the world a taste of what another world war would be like. In 1937, German planes destroyed the city of Guernica in northern Spain, killing perhaps one thousand civilians.

Illustration 39: Hitler: "Scum of the Earth, I presume?" Stalin: "Bloody assassin of the workers, I presume?"

On September 1st, 1939, Hitler ordered his troops into Poland. On September 3rd, France and Britain declared war on Germany—WWII in Europe had begun. On September 17th, the Red Army of the Soviet Union invaded and occupied the eastern portion of Poland per their agreement with Germany.

The invasion of Poland showcased the "new" German Army (the *Wehrmacht*) and its powerful *Luftwaffe*. Most stunning of all to people around the world was the Germans' use of tanks. Though tanks had been used in the latter days of WWI, the machines of that era, along with the thinking of its generals, were slow, ponderous, and unreliable. The German tanks of 1939 were neither.

Using armor and aircraft (mostly dive bombers and fighter planes) in close coordination, the Nazis would attack one specific point in the enemy's lines, usually where it was weak. The tanks would break through the lines and fan out to surround the enemy's neighboring positions and drive deeper into enemy territory to disrupt supplies and communications. They would be closely followed by infantry units, which initially advanced behind short but intense rolling artillery barrages (a rolling barrage is one that strikes just in front of the advancing infantry, with the idea being that the barrage will disrupt and disorient the enemy so he is not able to effectively fight back).

Though the Poles fought bravely against both foes, they were doomed. The fighting went on for six weeks, with the Poles finally surrendering when the *Luftwaffe* began reducing the Polish capital, Warsaw, to rubble. The Poles were the first to succumb to the Nazi military machine, and as a ratio of their pre-war population, no nation suffered more losses during WWII and the Holocaust than Poland. Just under *20 percent* of Poland's people (and *90 percent* of its Jewish population) died during the war. That's almost one out of every five people.

In response to the Nazi invasion of Poland, France launched an invasion of the German border state of the Saar, which was a province they had occupied at the end of WWI. This invasion, which was met with little resistance, penetrated about six miles and then stopped and went no farther. No adequate explanation has ever been given for the halt. After the war, Field Marshal Alfred Jodl, when he was on trial for crimes against humanity, stated that if the British and French, who had had a total of 110 divisions along the front in the west, had invaded, the Germans would not have been able to stop them, having only 23 divisions facing westward when they invaded Poland. Hitler had gambled and won.

In November of 1939, Stalin demanded that Finland give up some of its crucial naval and coastal installations in the southern Baltic Sea and its southern coast, with its sizable area of the Karelian Isthmus that connects Finland to Russia near Leningrad (today's St. Petersburg). His reasoning was that since Finland had been aided by the Germans in its war of independence against Russia during WWI and since Hitler needed to keep Scandinavia secure because of the natural resources there, Hitler might ally himself with Finland in any future moves against the USSR.

The interesting thing is that in the German-Soviet Nonaggression Pact, Hitler had given Stalin free rein to deal with Finland as he wished, as well as giving Stalin the go-ahead to re-annex the Baltic states of Lithuania, Latvia, and Estonia, which had belonged to Russia until 1918. That was the price Hitler was willing to pay to be able to attack Poland without worrying about the Soviet Union.

The Finns rejected Stalin's demands, and shortly thereafter, the Soviet Red Army attacked Finland, starting what is known as the Winter War. In England and France, there was talk of perhaps having to declare war against both the Soviet Union and Germany, as it seemed the two totalitarian powers were aligning. However, the Finns mounted a stubborn defense, which cost the Soviets nearly a million men killed, wounded, and missing.

In the end, however, Finland could not hope to hold out against the numbers of the Soviet Union, so the Finns came to terms with Stalin in the early spring of 1940. This had several effects on the course of the war. First, the ineptitude of the Soviets, at least during the first half of the short war against the Finns, convinced Hitler that the Red Army was a paper tiger and that it was poorly led, poorly trained, and badly equipped. The Finns' stand convinced Hitler that it was possible to defeat the Soviets.

Second, though the Western Allies by no means supported the USSR in its invasion of Finland, they did not need to concern themselves with questions about declaring war on the USSR as well as Hitler. The Winter War ended quickly, and by the time it ended, Hitler was already making threatening moves in the west.

And lastly, by the time the Finns gave in to Stalin's demands, there were small signs that the agreement between Germany and the USSR was beginning to fray, and over time, these signs would get bigger. Though it would be another year and some months before Hitler launched his invasion of the Soviet Union, the Allies were gathering information from its own intelligence agents within Germany and the USSR that things were not going swimmingly between the two dictatorships. This information was corroborated by informants within the German Army and government, as well as increasingly "undiplomatic" language coming from the German Ministry of Propaganda. As time went by, the Germans would begin to renege on much of their agreement, such as holding onto shipments that were supposed to go to the Soviets. The Soviets likewise reneged, sending raw materials westward, for example. However, this was a relatively slow process, and it would take until the spring of 1941 to hit its high point. By that time, Hitler had already ordered his invasion of the USSR to begin by the middle of May (it would be delayed for several reasons until late June).

All of that was in the future in 1939 and early 1940. On the Western Front, where nearly a million French soldiers sat in the fortifications of the Maginot Line (their incredibly expensive and highly technical defense line with Germany) along with the British Expeditionary Force (BEF), the soldiers took to calling the war the "Phony War." From September 1939 until May 1940, nothing of note happened on the Western Front.

In the early part of the war, Hitler was happy to have his general staff plan his campaigns. He would occasionally interfere or make suggestions, but, by and large, the campaigns against Poland, Western Europe, the Balkans, and the first part of the invasion of the Soviet Union were left to the generals. It was only after things began to turn for the Germans that Hitler got involved in the minutiae of the war, making things far worse for the German Army.

So, in 1939 and 1940, the German General Staff planned the campaigns under the general direction of Hitler. Many in the German Army were hesitant to attack France, but some of the younger, bolder, and more innovative generals believed it was possible to not only beat the French but also beat them swiftly.

From the early 1920s until almost the war began, the French had invested hundreds of millions of francs (an estimated seven to ten billion US dollars in 2021) in the most innovative and powerful line of defense ever seen. The Maginot Line ran along the Franco-German border, and many considered it impenetrable, including the Germans.

The problem for the French was Belgium. During WWI, the Germans had stormed through Belgium, violating its neutrality, to attack France. Throughout the 1920s, no appreciable work was done on fortifications on the Franco-Belgian border. Firstly, it was believed, or rather hoped, that Germany would remain a peaceful democratic power far into the future after having "learned its lesson." Secondly, it was hoped that should there be a threat of war from Germany again, Belgium would tie itself with the Allies after having experienced a harsh German occupation from 1914 to 1918. Building a strong defensive line of fortifications on France's border with Belgium would signal to the Belgians that the French had no intention of defending them and would instead stay behind the Maginot Line.

Throughout the 1920s and into the 1930s, the French and British assured the Belgians that should Germany attack again, they would immediately come to Belgium's aid as they had in WWI. However, after Hitler took power and especially after the British and French had abandoned Czechoslovakia, the Belgians began to waver and went back and forth in diplomatic circles, discussing whether they should declare neutrality once again and if Hitler would even respect it if they did.

Naturally, Hitler assured the Belgians as much as possible that he would respect their neutrality. However, the Belgians continued waffling, which only added to French insecurity. Thus, the French, belatedly, continued building the Maginot Line along the Franco-Belgian border. By the time of the German invasion, this addition consisted of a small number of forts that were widely spaced apart—the perfect position for an attacker.

While the Germans were planning their attack on France, developments in Scandinavia distracted both the Allies and Germany. Britain received word that Hitler intended to invade Norway, both to protect his northern flank and to protect the massive iron, nickel, and timber resources he received from Sweden. The British were also concerned that the Germans could use Norway's hundreds of fjords to hide their growing U-boat fleet, which was already beginning to take a serious toll on British shipping.

Hitler had thought of a Norwegian invasion, but he instead offered the Norwegians a nonaggression pact, part of which would allow German naval vessels to use Norwegian waters. This would be intolerable to the British, whose security lay at sea, so the British, along with a small number of French forces, launched a preemptive invasion of Norway. After receiving a negative reply to his overture from the Norwegians and having gotten word of British plans, Hitler launched an invasion of Denmark and Norway on April 9th, 1940.

The German assault on Norway happened on the same day the Allies landed at various strategic points in central and northern Norway. Though the battle lasted until June 10th, it was all but over by the middle of May, with the Germans, having sustained significant naval losses, successfully forcing the Allied troops to evacuate. (Denmark was overrun in a day, and it was used as a stepping stone for German troops to move to Norway and to assert German control over access to the Baltic Sea.)

The Norwegian campaign did not affect Hitler's plans to invade France in any significant way, except perhaps to raise the morale of the German armed forces and the German people while the Allies' morale took a significant hit.

On May 10th, 1940, Hitler ordered his generals forward. The German attack was launched all along Germany's western border. Holland, which had been neutral and unmolested in WWI, declared its neutrality again, but that did not save it. And the Dutch were no match for the Germans, who, along with the first airborne (paratrooper) attack in history, had also firebombed the major Dutch city of Rotterdam, reducing much of it to ashes. Five days after it had begun, the war in Holland was over.

To the south of Holland, the Germans invaded Belgium, just as everyone had expected. When they did, the BEF and much of the French Army moved into Belgium to meet the German attack, which was exactly what they had promised the Belgians and exactly what the Germans had hoped they would do.

To the south, along the Franco-German frontier, large numbers of German troops, cannons, and planes made a show of attacking in a number of places along the Maginot Line, holding the French in their tracks, just as the Germans had hoped.

In between the Franco-Belgian border and the start of the Maginot Line proper was the thick, hilly, and difficult-to-traverse Ardennes Forest. It was difficult to traverse since there were few roads, and the roads that existed were many times in poor condition or not very wide. "Surely," the French thought, "the Germans can't move tanks and large cannons through the Ardennes." Of course, you either know already from prior reading or can guess that was exactly what the Germans did, as you can see on the excellent map below.

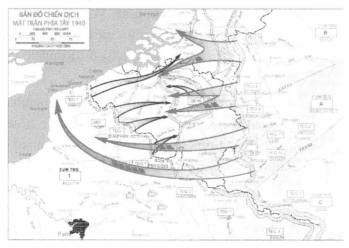

Illustration 36: The German moves north of the main part of the Maginot Line (blue hash marks). Though this map is in Vietnamese, it is an excellent and clear overview of the German attack in the west. Once the Germans reached the English Channel, they turned southward to attack or fend off French countermoves coming from the area of the Maginot Line.

The bulk of the German armored forces were in the Ardennes spearhead. Once they cleared the forest, they made a rapid dash to the English Channel, and once they were there, the main British and French force in Belgium was trapped. French forces to the south launched several counterattacks but, with only one real exception, did not make any progress.

What's interesting about the German tank (*Panzer* in German) spearhead is that, for the most part, German tanks were inferior to their French counterparts. Since the end of the war, a legend about the German tank forces of WWII has taken hold. What's odd about this is that, generally speaking, the Germans Panzers were not better than their opponents' tanks until late 1942 and early 1943 with the advent of the Panther, Tiger, and the up-gunned Panzer IV.

What the Germans did have, almost throughout the war, was better tank commanders, and that was most clearly the case in the French campaign. Germany's most famous WWII general, Erwin Rommel, was one of those leading the spearhead into France. Another was Heinz Guderian, who had helped formulate German tank doctrine before the war began.

The Germans used their tanks as a relatively independent arm of their armed forces. Tanks would break through the front lines, with mobile infantry in support to deal with anti-tank infantry. The German attack, dubbed *Blitzkrieg* ("lightning war"), called for deep armored penetration of enemy lines and/or the envelopment of their front-line forces. The Germans used the tank as their main weapon of war, whereas the French and British used theirs as infantry support weapons, dispersing them throughout their forces and thereby weakening their effect.

The campaign was basically over before it began. The BEF, along with some French and Belgian troops, were surrounded at the French coastal town of Dunkirk, from which they were evacuated through a Herculean effort on the part of the British Royal Navy and Royal Air Force, along with French troops, helping to prevent a German breakthrough. The successful evacuation of over 350,000 troops may have saved Britain, whose prime minister was now Winston Churchill. Churchill had taken office on the very day the Germans invaded France, and although he was faced with the greatest military disaster in British history, he vowed to fight to the end.

On June 25th, 1940, the French officially surrendered to Hitler and Mussolini, whose troops belatedly attacked in southern France. This armistice was signed in the same train car that the WWI armistice had been signed in. The French were "lucky." To avoid the cost in money and manpower it would take to occupy all of France, Hitler allowed the French to run a semi-autonomous region in the south, which was run by a former French war hero turned fascist named Marshal Pétain. This regime was centered in the city of Vichy.

Hitler visited Paris only once. He took a speedy tour through the city, which was filmed and which you can easily find on the internet or TV, seeing the Eiffel Tower, Notre-Dame, and, what was the most important spot to him, Napoleon's tomb. He never visited France again.

In Germany, even people who had been quietly on the fence about Hitler now had to admit there was something to the man. He had taken Germany from being the pariah of Europe to its most powerful state and its master. Germans began to enjoy the fruits of conquest as well, as looted, seized, and surrendered goods of all kinds began making their way into Germany.

The amazing thing was that all of this happened just as Hitler had predicted, which was also the problem. Hitler was powerful before the war, but now his position was unassailable. He would not be removed except through assassination or defeat, neither of which seemed likely in 1940.

The other problem was this, though it did not seem to be a problem at the time: Germany's economy had not even gone over to a war footing. Defense had taken up a great part of the budget before the war, and it continued at almost the same level through 1940 and arguably until the start of 1942. Germans had enough of everything and had not been asked to sacrifice in any deep way, at least economically. Even the casualties of the Polish and French campaigns had not been high, especially when compared to the Great War. It seemed as if Hitler had pulled off a miracle.

Illustration 37: Hitler and Göring on the balcony of the Reich Chancellery after the defeat of France in 1940.

Yet, within all this success was the kernel of the seed of defeat. Hitler, along with his lieutenants, especially Hermann Göring, the head of the *Luftwaffe*, began to believe they were both infallible and invincible. They got their first taste of how wrong they were when Hitler attempted to bring Great Britain to heel.

From late July and increasing through August and into September, the *Luftwaffe* and Britain's outnumbered Royal Air Force battled for air supremacy over southern England and the English Channel. Hitler planned on conquering Britain or, at the very least, forcing her out of the war to have a secure rear flank when he attacked the Soviet Union, which was his life's goal at that point.

To do this, he needed to do several things. He had already launched the U-boats against British and merchant ships arriving and leaving the UK. This attempt to starve Britain into submission and prevent aid from the US would continue throughout the war, but it would reach its height in 1942. After the war, Churchill would say the only thing that truly frightened him throughout the war was the U-boat campaign. At one point in 1941, the British had only enough food for two weeks.

Hitler also needed to establish control over the English Channel, at least for a short time, in order to move his planned invasion force to the British Isles. The Royal Navy was too powerful for the German *Kriegsmarine* to take on, though Hitler, like Kaiser Wilhelm II before him, attempted to rival it, at least for a time. However, if the *Luftwaffe* could destroy the Royal Air Force, he could send his invasion force across the Channel with an unrivaled air escort to fend off British ships.

That meant he had to destroy the Royal Air Force, though. Hermann Göring assured Hitler that it would only take a matter of days, weeks at the most, and at first, it seemed like this might happen. The Germans concentrated on bombing British airbases and destroying hangars, runways, and aircraft on the ground.

Though the British brought down a higher number of planes in comparison to the Germans, the Germans could afford to lose them—the British could not. For a time, the British were able to repair the damage to their airfields and continue, but by the end of August and beginning of September, they were on their last legs and were not able to keep up with the destruction.

It was at this point that fate stepped in. In late August, a German bomber crew made a navigational error and dropped its bombs over London. Hitler had expressly forbidden attacks on British cities. He had an affinity for the British as fellow "Germanic" peoples, and he wished to use his hesitancy to bomb civilians as a bargaining chip if the British sought terms. However, the next night, Churchill, who had forbidden attacks on German cities as well, ordered a small number of bombers to Berlin as revenge. Neither raid did much damage, but both infuriated the other side.

From that point forward, German planes began to concentrate on the destruction of British cities and the morale of their civilians.

Though "the Blitz," as the British called it, ultimately cost the UK forty thousand people (twenty thousand in London alone) from 1940 to 1941 (they lost seventy thousand throughout the whole war), the change in German tactics allowed the Royal Air Force to repair its airfields unmolested, build more planes, and mount a concentrated resistance to German attacks.

In this, they were helped by the advent of radar, a British invention that was totally overlooked by the Germans, though they shortly developed their own. Radar, combined with ships at sea, "coastwatchers" (civilians watching the air over coastal England), and intelligence sources and spies in Western Europe, helped the British anticipate German attacks.

This was also helped by an incredible fighting spirit. It was not unknown for two or three British fighters to attack German formations of twenty or more planes. Also aiding the British was the fact that they were flying over their homeland. They could attack a German formation flying over the coast, land and refuel, and then attack the same formation as they flew home. Naturally, this caused more damage to the Germans, and it also made them think the British had many more planes than they actually did. Additionally, British pilots who managed to bail out of damaged planes landed over friendly territory, sometimes even returning to base and flying again the very same day. Those shot down over the Channel, if they survived the impact, were often picked up by the Royal Navy. The Germans had a limited amount of fuel and could only spend minutes over their targets, and those who survived a dogfight and bailed out came down on British soil or were picked up by the British navy.

The Blitz went on until the spring of 1941 and continued again in 1944 with the advent of the V-1 and V-2 rockets, but by mid-September, the German effort had weakened. By the spring, most

German aircraft were deployed eastward for the coming invasion of the USSR. Hitler dismissed his defeat over Britain as inconsequential. To him, the English were all but defeated, and he would deal with them in his own good time. Many of his more insightful officers were sure this was not the case. They knew the English would not give up, and what's more, an unconquered England meant supplies (and perhaps even troops) from the United States would increase month by month.

But the Führer ordered them to prepare for a war against the Soviets, and orders were meant to be followed.

War in the East

Hitler launched his attack against the Soviet Union on June 22nd, 1941. He originally ordered his generals to be ready to launch the offensive on May 15th, but several factors caused a delay.

For many years, people believed that the delay was due to Hitler having to come to the aid of his ally Benito Mussolini in the latter's disastrous invasion of Greece. Though this did play a role in the delay, other issues contributed to it as well, the most important of which were a lack of oil and gasoline and the Germans needing more time to gather transport for the campaign.

This latter fact was dismissed for many years, partly due to the successful propaganda put out by the Nazis themselves. During the war and for years afterward, the image of the German Panzers thundering across Europe was what people thought of when they pictured the German Army in action, but in reality, most of the German Army moved by horse and wagon. This remained the case until the end of the war. Literally hundreds of thousands of horses and their fodder had to be gathered before the invasion of the Soviet Union, and this, combined with a lack of fuel and oil for their machines in the spring of 1941, which was only made worse by the invasions of Yugoslavia and Greece, delayed the Soviet operation until late June.

That delay came about because Mussolini was jealous of Germany's imperial gains. Mussolini fashioned himself as a modern-day Caesar and wished to establish a new Roman empire in southern Europe and North Africa.

In North Africa, Mussolini had launched an invasion of British-controlled Egypt and Kenya from his colonies in Libya and Somalia only to be humiliated by the smaller but better led British forces. Hitler had to come to his friend's rescue then as well, sending the Afrika Korps under Erwin Rommel to Africa, where he fought an intense campaign against the British and later the Americans until the spring of 1943.

In October 1940, Mussolini launched an invasion of Greece and was humiliated when the much smaller Grecian armed forces pushed him back into Albania, which was an Italian colony and Mussolini's starting point. Hitler, worried that the British would use Greece and the Balkans as a second front against him to penetrate his southern flank, sent a sizable number of divisions and planes southward.

At the start, he had gotten permission from the Yugoslavian regent Prince Paul to move his troops through that country, but at the last minute, pro-British forces overthrew the regent and replaced him with the fifteen-year-old Peter II. Peter and his advisors immediately refused Hitler passage. In response, Hitler launched Operation Punishment (also known as Operation Retribution) against the Yugoslavs.

Though Hitler successfully defeated the Yugoslav Army in the field and moved his troops on to Greece, the occupation of Yugoslavia was resisted fiercely throughout the war, forcing Hitler to keep between 250,000 to 300,000 troops in the country, which could have been of use to him elsewhere. The occupation of Yugoslavia was incredibly brutal, even by Nazi standards, and it also devolved into a civil war between rival Yugoslavian groups based on ideology, ethnicity, or both.

With the occupation of Yugoslavia done, Hitler moved into Greece on April 6th, 1941, which, by that time, had seen the arrival of sizable British and British Imperial troops. Despite a stubborn defense, the Greeks and British troops were no match for the Germans, and by June, the Germans occupied the country, including the large island of Crete, which saw a major battle between British and Imperial forces (notably troops from New Zealand and Australia) and German paratroopers. This was the largest use of paratroopers at that point in the war, and the casualties suffered by the Germans caused Hitler to forbid the use of paratroopers for the rest of the conflict, though they did fight with incredible tenacity in Italy and France.

By June 22nd, Hitler was ready to invade the Soviet Union, despite his agreement with Stalin in 1939. Stalin received many warnings about Hitler's intentions, but he inexplicably chose to ignore them. Goods still streamed to Germany, even as German troops were moving to take their positions for the invasion, and literally hundreds of German planes had been seen behind Soviet lines scouting Red Army positions. Additionally, spies from all over the world had sent Stalin warnings of an impending invasion, and Winston Churchill himself, who was privy to information gleaned from one of the most successful code-breaking operations in history, warned Stalin an invasion was coming. In the latter case, Stalin chose to believe that Churchill, who was an anti-communist if there ever was one, was trying to bait him into attacking Germany. When the German invasion did come, Stalin at first refused to believe the reports he was getting from his own commanders. Stalin only believed it when the evidence became absolutely irrefutable, and when he did, he went into a depression that lasted weeks, which only helped the German cause.

The German invasion of the USSR involved almost four million men, over 3,500 tanks and assault vehicles, nearly 5,000 planes of all types, nearly 30,000 cannons and mortars of all sizes, more than half a million horses, and an equal number of trucks and other transport vehicles.

Facing the Germans on the Soviet western border were nearly three million men, more than ten thousand tanks, and an equal number of aircraft of all types. Unfortunately for the Soviets, a variety of factors hindered their defense. First and foremost, Stalin had killed many of the Red Army's top commanders in the purges of the late 1930s, believing them to be part of a conspiracy against him (they were not). This meant that that the top commanders in both the field and to the rear were hesitant to act on their own lest it result in their own deaths. In addition, many of those commanders had been junior officers during the purges and were not prepared for the responsibilities thrust upon them. So, when they did act, it was frequently the wrong thing to do.

Though a new training regimen had been put into place following the Winter War against the Finns, most Soviet troops were poorly trained, poorly led, and poorly equipped. Though in many cases they fought to the death, just as many or more were captured in the huge envelopment battles that took place when the Germans invaded. This situation would continue at different times and places throughout the first part of the German campaign, known as Operation Barbarossa.

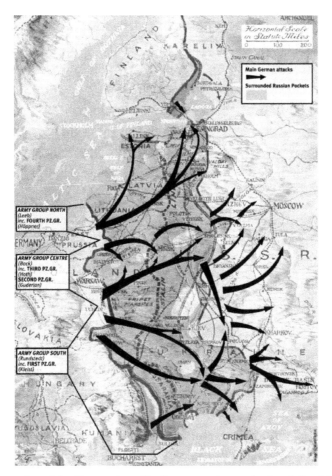

Illustration 38: Operation Barbarossa through the fall of 1941.

Hitler and several of his generals believed they could employ the same blitzkrieg tactics in Russia that they had elsewhere and win the war within weeks or at least before the onset of winter. An equal number of his generals believed that was wishful thinking in the extreme, but, of course, for the most part, they kept that to themselves or among trusted associates.

The progress of the invasion through August and the beginning of September seemed to reinforce Hitler's beliefs. As you can see on the map above, the Germans penetrated deep into the Soviet Union in the summer and early fall. If you look carefully at the map, you will notice large circles behind the arrows of the German advance. These indicate the surrounded Soviet forces, sometimes numbering almost half a million men or more, and those shown on the map are only the larger examples. Throughout the summer, the Germans, through leadership, fighting skill, and tactics, surrounded astounding numbers of Red Army troops and, in most cases, forced them to surrender. By the end of the campaign in the early winter, the Soviet had lost a million men or more captured, not to mention killed or wounded. It looked as if Hitler was right, once again.

However, the western Soviet Union was not France. Distances were vast, roads were poor if they existed at all, and accurate maps were in limited supply. The front-line combat troops and their vehicles had a difficult time traversing the USSR because of this, and the distances made supplying them a very slow and tenuous thing. The German movement was made worse in the fall (as well as the early spring) by the onset of the rainy season and the *Rasputitsa*– (Russian for "the season of mud").

The vast countryside of the USSR, most of which did not have modern drainage or even trees, to say nothing of the dirt roads, turned into a literal sea of mud twice a year, slowing movement to a crawl. Thus, beginning in the early fall of 1941, the Germans were forced to slow their advance along the entire front. The good news, for the Germans at least, was that the mud froze when the weather got cold, and in late October, the Germans began their march on Moscow once again. Of course, you likely know that it gets very, very cold in Russia.

The delay gave the Russians some time to reorganize, and more importantly, in December, they were able to move reinforcements from the Soviet Far East to the front in the west. The latter was due to Stalin's spies in Japan, whom he now trusted. They had told him that the Japanese were going to attack the United States and that they did not plan to invade the USSR from the east. And on December 7th, 1941, this was borne out by the Japanese attack on the US Pacific Fleet at Pearl Harbor. This allowed Stalin to move nearly one million trained troops to the front against the Germans, where, on December 5th, the Soviets launched a counterattack outside Moscow and other places along the front, pushing the Germans back over one hundred miles. The Nazis would never come as close to Moscow again, and the Germans' situation was made even worse by Hitler's decision to honor his alliance with the Japanese by declaring war on the United States on December 11th.

The number of Soviet troops took the Germans by surprise. They had already been shocked by the fighting in the summer and fall when it seemed that despite killing and capturing millions of Soviet troops, there were always more to replace them. This time around, at least outside Moscow, many of the replacements actually knew how to fight.

What's more, the Germans were stunned by the number of Soviet tanks they encountered. Most of them were subpar; they were either obsolete or poorly designed. However, two series of Soviet tanks, the KV (Mark I and II) and the T-34, completely took the Germans by surprise. The heavy KV series was able to sustain an incredible amount of damage before being destroyed or breaking down, and though they moved slowly, they packed a powerful punch. The T-34 surprised the Germans even more, and they even forced the most ardent of Nazis to admit that the machine was better than anything the Germans had at the time. Luckily, for the Germans, in late 1941 and early 1942, the T-34 was not rolled out in the incredible numbers that it would be in the latter part of the war. Still, the appearance of these tanks forced the Germans to both revisit their assessment of the Soviets and also hurry to the drawing board to design a tank that could rival the Soviets' machines.

In the spring of 1942, the Germans were no longer strong enough to launch an offensive all along the front as they had the previous year. Despite having defeated the Soviets in most of the battles of 1941 and having stabilized the line after the Soviets' counterattack outside Moscow, German tank forces and manpower were limited. Toward the end of 1942, the Germans would not be able to replace the losses they were sustaining, whereas the Soviets (and, since December, the US) had an almost unending supply of manpower.

The Germans also had a vast empire to defend now. Over the two years, increasing numbers of troops would be sent to guard the French coast. Over 200,000 men were stationed in Norway, for Hitler believed that the British might try to invade the Nordic country once again. Hundreds of thousands of men were stationed in Yugoslavia and Greece, fighting against resistance movements there, and over 100,000 men were fighting the British and soon the Americans in North Africa, not to mention occupation troops throughout Europe. The Soviets, who had more than twice the population of Germany at the beginning of the war, put every eligible man (and, in many cases, boys) into the effort against the Germans.

The German plan for the spring of 1942, dubbed *Fall Blau* ("Case Blue"), called for an armored strike deeper into Ukraine, with its target being the city of Stalingrad (now Volgograd). Simultaneously, they would continue to hold the rest of the Eastern Front and continue to besiege the city of Leningrad (today's St. Petersburg) and strike into the Caucasus in an attempt to seize the vast oil reserves at the city of Baku. Just about one million men and 1,500 tanks would attempt to take the city that bore Stalin's name and cut off the vital Soviet supply line of the Volga River.

The offensive began in late June 1942, and by the last week of August, German troops were fighting in the outskirts of Stalingrad. By the end of September, Hitler's forces held 90 percent of the city, and the Führer announced that the battle was essentially over. However, it wasn't. The Red Army, digging in and under orders to fight to the death, had stiffened their resistance the farther the

Germans penetrated into their country. They held that last 10 percent of the city while sustaining and inflicting incredible casualties in what might perhaps be the most brutal street fighting of the war.

Some Soviet reinforcements were sent over the Volga River under almost constant attack by German planes. A plan developed in the Soviet General Staff, calling for just enough troops to be sent into Stalingrad to be able to hang onto the foothold they had in the center of the city along the river. The rest of the reinforcements would be sent to the fronts in the north and south of the city under cover of darkness to wait until the order to attack was given. The placement of Soviet troops was no accident. Aside from being strategically brilliant, the Axis troops to the north and south of the city were mostly Hungarian, Romanian, and Italian troops, whose hearts were not at all in the fight. This was made worse by enmity between the Germans' allies and their poor equipment.

By mid-October, the temperatures in the Soviet Union had begun to drop, as had increasing amounts of snow. Amazingly, the Germans, who had a bad experience during the previous winter in Russia, were still not equipped with enough winter clothing. By November 19th, when the Soviet counterattack known as Operation Uranus began, temperatures were falling far below zero and would drop to as low as -40°F for much of the winter.

Within days, the Soviet counteroffensive had broken through the weak lines to the north and south of the city and surrounded the German 6th Army. Though Hitler insisted that the city would and could hold out, most of the generals in the German Army knew that was impossible. An abortive relief effort began some days after the Soviet attack, only to be stopped after about a twenty-mile advance.

For the Germans inside Stalingrad, it was only a matter of time before the end, which came in late January and early February 1943. For the month and a half they had to wait, they suffered frostbite and the lack of food, medicine, and warm clothing. The horses they had brought with them were killed for food shortly after the Soviet attack. Soon, the men were eating rats, if they ate at all. When the Germans at Stalingrad surrendered, ninety thousand men went into Soviet captivity. Five thousand survived to return to Germany about ten years later.

Stalingrad was a pivotal point in the war. Though the Germans would mount one more major attack at Kursk in July and a number of local counterattacks, for the most part, Hitler's forces were on the defensive in the east for the rest of the war.

Stalingrad cost over a million Soviet and German lives. The entire war in the Soviet Union and on the Eastern Front during the war cost the Soviet more than twenty million people, both military and civilian. It would not end until the Soviet's Hammer and Sickle flag flew over the Reichstag building in Berlin.

Of course, this is just an overview of the war, both in the east and in the west. For a more detailed study of the war between Hitler and Stalin, please see Captivating History's *The Eastern Front*, available on Amazon.

The War in the West

While Hitler and Stalin were fighting to the death in the Soviet Union, the war in North Africa and the Western Front continued, though in a much different form, at least from 1941 to late 1942.

In 1941 and 1942, the British stood alone against Hitler in the west, and though they sometimes engaged in heavy fighting in the North African desert to prevent Hitler from capturing the vital supply line that cut through the Suez Canal, the war on the Western Front was limited to the Battle of Britain, which continued in fits and starts through the spring of 1942, the commando raids on the French and Norwegian coasts, and the Battle of the Atlantic.

The Battle of the Atlantic was the only thing that truly frightened Winston Churchill throughout the war, for if the British did not win the battle on the ocean, Britain would starve and run out of enough arms to defend itself.

From 1940 until late 1942, the German U-boat offensive took a great toll on British and Allied shipping, at one point leaving Britain with only enough food to feed itself for two weeks. Fortunately, the British were helped in their struggle in several ways.

First, they had a massive navy with experienced crews and leaders motivated by the desire to keep their country free. Second, they developed and refined a tactic that had proved useful to them during WWI, that of the convoy system, in which fast anti-submarine vessels would escort large numbers of merchant ships across the Atlantic. Third, they developed sonar, which allowed them to search the ocean depths for U-boats rather than rely on seeing or detecting them with radar at the surface, which often proved too little, too late. Fourth, the British, in one of the war's most secret efforts, began to break German codes, especially naval codes, in a top-secret project called "Ultra." Many times, from 1942 onward, the British knew where German submarines were before the German High Command did.

Lastly, the British were aided by the United States. Even before the Americans' entry into the war in December 1942, they were escorting merchant convoys halfway across the Atlantic and "handing them off" to the British, who would take them the rest of the way. Hitler ordered his submarines to refrain from attacking American and neutral shipping in the western Atlantic, and despite a couple of isolated instances, this held. It seemed the last thing Hitler wanted was a war that included the United States, which makes his declaration of war on America on December 11th even more inexplicable.

America's massive industrial complex had begun to ramp up even before its entry into the war, and the nation supplied Britain with weapons, ammunition, planes, tanks, ships, fuel, food, and much else. By the time the war ended, the United States would become the richest and most powerful nation known in human history, possessing the largest industrial plant in the world, a navy many times larger than even the Royal Navy, twelve million men under arms, and the sole ownership of the atomic bomb.

However, in late 1941, that was a long way away. The United States' entry into the war and their insistence on doing things "their own way" cost them millions of tons of shipping sunk off the coast of the United States in what the German U-boat crews called the "Second Happy Time" (the first being the beginning of the war).

Additionally, when US troops did enter combat against the Germans at Kasserine Pass in Tunisia in February of 1943 after the Anglo-American invasion of North Africa, the quality of their troops, tanks, and leadership was brought into question after a hard defeat at the hands of Erwin Rommel.

Still, they learned fast, and with the additional strength of their navy and increasing numbers of merchant ships bringing troops and supplies to Europe, overwhelming the relatively small number of U-boats in the Atlantic, the strength of the Americans increased by the day, as did the British and their Imperial forces.

In July 1943, just days after Hitler launched his last major counterattack in the USSR at Kursk, the British and Americans invaded the Italian island of Sicily, forcing Hitler to order troops to Italy when he could not spare them after the defeats he had sustained in Russia.

In September 1943, the Allies landed in multiple places on the Italian coast, and though the fighting was incredibly difficult (much more difficult than had been thought), British and American troops fought their way to the gates of Rome in the first week of June 1944. Rome itself was liberated on June 5th, 1944. It was a great victory that was overshadowed by what happened the next day in France: the D-Day landings.

All the while, the Allies had been mounting ever-stronger bombing attacks against German cities and industries. This campaign, which would eventually destroy every major German city, was costly, with the Germans fighting with both fighter planes and tens of thousands of anti-aircraft guns. In both the British and American armed forces, no branch sustained more deaths as a ratio of its strength than the air forces.

With the successful Allied landing on the French coast on June 6th, 1944, Hitler's fate was sealed. If the Allies had failed on the Western Front, he would've had the ability to move many hundreds of thousands of troops to the Eastern Front before the Allies were able to mount another effort. What might have happened if these German troops had been moved to the Eastern Front has been debated since 1945. Would Hitler have been able to defeat Stalin? It is doubtful, especially when you consider the size of the Red Army and the fact that the United States was still developing the atomic bomb, but at the very least, the war would've been prolonged, and hundreds of thousands or perhaps millions more people might have died.

As it was, it took a Herculean effort for the Allies and the Soviets to drive into Germany in 1945. In the east, the Germans inflicted many more times the number of casualties on the Soviets as the Soviets did them. In the west, the limited size of the front condensed German manpower and firepower; at times, for instance, in the late fall of 1944, the front resembled that of WWI to a degree (for those interested, look up the Battle of the Hürtgen Forest). Hitler was also able to secretly amass a quarter of a million men for his Ardennes Offensive in December (also known as the Battle of the Bulge) and launched thousands of the first ballistic rockets in history at Great Britain, Holland, and Belgium. What's more, despite the massive Allied bombing campaign, German industrial output actually increased in 1944, though that was temporary.

Still, the end was inevitable. Though Hitler survived an assassination attempt on July 20th, 1944, on April 30th, 1945, ten days after his fifty-sixth birthday, he committed suicide in his underground bunker in Berlin, spending his last days in madness and delusion. On May 8th, 1945, the German High Command surrendered to the Allies, and German history would enter a new phase.

Illustration 39: Last known picture of Adolf Hitler, at the entry to his bunker; Berlin, 1945.

Chapter 10 – The Holocaust

During the war, trains, men, and much materiel were used by the Germans to transport and kill the Jews of German-occupied Europe rather than utilize them in the war effort. Since the end of the war, historians have studied this and have come to essentially the same conclusion: the extermination of the Jews was more important to the Nazis than actually winning the war. In more than a few instances, German troops that were needed immediately at the front lines had to walk or wait while hundreds of trains transported Jewish people to the camps.

That sounds heartless, but it is the truth. To Hitler and Himmler, their deaths were more important than the war at the front. In the twisted minds of Hitler, Himmler, and the Nazi true believers, the "threat" that the Jews posed for Germany and Europe was greater than the threat posed by the war.

However, though the Germans developed a reputation for efficiency during the war, a deeper look into the German war effort shows that the Nazis were not as efficient with their resources and manpower as one might think. The example above comes to mind, but two other examples illustrate the point well.

In February 1943, after the defeat at Stalingrad had been announced to the nation, Propaganda Minister Josef Goebbels stood in front of a packed house of thousands at the Berlin Sportpalast and gave one of the most rousing and intense speeches of the Nazi era. The people in the audience went wild. At the end of his long speech about the war and its causes, he asked the crowd and the millions listening on the radio, "Do you want total war? If necessary, do you want a war more total and radical than anything that we can even imagine today?" He was pumping up the crowd, but he also had extolled them to work fourteen-, sixteen-, and twenty-hour days for the war effort. There were still areas of the German economy that were not at full capacity, as 1944 would show.

The other example that shows how inefficient the Nazis could be was the V-1 and V-2 efforts. Instead of developing those weapons, the Nazis could have built five more battleships, thousands of more tanks and planes, and much else. Hitler insisted on their development, even though they carried only a bit more than most conventional bombs, were wildly inaccurate, and did not even dent the Allied war effort. Had the Germans built one or two good all-purpose tanks, planes, or vehicles rather than a huge, highly technical assortment like they did with the materiel that went into the V-program, the war truly might have ended differently.

However, the war against the Jews increased full steam from the late 1930s onward, and it never stopped. In actuality, most of the six million Jewish victims of the Holocaust had been murdered by the end of 1944, with the peak of the killing having been reached between the years 1942 and 1944.

Before we begin, let's make one thing clear. Though the Jews were by far the largest group singled out by the Nazis, there were others. It is estimated that a further two million Roma, homosexuals, Jehovah's Witnesses, political prisoners, and others died in the camps. This figure does not include the Russian prisoners of war who died by the millions in German captivity, which are estimated to be over three million. Though most of these victims died in prisoner-of-war camps or in the field, it should be noted that the first victims of the Auschwitz gas chambers were Soviet prisoners of war.

Previously, we told you of *Kristallnacht*, the Night of the Broken Glass, in Germany and many of its consequences. The persecution of the Jews in Germany accelerated after *Kristallnacht*. Within days, the requirement of the German Jews to transfer all retail businesses to Germans was issued. This included mom-and-pop stores as well as department stores, a particular enemy of the Nazis and many of which were Jewish-owned. Department stores, as the Nazi thinking went, lowered prices on the same goods sold by the "more traditional" local shop, which the Nazis saw as a stable of village and town life, never mind that small Jewish shop owners were sometimes affected by this as well.

A few days after this, all Jewish children and young adults were expelled from German schools. The worst insult took place on December 12th, 1938, when it was ordered that the Jews of Germany pay for the property damages that occurred during *Kristallnacht*.

The Holocaust is, unfortunately, a broad subject, and we can only touch upon it here, but at this point, the main purpose of the Nazi persecution of the Jews in Austria and Germany seems to have been to force the Jews out of the country. However, that was fraught with problems. The Jews were required to pay enormous sums for exit visas, money that most did not have. In addition, the offices handling the exit visas and other paperwork were understaffed and moved at a glacial pace. Also, sadly, many Jews believed that the worst of the persecution was over and that life would soon return to somewhat "normal" after Hitler solidified his power.

Perhaps worst of all was the lack of cooperation and the willingness to take Germany's Jews among the other countries of Europe and the United States. The Swiss, where many desired to go, requested the Germans stamp German-Jewish passports with a "J" so they could restrict the number of Jews coming into their country. Poland, which was once one of the most accepting countries toward Jewish immigrants in the past, was at the same time extremely anti-Semitic; almost twenty thousand Polish Jews living in Germany were expelled shortly before *Kristallnacht* but were refused entry into the country. Nearly nine thousand of them were stranded in a border village until the beginning of the war the following year. Other nations of Europe had quotas on both immigration in general and Jews in particular, but it should be noted that Holland and France did take sizable numbers of German Jews.

Sadly, a strain of anti-Semitism ran deep through the US Department of State, which, at the time, dealt with international matters, including refugees and immigration. The State Department had an immense influence on President Franklin Delano Roosevelt, who was from the same social strata and ethnic background as many leading State Department figures and harbored some of their anti-Semitic beliefs as well, though he did include Jewish-Americans in his inner circle. The most infamous incident occurred in June of 1939 when the ocean liner *St. Louis* arrived off the coast of Miami, carrying some nine hundred Jewish refugees, and was refused entry. To be "fair," the ship was also denied entry into Cuba and Canada, though several countries did negotiate with the Jewish Joint Distribution Committee, a humanitarian organization, which still exists today, for cash payments to take in a number of the *St. Louis*'s Jewish refugees. Sadly, the ship eventually returned to Europe, and most of the remaining Jews on board (254 of them, including young children) were eventually killed by the Nazis.

On January 30th, 1939, in a speech to the Reichstag commemorating the Nazis' seizure of power, Hitler uttered the words that many believe directly pointed to the future. In his speech, he said, "if war erupts, it will mean the extermination of European Jews."

At the time, very few outside Germany believed this literally, thinking it another of Hitler's ranting speeches, but inside the Reich, the words of the Führer were gospel. Those outside Germany couldn't fathom the possibility of killing *all* the Jews of Europe. To people in Hitler's inner circle who brought up the subject, he simply replied, "Who, after all, speaks today of the annihilation of the Armenians?" History forgets that German General Liman von Sanders played a supporting role in the Turks' persecution of the Armenians during WWI.

Hitler's goal before the war seems to have been the expulsion of the Jews from Germany or German-controlled territory. However, that goal was made virtually impossible by the German conquest of Poland in 1939. The pre-war Jewish population of Poland was about three million, more than four times the size of Germany's 700,000. Indeed, more Jews lived in Poland than any other European nation. With the addition of Polish territory in 1939 and eastern Poland in 1941 during Operation Barbarossa, Hitler increased the number of Jews under his control manyfold.

This was the beginning of the Nazis' earnest conversation to begin some sort of "Final Solution to the Jewish problem," which was what the Nazis later euphemistically called the murder of millions of innocent people.

Inside Poland, as in Germany, the Jews tended to live in their own neighborhoods in cities and towns. In smaller villages and the countryside, everyone knew who the Jews were, even if they were not distinguishable by their unique clothing, as many Jews in Eastern Europe were. Also, within Poland, as in Germany, Jews, generally speaking, had particular names with particular spellings and were kept track of by the authorities. When the Germans moved in, it was a relatively simple matter for them to identify and round up Poland's Jews. In many cases, Jews were ordered to assemble at a specific place at a specific time or face serious consequences. In this, the Nazis were aided by anti-Semitic Poles or Poles who simply wanted to "get in good" with their new rulers.

Within a relatively short time, the Jews of German-controlled Poland had been herded into small and grossly overpopulated sections of the major Polish cities into what were called ghettos. "Ghettos" is actually a word of likely Italian origin, meaning "foundry," as the first "ghetto" was said to be around a forge in Venice in the 1600s. Soon, the ghettos of Poland were being crammed with additional refugees from Germany, Austria, and Czechoslovakia.

Almost immediately, the Germans set up a program designed to kill the Jews in the ghettos by neglect. Food was at a minimum, and it was frequently rotten. The crowded conditions overwhelmed what sanitation and water systems did exist, and diseases of all kinds ravaged the population, as did starvation.

When the Germans invaded the Soviet Union, they realized that it would be impossible to house the nearly three million Jews of the Baltic states and the Soviet Union in the ghettos of Poland. Before the invasion, Himmler and his righthand man, Reinhard Heydrich, the head of the SD, had their subordinates organize "special action groups" (*Einsatzgruppen*) to "deal with" the Jews they found as they followed the front line troops.

The commanders of the *Einsatzgruppen* were SS officers, and while many of the men of these special action groups were also SS men, there were many who were not. They were generally older men from the *Ordnungspolizei* or "Order Police," the uniformed police of Germany. Christopher Browning's best-selling and well-regarded bestseller *Ordinary Men: Reserve Police Battalion 101 and the Final Solution in Poland* describes these men as, well, "ordinary." They, by and large, were not men with delinquent records or histories of brutality. Most of them were lower-middle-class career policemen with a high school or sometimes a college diploma, yet they engaged in one of the worst atrocities that mankind has ever known.

Another historian named Daniel Goldhagen, in his *Hitler's Willing Executioners*, makes the argument that these men were not "ordinary" but conditioned by years of anti-Semitism in Germany, both before and during Hitler's reign. Both Browning and Goldhagen, as well as others, argue that the perpetrators of the Holocaust and other crimes against humanity since then were encouraged by the fact that their actions were "legal" or commanded, thereby abstractly "giving them permission" to murder.

Throughout 1941 and early 1942, the *Einsatzgruppen* fanned out over the Baltic states and then the Soviet Union, carrying out massacres in what has lately been labeled "the Holocaust by bullets." At Babi Yar on the outskirts of Kiev (Kyiv), Ukraine, they gunned down over thirty thousand people in plain sight of onlookers. At Rumbula Forest in Latvia, an estimated twenty-five thousand Latvian and other Baltic Jews were gunned down and buried in huge pits. This occurred in smaller numbers (sometimes dozens, sometimes hundreds, sometimes thousands) throughout the Baltic states and the western Soviet Union. Even today, people are discovering previously unknown mass-killing sites in Ukraine.

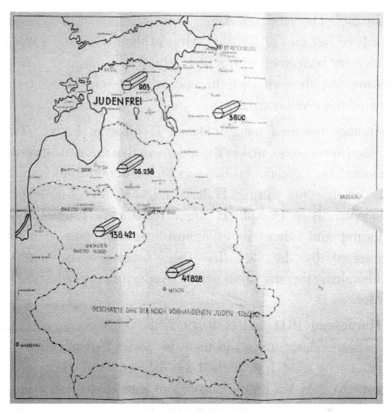

Illustration 40: Map of the Jews killed in the Baltic states and the western USSR, with the total of those murdered next to the site. This map was submitted by Einsatzgruppe "A" commander Franz Stahlecker. Note that Estonia is labeled Judenfrei—"free of Jews."

From the Nazi viewpoint, there were several problems with this method of eliminating the Jews. First, it was very public; on a few occasions, onlookers from the non-Jewish population saw the killings firsthand. Unfortunately, many of them also took part, which the Nazis were all too willing to allow. Related to this, a number of German soldiers took photos and home movies of the slaughter and mailed them home. Since the war, several undiscovered photo albums have been discovered by relatives in attics and basements after the deaths of their older relatives.

Second, in the eyes of the Nazis, the system of hunting down and killing the Jews was inefficient. Having them "voluntarily" rounded up for "resettlement in the east" was more effective and less likely to cause rebellion and/or panic.

Third, Himmler, though he wasted no tears on the Jews and others whose deaths he was ordering, was concerned about the psychological effect of these mass killings on his men. Though this reason has often been pushed aside among historians, especially in light of the suffering inflicted on their victims, this was a concern for Himmler and the SS leadership. Cases of alcoholism, suicide, and mental breakdown among the personnel of the *Einsatzgruppen* grew dramatically as time went on.

All of these, but particularly the last, were the impetus behind the construction of gas chambers at existing and partially built camps in Poland.

The camps themselves and their method of killing by gas have a tragic prelude within Germany. In a program known as T4, the Nazis began to kill off patients in mental hospitals throughout Germany in the late 1930s. This was done by using poison gas, with the patients under the illusion that they would be taking a shower, or by lethal injection. In six camps in Germany and Austria, the mentally challenged, the insane, and people with severe epilepsy were killed by physicians and nurses, who were supervised by SS officers. The parents or relatives of the victims would receive a letter stating that their loved one succumbed to natural causes, such as a heart attack or stroke.

These "mercy killings" were an open secret, and they were protested by a variety of people, most notably the bishop of Münster, August von Galen, who publicly condemned them and caused them to be halted, albeit temporarily. The general lack of outcry among the German public, however, caused the Nazis to believe that little if anything would be said about the deportation of the Jews "to the east."

The first extermination camp was located at Chelmno (known by the Germans as Kulmhof), near the city of Lodz in western Poland. There, victims were brought to the large former estate of a Polish nobleman. And there, they were killed by asphyxiation caused by the pumping of carbon monoxide exhaust from large trucks. This account by SS sergeant Walter Burmeister after the war explains what happened:

> As soon as the ramp had been erected in the castle, people started arriving in Kulmhof from (Lodz) Litzmannstadt in lorries...The people were told that they had to take a bath, that their clothes had to be disinfected and that they could hand in any valuable items beforehand to be registered. When they had undressed they were sent to the cellar of the castle and then along a passageway onto the ramp and from there into the gas-van. In the castle, there were signs marked "to the baths." The gas vans were large vans, about 4-5 metres [13-16 ft] long, 2.2 metres [7.2 feet] wide and 2 metres [6.6 feet] high. The interior walls were lined with sheet metal. A wooden grille was set into the floor. The floor of the van had an opening which could be connected to the exhaust by means of a removable metal pipe. When the lorries were full of people, the double doors at the back were closed and the exhaust connected to the interior of the van.

—Walter Burmeister, *The Good Old Days*

The bodies would then be trucked to a nearby forest and burned. An estimated 150,000 to 200,000 people were killed at Kulmhof, but Himmler and others considered it inefficient, and they thought the same of the murders at Belzec, north of Lwow (over 600,000 victims), and Majdanek, south of Warsaw (80,000 victims).

At Treblinka and Sobibor, both Jews and Red Army prisoners were killed. Many of the killers were Ukrainian collaborators who blamed Jews for the hated Soviet communist regime in their home country. At both Treblinka and Sobibor, the killing was done by piping in carbon monoxide exhaust from captured Soviet tank engines. This reduced the time it took to kill the prisoners when compared to the other camps at Belzec, Kulmhof, and Majdanek. Additionally, experience with killing in large numbers had essentially created experts in mass murder, and, especially at Treblinka, the time from arrival to one's death was about an hour. Deportees would arrive at a fictional train station, equipped with a painted clock that never moved, and then driven up to a large field surrounded by guards, dogs, and barbed wire. Though they were treated roughly, they were told they were being sent to the showers, and from there, they would be given work assignments. Treblinka was the home of the horrific "tube" (*Schlauch* in German), which funneled naked prisoners through a camouflaged, barbed-wired path leading to the gas chambers. Inside the tube, they would be whipped and beaten like animals, having no idea what lay in store for them. Minutes later, they would be dead, their bodies then transported to open pits crisscrossed with steel railroad ties. This place was euphemistically called "the grill" by the guards. There, specially chosen workers would throw bodies on the ever-burning pyre. In many cases, those who did not move fast enough were kicked or thrown onto "the grill" alive.

Despite Treblinka's death toll of nearly one million people and Sobibor's 625,000 people, Himmler and his SS cronies believed that the killing process could be both more efficient and "more humane" for their guards. Sobibor was eventually shuttered after a mass revolt by Soviet prisoners of war, which resulted in the deaths of SS guards and the escape of many of the rebelling prisoners.

The result of Himmler's insistence on efficiency was the notorious death camp at Auschwitz-Birkenau. Birkenau was actually the second of three camps at the Polish town of Oswiecim. Auschwitz I had been built shortly after the invasion of Poland and housed political prisoners, habitual criminals (who were used by the SS to keep the other prisoners "in line"), members of the Polish resistance, intellectuals, and others. Even before the erection of Auschwitz-Birkenau, Auschwitz I built a notorious reputation for cruelty—the list of diabolical types of physical and mental abuse doled out there would take up pages.

Auschwitz III, or Auschwitz-Monowitz, was located to the east of the main camp in a factory complex converted by the Germans into a lab and factory for the study and production of synthetic resources like oil and rubber. Thousands were worked to death at Monowitz, and not a single effective materiel was ever produced there.

The largest part of the Auschwitz complex was Auschwitz II Birkenau (*Brzezinka* in Polish for "place of birches," named for the birch groves that grew there and which were often the waiting places for people when the gas chambers were "too busy"). Building began at Birkenau in the fall of 1941, shortly after the beginning of Operation Barbarossa.

As was mentioned previously, the first victims of the gas chambers were Soviet prisoners of war in late August 1941 in a small chamber at Auschwitz I. These were the first victims killed using prussic acid, chemical pellets that turned to gas when exposed to oxygen and sold under the now-infamous name of Zyklon B, which had previously been sold to kill rats and other vermin. The killing time of Zyklon B was about fifteen minutes compared to the half-hour to an hour it took using carbon monoxide.

A second and larger gas chamber was built in the spring of 1942, just outside the gate of the camp, which underwent rapid construction. The first gas chamber was built inside a farmhouse, from which the owner had been expelled. It could fit eight hundred people inside at one time. It was deactivated after the construction of the larger three gas chambers inside the camp, which could hold two thousand people at a time.

These new gas chambers could kill so rapidly that specially designed crematoria had to be designed to dispose of the bodies. However, the death toll was sometimes so high that burn pits were used at Auschwitz as well. The pits were also used when crematoria broke down or were destroyed, as happened during a prisoner's revolt on October 7th, 1944. A movie based on this revolt, *The Grey Zone*, is listed in the bibliography at the end of this book (it is for mature audiences only).

At its peak, Auschwitz-Birkenau was killing an estimated twelve thousand to fourteen thousand people a day. Most of the murders at Auschwitz took place from 1942 to 1943, though a new high was reached in the summer of 1944 when Hitler's Hungarian allies, who had been reluctant to send their Jews into German custody (more out of a question of national sovereignty than for any love of their Jewish population, at least among the fascist-dominated government), sent over 400,000 people to their death by allowing the Germans to transport them to Auschwitz.

(The story of Auschwitz is long and brutal, and this e-book is meant as an introduction to German history, not a history of the camps. Please see the bibliography at the end of this book for some authoritative and exhaustive reading on this topic.)

As the war turned against the Nazis and they were forced to retreat toward Berlin, they made attempts to destroy the evidence of their crimes. In places like Babi Yar and Rumbula, surviving Jews were made to dig up what remains were left intact and burn them on large pyres, sometimes fueled by cranes or bulldozers dropping bodies onto them. The intense heat was too much for people to approach.

Though there were six extermination camps—Auschwitz, Treblinka, Sobibor, Kulmhof, Majdanek, and Belzec—there were hundreds of concentration camps throughout the German Empire where death took place on a massive scale, usually by working inmates to death, disease, or starvation. As the Soviets approached from the east and the British and Americans from the west, some of these camps were destroyed. Others, like Belsen or Buchenwald, among others, were left intact by fleeing guards. Battle-hardened troops from the liberating armies were reduced to dumbfounded tears at the sight of the dead, the remaining gas chambers, and the starved skeletons of the living. In many cases, SS members who could not flee attempted to disguise themselves as inmates. Many of them were beaten to death or severely injured by the inmates themselves. In at least one case, twenty-five to thirty-five captured SS guards were openly gunned down at Dachau by the liberating US troops, though this news was suppressed for decades. Only the Russians know how many guards were killed in the east, but unfortunately, many of the executioners, their leaders, or their enablers escaped judgment, either through suicide or by a world unwisely wishing to put an ugly chapter behind it with the coming of the Cold War.

Illustration 41: Image taken by SS guard of the "selection" of victims for the gas chambers at Auschwitz, likely summer 1944. Notice the smoke from the crematoria in the background.

Chapter 11 – Post-War Germany to the Present Day

Alfons Heck, the Hitler Youth member that was mentioned in a previous chapter, was among those Germans fortunate enough to have survived the war. He was one of the young men you see in one of the last pictures of Hitler outside his bunker; he was being given an award for bravery from the Führer himself. Even after the death of Hitler had been announced, Heck and millions like him were true believers. In a prisoner-of-war camp after the ceasefire, Heck and other boys were shown films of the concentration camps, with piles of bodies stacked like wood or strewn about the grounds. Heck and the other boys began to snicker and thought, "Who do they take us for? This stuff is staged!" With that, their guards lit into them, beating them with fists and truncheons and telling them, "You damn Nazis! This is what you've done!" It was not until Heck saw his Hitler Youth leader, Baldur von Schirach, on trial at the Nuremberg trials that he started to believe that the Holocaust had actually happened. And this was only because he heard it directly from his leader and other top Nazis on trial for their crimes against humanity.

Other Germans did not take so long to believe, for the Allies marched local civilians through the camps to see what Nazism and the support of Nazism had done. In many cases, German civilians and surviving guards were forced to bury the thousands of bodies lying about.

Illustration 42: German civilians marched through the Neuengamme camp near Hamburg by the US 82ⁿᵈ Airborne Division.

As Heck had, Germans throughout the country were sometimes "required" to attend screenings of newsreels of the Nuremberg trials. What they didn't see and hear, they read in Allied newspapers and the many free German newspapers that quickly sprung up.

The Nuremberg trials were important for several reasons. First and foremost, they showed the world exactly what happened under Hitler. Second, it was done as a hopeful deterrent to anyone so inclined to engage in atrocities in future years. Third, it was a punishment, plain and simple. At the Tehran Conference in 1943, Joseph Stalin had half-kiddingly proposed killing a random fifty thousand German officers as a lesson and as a punishment. It is true that great numbers of German officers and soldiers disappeared into the Soviet Gulag camp system, never to be seen again. However, British Prime Minister Winston Churchill and US President Franklin Delano Roosevelt pushed Stalin into holding the Nuremberg tribunal as a public exhibition of Nazi horror and Allied power.

Nuremberg was chosen purposely. It was where Hitler and the Nazis held their huge rallies every year, and by holding the trials here, it was a very clear sign that those days were not only over but were never coming back.

The first of the Nuremberg trials included some of the most famous names in the Nazi world. Unfortunately, both Hitler and Himmler had escaped justice by committing suicide. Reinhard Heydrich, who had been ordered to implement the "Final Solution to the Jewish problem" in Europe by Himmler, had been assassinated in Czechoslovakia in 1942. However, Hermann Göring, who was once Hitler's number two man and the head of the *Luftwaffe*, was captured. In addition to his other duties, Göring had signed off on some of the most important documents and orders that put the Holocaust into motion.

Among the others at the trial were Albert Speer (Hitler's architect and eventual minister of munitions), Field Marshal Albert Jodl (a *Wehrmacht* yes-man at the head of the General Staff), the aforementioned Baldur von Schirach, Karl Dönitz (the head of the German Navy and Hitler's successor after he received word about Göring attempting to make peace without his authorization), Rudolf Hess (Hitler's "deputy Führer" until he flew to England in 1940 in a bizarre attempt to make peace), and about a dozen others. Of the twenty-two defendants in the first round of trials, twelve were sentenced to death by hanging, three were given life sentences, four were given sentences of ten to twenty years in prison, and two were found not guilty. Hermann Göring, due to either a security lapse or with the aid of a sympathetic American guard, was able to cheat the hangman by ingesting a cyanide pill in his cell. Martin Bormann, the head of the Reich's Chancellery and Hitler's secretary, was tried in absentia and sentenced to death; his remains were found in the 1980s in Berlin, and they were confirmed to be his in the 2000s. The trials at Nuremberg and several other places, both in the west and the east, continued for a number of years.

The question facing the world was what should be done with Germany. One American plan floated during the war by Roosevelt's Secretary of the Treasury Henry Morgenthau Jr. (who himself was Jewish and had helped (or attempted to help Jewish refugees before, during, and after the war), developed the Morgenthau Plan for post-war Germany. Put simply, the Morgenthau Plan would have reduced the size of Germany, removed all industries, and created a new and unarmed state of farmers who would be unable to go to war ever again. Given the nature of the Nazi regime, the Morgenthau Plan underwent serious consideration, but in the end, it was refused.

It was refused because the Allies had seemed to learn their lesson after the disaster that was the Treaty of Versailles. Not only would it be practically impossible to force the Germans to become farmers for who knows how many years in the future, but when they began to rebuild, once again, there would be tremendous resentment, just as there had been in 1918, which was something the Allies wished to avoid at all costs.

More importantly, however, were the geopolitical developments taking place in Europe and around the world after the war. By the end of 1945 and into 1946, the Soviets, despite their promises to hold free, fair, open, and democratic elections in the nations occupied by their troops, were already celebrating communist victories in every country in Eastern Europe, with the exceptions of Yugoslavia and Albania, which had largely liberated themselves and were determined to be independent. (Stalin, for his part, knew that the Yugoslavs had fought over half a million Germans during the war largely on their own and would not stand for Soviet interference. And to get to Albania, the Soviets had to go through Yugoslavia.)

While the Western Allies had made promises to the various Eastern European governments in exile in the West, which were mostly democratic in nature, the Soviets had their own Polish, Czech, Bulgarian, Romanian, and Hungarian governments in exile, which were all communist. More importantly, in their home countries, those coming from the West-leaning governments in exile were either refused entry or "disappeared" into the Gulag on their return home. The fact is, short of war, there was nothing the Allies could do to affect anything the Soviets were doing in Eastern Europe.

After the ceasefire, the wartime Allies (the US, Britain, and France in the west and the USSR in the east) had hoped that a united Germany, one neutral in outlook, could be reconstructed, but both sides held suspicions of each other and of the Germans, which kept that from becoming a reality. The division of Germany, which had been devised during the war, was to be a permanent thing.

From 1945 to 1949, Germany was divided into four zones of control: the American, Soviet, British, and French. The capital city of Berlin was likewise divided into four areas.

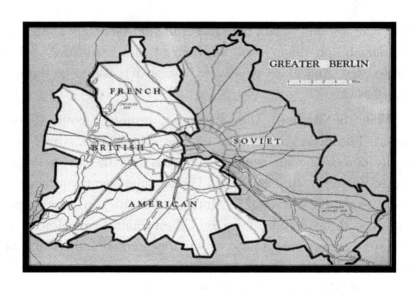

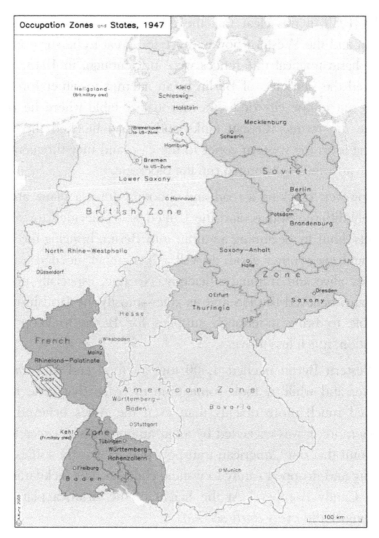

Illustration 43: The division of Germany between the Allied Powers, 1945 to 1949. The striped Saarland was administered by all four nations.

Western Germany began rebuilding itself almost as soon as the war ended. American and British soldiers could not get over the speed with which the Germans began to clean up and rebuild, and truth be told, they got, for the most part, a much better reception in Germany than they did in many of the lands that had been occupied by the Germans.

By 1949, it was clear that the differences between the Soviet Union and the Western powers were too great to be surmounted. As if basic political differences were not enough, in 1948, Stalin ordered the blockade of Berlin in an attempt to either force the Allies out of the city or to the negotiating table where he could dictate the terms. Russian tanks and troops blocked the roads leading from the western zones to the east, and they threatened to fire on anyone attempting to run the blockade.

However, blocking a road and shooting down a plane are two entirely different things, and the United States decided to call the Soviets' bluff by beginning an airlift into Berlin, bringing the food, fuel, and every other good, as well as personnel, needed to keep the city alive and running efficiently. No one, especially not the Russians, believed the US and its allies—mostly the British—would be able to bring in enough supplies for Berlin to keep from starvation, much less thrive.

Western Berlin needed 4,500 tons of food and fuel *daily* to survive, and while it took some time to reach that goal, it was reached much more quickly than even the Allies believed, and what's more, it was exceeded by a fair amount. It was exceeded to the point that one American transport pilot flew extra sorties over the city and dropped candy to waiting children. His nickname was "The Candy Bomber." At the height of the airlift, a plane was reaching Berlin *every thirty seconds.*

The Berlin Airlift lasted for nearly a year until Stalin relented and opened the roads. The airlift was a public relations disaster for the Soviets, who were having trouble keeping famine at bay in their own war-ravaged country, much less in Eastern Europe.

Not only did the Berlin Airlift bring in food, fuel, clothing, and much more, it also brought hope and tremendous regard for the Allies, especially the Americans who flew the bulk of the flights. The Germans also knew that over one hundred British and American airmen had died trying to keep their city alive. What's more, many Berliners were employed during the period, and they were able to keep themselves warm and full during a very trying time.

Illustration 44: One of the famous pictures from the Berlin Airlift in which German children watch the landing of an American C-54 bringing in supplies to the surrounded city.

In 1949, with increasing tensions between the Allies and the Soviet Union in what was supposed to be a joint administration of Germany, including not only the blockade but also the introduction and success of the new currency in Western Germany, the failure of Eastern Germany to make the same progress and the Soviet attempts to pressure Western German politicians culminated in the announcement that a new country, the Federal Republic of Germany (*Bundesrepublik Deutschland* or "BRD"), was going to be established in the west on May 23rd, with the western city of Bonn as its capital.

In October, the Soviets announced the establishment of the German Democratic Republic (*Deutsche Demokratische Republik* or "DDR") in the east. Berlin was divided between the west and the east, with the DDR naming the eastern half of the city as its national capital.

Throughout the 1950s and 1960s, West Germany underwent what is called the "German economic miracle." From a nation that had been totally defeated and most of its cities completely destroyed, the West Germans, with significant help from the United States in the form of the Marshall Plan, began rebuilding their economy to the point that, by the early 1960s, it was rivaling France as an economic power.

The dominant political party was once again the SPD (Social Democratic Party), but at times, it was forced into coalition governments with the CDU (Christian Democratic Union, a conservative party based in the south) or the Liberals. The first West German chancellor, Konrad Adenauer (1876–1967), known as *Der Alte* ("the old one"), was from the CDU, and he governed the country from 1949 to 1962. The best-known post-war chancellors of Germany are Adenauer, Willy Brandt, Helmut Schmidt, Helmut Kohl, and Angela Merkel, who has announced her retirement after over fifteen years in office as of this writing in 2021.

In 1955, West Germany joined NATO, the North Atlantic Treaty Organization, which was first put together to defend Western Europe from the Soviet Union. In response, the Soviets admitted a newly rearmed East Germany into the Warsaw Pact, its organization to defend itself from an attack from the West.

Western Germany soon became known for its liberal and vibrant political life, as well as a booming cultural life, which included film, music, literature, and art. In some ways, life in West Germany, at least culturally and especially in Berlin, resembled the Weimar period, with the people once again enjoying the freedom of expression after the Nazi era.

Conversely, in East Germany, life stayed hard, and it remained that way. The one-party system under the Socialist Unity Party

(*Sozialistische Einheitspartei Deutschlands* or "SED," which was really the "Communist Party" by another name) mirrored Stalin's Soviet Union: repressive and economically backward. Cultural life was dictated by the party, and deviation from it was punished in many ways, including incarceration, forced employment or unemployment (depending on the situation), and social ostracism. Watching its citizens was the Stasi, the secret police ("Stasi" is an acronym of the *Ministerium für Staatssicherheit* or "Ministry for State Security"), which was a little less brutal than the Gestapo. A little.

Life in East Berlin was so miserable and the future so bleak that between 1945 and 1961, tens of thousands of East Berliners defected every year. Between 1960 and 1961, this became thousands every month. Until 1961, East Berliners had the ability to cross into West Berlin, more or less, at leisure, but for the most part, they did not work there. They could see the freedom and economic success of the West firsthand, which was exactly the opposite of what SED propaganda told them it was like. Facing an exodus of labor and intelligence, the East German government, at the strong "urging" of the Soviet Union, took drastic measures to stop the flood and limit contact with the West.

Virtually overnight, on August 13th, 1961, the Berlin Wall went up. At first, it consisted of cinder blocks topped with barbed wire running just inside the East German border. This was done so, in theory at least, East German guards could go over the wall and still be within East Germany to retrieve the dead or those wounded while attempting escape. At first, the border was relatively porous, and people literally broke their legs jumping from buildings overlooking the wall into West Germany. Soon, however, the authorities moved everyone out of the border buildings and bricked up the windows.

When the Berlin Wall was finished, it was hardly made of cinder blocks. Most of it consisted of a ten-foot smooth concrete wall with smooth cement "rollers" on the top, both of which made the wall hard to climb. Of course, to get to the wall, one had to first get by several security checkpoints, floodlights, barbed wire, police dogs, minefields in ever-changing places, ditches, and more. The Berlin Wall didn't just divide Berlin; it was erected down the main East and West German border, and it went on for hundreds of miles.

I personally visited Berlin twice during the Cold War, in 1980 and 1981, legally crossing into East Germany on my first trip. The Berlin Wall was not only physically but also psychologically daunting, and East Berlin was an experience in what can best be called "greyness"—it was a city that seemed to have a pall over it even on a sunny day. When myself and two friends responded to the smiles of a group of young people in a park near the wall, we were soon stunned by the rapidity with which they dispersed. Unseen by us, a group of police (known as "VoPos" for *Volkspolizei* or "People's Police") had approached. The East German teenagers fled like a school of startled fish before we knew the police were even around, as they did not want to be seen talking to Americans.

Despite the daunting obstacles, many East Germans escaped or attempted escape from the repression in their home country. An estimated total of over five hundred people was killed trying to escape East Germany, one not long before the wall came down in 1989. Over five thousand people did manage to escape, however. Some literally climbed over the wall. Many tunneled underneath it. A few even used makeshift hot air balloons to cross. The ways in which people in East Germany escaped are amazing, and many of their stories are told in the Haus Am Checkpoint Charlie Museum, which is still standing in Berlin and has a great online presence.

When Mikhail Gorbachev became the premier of the Soviet Union in 1985, he almost immediately signaled that many changes would be coming to the Soviet Union and the nations of the

Warsaw Pact (or Eastern Bloc). Gorbachev realized that the Soviet system was not creating the "socialist paradise" the regime had been promising for decades. Actually, during most of the 1960s through the mid-1980s, the Soviet economy stagnated due to the lack of economic freedom and technical skill, as well as having been forced to compete with the United States in the arms and space races, something which was hitting new heights under President Ronald Reagan.

Gorbachev announced two new massive policy shifts: *perestroika* and *glasnost* ("restructuring" and "openness," respectively). The Soviet economy would be reconstructed to become more efficient and competitive, and the government would be more open with its people about what was truly happening in the country (this last policy was spurred on by the Chernobyl nuclear disaster). While he was at it, Gorbachev "suggested" that the nations of Eastern Europe adopt these changes as well, something many of its rulers were not inclined to do. What's more, Gorbachev announced the USSR would not be able to send economic aid to its allies any longer, as it was barely getting on by itself.

For the leaders and regimes of Eastern Europe, this was the end. Without Soviet aid and Soviet soldiers, their unpopular regimes would fall, and in 1989, that was exactly what happened. Throughout Eastern Europe, "people power" successfully and peacefully, apart from Romania, overthrew their governments or forced them to slowly change from within.

East Germany's leader at this time, Erich Honecker, was among the most hardline communist leaders and actually contemplated firing on the many demonstrations that were taking place within his country, as had been done in 1953 when East German workers went on strike; hundreds, perhaps more than a thousand, were killed. But times were different. Not only would many of

Honecker's generals not support this order, but the Soviets also made it clear that they might actually interfere should this begin.

At the end of October and the beginning of November, the East German government slowly then rapidly came apart. Amazingly, on another November 9th in German history, the Berlin Wall fell. Less than a year later, East Germany voted itself out of existence and united with its western counterpart. Germany was one again.

Illustration 45: East and West Germans on the now-defunct Berlin Wall, 1989.

Conclusion

In the years since the reunification of the country, the Germans have had to face a variety of problems. The first one was the absolute poverty of East Germany. Over the years, billions of marks have been allocated to help support and train Eastern Germans while they helped build and form a modern economy, build new infrastructure, and integrate East Germany into the fold.

This has not been without problems. In West Germany, significant resentment against the "hand-outs" given to the *Ossis* (a play on the German word for "easterners") built up. Conversely, those in East Germany felt that the *Wessis* (a play on the word for "westerners") were snobs and looked down at those in the east. Additionally, many in the east found the world of cutthroat capitalism in the western half difficult and repulsive, while westerners saw the easterners as without ambition. Despite the passage of time, some of these attitudes still exist.

Worse still, with the end of the East German police state under communism, old hatreds and bigotries, having been suppressed but not addressed, have reared their ugly head in the form of neo-Nazism and racism in what was once East Germany. What's more alarming is that this was seen as mostly an *Ossi* problem until recently.

Because of its WWII history, West Germany has felt a particular need to help in humanitarian causes throughout the world but especially in Europe. One that made headlines was the German-led bailout of Greece in the early 2000s when the latter country was on the verge of economic collapse.

In 2011, Germans took refugees from the Arab Spring uprising in the Middle East, and in 2015, Chancellor Angela Merkel allowed hundreds of thousands of Syrians fleeing the civil war in their country into Germany. Germany had been a refuge for those fleeing war and persecution for years, and, in the case of Germany's large Turkish population, it was partly done for economic gain. In recent years, Germany has taken in more refugees than any other country.

While most Germans have been welcoming, an increasing number have called on a moratorium or a law to limit the number of foreigners allowed into the country. Several attacks on German women by Arab youths alarmed the country, as have increasing numbers of right-wing attacks on Arabs by Germans. A new party, known as the *Alternativ für Deutschland* ("Alternative for Germany" or "AFD"), which at times uses rhetoric very similar to that of the 1930s, has gained influence. Its presence, along with popular support for limiting refugees, has caused a shift to the right in Germany, which has alarmed some.

Still, every year, Germany ranks among the wealthiest, happiest, healthiest, and most free nations on Earth, which is a far cry from 1945.

Part 2: Germania

A Captivating Guide to the History of a Region in Europe Where Germanic Tribes Dominated and How It Transformed into Germany

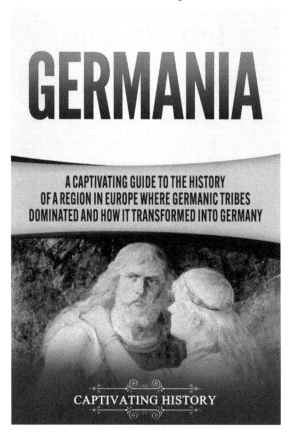

Introduction

Germany is a relatively young nation-state. United in 1871, it's even younger than the United States. However, the territories inhabited by the Germanic people have a rich history that reaches far back in prehistory and antiquity. Located in the heart of Europe, Germany witnessed centuries of conflicts, immigration, and negotiations. Consequently, its shape, size, and ethnicity changed throughout history. The territories which constitute Germany today were often war zones, and at times they would join forces against a common enemy or break apart due to internal conflicts. Because of these conflicts, Germany's boundaries, as well as what it means to be German, fluctuated throughout history and, in some way, are still evolving. The region's long and troubled history influences its present, its politics, and its nationality.

Today's Germany is situated on a historic migratory path. The first evidence of humans traces back fifty million years. First, distant relatives of modern humans migrated into these parts of Europe. Soon, they were followed by the Neanderthals, who were named by the valley in Germany where they were first discovered. Within the last few years, some of the biggest and most important prehistoric findings happened in today's Germany. Modern scholars believe that southern Germany could be the birthplace of music (and art in general) over 35,000 years ago. But the migration didn't stop with the arrival of the Cro-Magnon, the early humans. It continued through the centuries and even millennia. The Bronze Age saw the arrival of the Celtic people, whose civilization in central Europe survived centuries. At approximately the same time, the first Greek and Roman writers started describing the peoples occupying the territories of central Europe and, with these writers, the historical records of the area begin.

From around 300 to 500 BCE, the first Germanic-speaking groups of people started arriving in this region. They came from the east, and they encountered the Celts already living in the territory of modern-day Germany. Even though there were some similarities between the two ethnicities, the Germanic peoples slowly pushed the Celts back and started occupying the territories along the Rhine and Danube, previously controlled by the Roman Empire. According to the Romans, the Germanic tribes were warmongering people, determined to inflict fear and destruction upon the civilized world. The various peoples of Germania, the shadowy land beyond the borders of the civilized Roman Empire, were simply placed under the common name barbarians.

Once the conflict with the Romans was over, the Germanic tribes took the opportunity to rise into a new European civilization. The Franks were the first to attempt unification, and they managed to bring some of the Germanic tribes under their direct or indirect authority. At the same time, the Christianization of the pagan Germans began. Believing they were the heirs of the Roman Empire, the Frankish rulers built the foundation for the Holy Roman Empire. Starting in the 800s, the political structure of this empire that gathered various Germanic tribes into a loose confederation would shape the politics of Europe until modern times. With the dissolution of the Carolingian Empire, a new ruler, Louis the German, rose to power in the east, founding the first Germanic state in central Europe. His successors would become

Holy Roman Emperors and lead the German-speaking people into a modern future.

But the unity of the Holy Roman Empire was shattered during the 16th century when Martin Luther protested the Catholic Church. This conflict divided Germany and, with it, the whole of Europe into two rival factions: the Protestants and the Catholics. The Thirty Years' War of the 17th century was the culmination point of this conflict. The German territories suffered devastation and depopulation, and at the end of the war, the authority of the Holy Roman Empire diminished. Unable to control the territorial autonomy of each Germanic region, the emperor allowed his empire to become an arena in which various princes fought for dominion. Because of these conflicts, Prussia emerged as a military state in the north and Austria as the powerful Habsburg heartland in the south. At the same time, the waking of the German nation occurred. This rise of German nationalism would seal the fate of Europe in the future.

The modern history of Germany starts with the Napoleonic Wars and the resulting revolutionary army, which brought the Holy Roman Empire to its end. In its place, the ambitious German nation-state was founded by the Prussian ruler. The country went through rapid industrialization and soon emerged as the second industrial powerhouse of Europe, after Britain. But the 19th century was ruled by militant German nationalism, which brought about new conflicts and the start of World War I. After the Great War, Germany was devastated, and under the Treaty of Versailles, the new nation-state was forced to accept a humiliating peace. The trauma of war and the humiliation it brought paved the way for the rise of fascism, as discontent with the ruling parties grew due to poverty and overall economic depression. Once Adolf Hitler was appointed as chancellor of Germany, the totalitarian Nazi dictatorship and racist oppression of the Jews and other people groups began.

Hitler's vision of a "Thousand Year Reich" ended after only a decade but left scars on Europe still visible even today. World War II and the genocidal madness of one dictator brought Germany to its knees. After the war, the victorious forces partitioned Germany and paved the way towards the Cold War. While the western parts of Germany managed to exit the post-war crisis with the help of the allied USA, France, and Britain, the eastern parts suffered under the Soviet Union and the iron heel of its leader, Stalin. West Germany returned to democracy, joined NATO, and laid the foundations for the future European Union. But East Germany was a part of the Warsaw Pact and under the strict control of the Soviet Union, which divided it from the west by raising the infamous Berlin Wall. But the communism of the east was doomed to fall, and in 1989 people started demanding changes.

During the peaceful revolution, the government of East Germany fell and opened the way to reunification. With the destruction of the Berlin Wall in 1991, the unification of Germany into the Federate Republic symbolically began. The country was ready to look into the future without being pulled down by the atrocities committed during World War II. Through hard work and cooperation, Germany earned the world's forgiveness and strode proudly forward to become a bastion of liberty and democracy at the front of the European Union.

Chapter 1 – The Early History of Germania

The archeological site which testifies to the earliest history of the region of Germany is the Hohle Fels cave in south Germany (near today's city of Ulm). There, two remarkable facts were discovered. The first is that the first Homo sapiens who migrated to this part of Europe from Africa settled near their genetic cousins, the Neandertals. The second one is that right here, in these caves, humans crafted the first musical instruments. Two flutes that were discovered carbon-dated as far back as 40,000 years. One was made from bird bones and the other from mammoth ivory. What an astonishing discovery! As soon as Homo sapiens came to the regions of today's southern Germany, they started developing art. And music wasn't the only artistic expression our ancestors of the Hohle Fels cave invented. Here the archeologists found some of the earliest examples of human and animal carvings and paintings. It is amazing to think that the first glimpses of culture, music, and art are a part of European heritage! The early humans quickly superseded and replaced the Neanderthals and silently became rulers of the surrounding territories. However, they would not remain the only settlers for long. Other groups of people migrated to the region, and they would all become the settlers of the area we call Germany.

The region today's Germany occupies is geographically unique. It is crossed by three mighty European rivers: the Elbe, Rhine, and Danube. However, it doesn't have natural barriers that would prevent people from migrating or invading. Because of this, a variety of people settled in Germania (the historical name for the region) and called it home. Germania and its history tell us the story of very fluid borders and the constant movement of people. It was only natural that these movements and migrations caused political instability and frequent conflicts. Accordingly, the region of Germania was fragmented, with different cultural and linguistic boundaries, which often changed. The earliest fragmentation we can trace is between Homo sapiens and their neighbors, the Neanderthals. We cannot say if they were ever in open conflict, but their cultures (and probably their languages) differed greatly. While Neanderthals produced crude tools and art, those belonging to Homo sapiens were much more sophisticated. The fragmentation between the two groups wasn't only cultural but also physical. The two peoples were also two different species. However, modern tests show that Neanderthals shared at least 99% of their DNA with Homo sapiens, leading to big questions posed by scholars: did the two species interbreed? Is that how the Neanderthal disappeared? Were they simply absorbed into the genome and culture of Homo sapiens? These questions remain to be answered, and once they are, they will cause many more new questions. This is the beauty of history—it never ends.

The Neanderthals were already long gone (approximately 40,000 years ago) when the Homo sapiens entered the Mesolithic period and roamed central Europe alone. This period began 10,000 years ago, and at that point, humans were a hunter-gatherer society. They remained such for several millennia, but an astonishing change occurred 5,000 to 3,500 years ago. The Homo sapiens of Europe gradually developed the ability to grow crops and produce food. They also learned how to tame animals and use them for farming, clothing, and food. Because there was no more need to move across central Europe in search of food and game, the humans established the first settled societies of Germania. These early people recognized the value of fertile lands, so the first settlements were built in the wetlands of Northern regions as well as along the banks of the Elbe, Rhine, and Danube. The people settled along other rivers, as well as lakes, but it seems that the first settlements in these locations were seasonal. During warmer days, people took their herds to graze in the fields. Society must have been divided, with some staying in the settlements to work the land around them. The first peoples of central Europe who started their settlements during the Mesolithic and Neolithic period are known to scholars today as the Linear Pottery culture, named after the specific decoration on the pottery they produced. But they weren't the only ones. Later excavations in lower Saxony, at the site known as the Dümmer, discovered a series of settlements ranging from 4,900 to 3,600 BCE. These people are known as the Funnel Beaker culture, and they transitioned from hunting and gathering to farming and herding animals. This specific culture persisted through the Bronze Age until its end (3,200–600 BCE). The Bronze Age saw the rise and fall of many cultures in Germania that worked metal, plowed fields, and grazed livestock. They all displayed different burial rites and included various everyday life items in their tombs, suggesting belief in some kind of afterlife.

The Celts came to the region of Germania sometimes during the Bronze Age and stayed for quite a long time. In fact, their DNA can still be traced in various European peoples from Ireland to the Mediterranean and from Spain to Hungary and even Romania. The Celts were the most influential people in Europe during the Bronze Age. Their origin remains obscure, but some scientific discoveries in their burial practices seem to point to the Urnfield culture as possible ancestors. For example, just like the Celts, people of the Urnfield culture cremated their dead and buried them in urns. The Urnfield culture disappeared somewhere between 700 and 500 BCE, giving way to several new cultures in Europe, most of them proto-Celtic. The earliest Iron Age civilization that succeeded Urnfield culture was the Hallstatt culture, which flourished between 800 and 450 BCE. They are named for a city in Austria where their culture was first discovered. With the end of Hallstatt culture, Europe saw the rise of another proto-Celtic culture, the La Tène culture. This one was so widespread that it reached Anatolia and Ireland, as well as the central Europe of Germania.

The Celts

The Celts' Expansion in Europe
https://upload.wikimedia.org/wikipedia/commons/a/aa/Celtic_expa nsion_in_Europe.png

From these early civilizations, the Celts developed their own culture composed of tribal groups whose society was based on warfare. As such, their aristocracy rose from the military ranks, but the whole group had a reputation for being fierce and warmongering. The classical world is filled with stories about Celtic raids. Romans have probably written the most about the Celts since they suffered the sacking of their city in 390 by the Gauls, who were nothing more than a Celtic group.

Celtic society had a strict class division: warrior elites, druids who practiced religion, and commoners who were pastoral and moved together with their herds. Interestingly, the women of Celtic tribes enjoyed more freedom during the classical era than their Greek or Roman counterparts, who thought of themselves as more civilized than the Celts. The women in Germania could choose their calling and could be warriors, just like men. They could also rule if their predecessor had no male heirs.

Unfortunately, Celts did not leave many written sources, and a large portion of our knowledge about them comes from their contemporaries, the Greeks and the Romans. However, these contemporary civilizations wrote mostly negative comments about the Celtic people since they were victims of their raids and couldn't possibly be objective. The most detailed literary work on Celts comes from a famous Roman military leader, Gaius Julius Caesar. Written between 58 and 50 BCE, the work was named *Commentarii de Bello Gallico*, or *Commentaries on the Gallic War*. (The Celts inhabiting regions of today's France, Luxembourg, and Belgium were named Gauls by Romans who conquered their lands.) But Caesar also led his army through the territory of what is today the German-speaking part of Europe, and he described the people living there. Caesar made a distinction between the Gauls and the Germanic people of central Europe, but his Greek contemporaries thought of them as one people. Culturally, they were similar, but their language was very different. Romans made the classification based on language, and thus the Germanic tribes were born.

Some of the Gaulish tribes were in an alliance with Rome and suffered attacks from Germanic tribes. In one such instance, the tribe known as Aedui, which had allied with Rome, was attacked and defeated by newcomers, the Suebs. Rome was called to aid the Aedui, so consequently, Caesar was the first to describe this new group of people. According to him, the Suebs were a distinct tribe, probably the most aggressive of all Germanic peoples. However, a later Roman historian, Pliny the Elder (1st century AD), thought of them as a larger entity consisting of smaller tribes such as the

Lombards, Semnones, and Marcomanni. Another group of Celtic people, the Helvetii, were being pushed from the north by migrating Germanic tribes, and they too fought Romans for their right to inhabit the territory of central Europe. Roman borders were endangered by all these moving tribes of Gauls and Germanic peoples. Caesar decided to protect the borders, and in 58 ADE, he mounted a military expedition to stop Helvetii and Suebi.

A series of conflicts over the years resulted in the expansion of Roman rule. Romans even reached the Northern and Baltic seas of today's northern Germany. In his Commentaries on the Gallic War, Caesar not only described military conflicts and his expedition to conquer Celtic and Germanic tribes but also provided detailed descriptions of the appearance, language, and culture of the peoples he encountered. He noticed similarities in society and culture among the Celtic and Germanic tribes who occupied the regions of Europe that were far away from the Roman influence. These similarities seemed to disappear with closer proximity to Roman territories. Caesar describes Celts and Germanic people of northern Europe as aggressive and fierce, quick to start a quarrel, and hard to fight. He also claims that the Gaul tribes Rome was fighting owed their bravery and valor to the Germanic tribes north of the Rhine with whom they were constantly battling.

The *Commentaries on the Gallic War* could be observed as one of the first ethnographic studies of the Celtic people, especially those living in central Europe. Celts were an enigma to Romans, and the Roman account of these fierce warrior people was biased and filled with negative comments. After all, they were enemies, and Caesar's work is only a fraction of the Roman attitude towards Gauls. For example, Caesar was repulsed by the clan-like structure of Gaul society, which was led by a warrior chieftain who would buy the loyalty of his warband with gifts and lavish feasts.

For Romans, it was the Druidic religion of the Gauls that posed the greatest enigma. Caesar describes Druids as religious leaders and a social class that enjoyed many privileges. Caesar found Druids to be of enormous importance, as one of their tasks was to encourage the battle and inspire valor in the Gaul warriors. Druids never went to war, and it seems they were exempted from paying tribute. Druid religion was oral, so one of their main tasks was to learn the stories and verses they would preserve and pass on to the next generation. Caesar noticed that Gauls used Greek letters for everyday writings, transactions, or public and private messages. However, writing down the Druidic lore was a sacrilege. This is probably because Gauls thought of writing as an inferior method of learning that makes people lazy. Caesar also wrote that Gauls believed in reincarnation and that, because of this, they never feared death. Instead, they were promised that if they died with valor, they would be reborn with a high social rank and many riches.

Pliny the Elder also described Druids in his observations of the religion. According to him, Druids worshiped nature and could read important moments in the future from various natural occurrences, such as stone formations and bird flights. They had no temples but practiced sacred rituals in groves, out in the open. The Druids also sacrificed animals, but in special cases, they would also sacrifice humans. However, no archeological examination confirms the practice of human sacrifice in Celtic society. Nonetheless, it was exactly this that Romans claimed prompted them to ban Druidic practices within the borders of Roman territories in the 2nd century BCE. This ancient Celtic religion died out a century later without leaving any written evidence of its existence.

Caesar's campaign against the Gauls of central and western Europe influenced numerous people groups. The Celts were subjugated to Rome and pacified, and their territories were opened to new migrations of people. It was the Germanic tribes who moved first and inhabited the territory of Germania. They were newcomers here, and they played a dominant role in the history of this region. They not only gave Germany its name but also its culture and language. However, they didn't call themselves Germani. This was a Roman word, probably just a Latin form of an ancient Celtic word that described people similar to themselves but speaking another language.

The Germanic Tribes

At the time of Caesar, the Roman Empire's northern borders were at the Rhine and Danube. But across these waters lived new tribes that posed an even bigger threat than the Gauls. These were the Germanic tribes that migrated from the east—wild, warlike people who wouldn't accept the Roman yoke. Their society was of an egalitarian nature, which Romans couldn't grasp. Fearing the newly-come Germanic tribes, Romans decided to prevent possible future conflicts by invading them. This mission started in the year 12 BCE and was a very small expedition at first. However, Romans soon realized it would take more men and resources to conquer the territories beyond the Rhine, so they sent thousands and thousands of people in the following years. It took them over a decade just to gain the upper hand in the conflict, and three decades after the initial invasion, a decisive battle took place in the Teutoburg Forest (9 CE). But the Germanic tribes were ready, and they united against the common enemy, the Romans. It was the worst defeat Rome experienced since their first endeavors to conquer the tribes of central Europe. The Germanic chieftain who united the tribes against the Romans was Arminius (18 BCE–19 CE). Previously, this chieftain fought in the Roman army as a mercenary. This gave him insight into their tactics and enabled him to plan an ambush and attack, butchering the Roman legions in the woodlands of the Lower Saxony. Roman Emperor Augustus (63 BCE–14 CE) decided to abandon the mission in Germania due to the heavy losses.

But who exactly were these newcomers? Latins would go on to call them *Germani*, but the Germanic peoples never had a common name to unite all the tribes that had migrated to the territory of modern-day Germany during the 1st century BCE. They shared a common language, and this is the main characteristic by which Romans defined them. Modern linguists share the opinion that the Germanic tribes came from northern Europe but were pushed southward with climate change, which made their homeland hostile to life. The tribes never formed a cohesive group. Instead, they warred among themselves, taking each other's territory, food, women, and riches. Once they arrived in central Europe, their first contact was with the Celts who already occupied the territory. They quickly realized the similarities between their two warlike peoples, but that didn't stop them from fighting for the right to occupy the land. Soon enough, the borders of the Roman Empire were occupied by people who spoke Germanic languages— from Eastern Europe (the Baltic region) to central Europe where today's Germany, Austria, and the Netherlands are, all the way to the British Islands in the northwest.

Germanic people also settled in the western provinces of the Roman Empire, which is today's Belgium and France. However, they were heavily influenced by the Roman culture there and quickly adapted, mingling and assimilating into the local population. Because of this spread out of Germanic tribes across the whole of Europe, Romans were very confused and had difficulty defining them. There were too many different tribes to count, and the Romans simply named them all *Germani*. At first, Romans used the term *Germani* only to refer to the people who lived across the Rhine, but in their inability to describe other peoples who spoke a similar language, Romans soon designated them all the same. It is unknown where this term comes from exactly. The widely accepted proposal is that it is of Celtic origin; however, some linguists suggest an Illyrian or even purely Latin origin. Another term Romans used to unite all the tribes who lived outside their borders and often attacked them was "barbarians." The *Germani* were the barbarians, but not all barbarians were

Germani. They could also be Celts, Gauls, Illyrians, and later, Slavs. Romans left writings in which they tried to identify and describe different ethnic groups, but they were often in disagreement. Modern scholars find it difficult to discern the truth from ancient Roman texts. Even today, we are unsure which among these diverse people represent distinct ethnic groups or at least a cohesive culture. Roman sources mention different tribes, each having their own names, such as Alemanni, Cimbri, Frisians, Franks, Suebi, and Saxons.

We already learned that Caesar confronted Suebi during his conquest of Gaul and wrote about them, extensively comparing them to the Celts. The main difference between the two groups of people, according to Caesar's observations, was that Germanic tribes gave priority to warfare, praising it above religion and domestic life. Just like the Celtic, the religion of the Germanic tribes was about worshiping nature. However, they had no organized priesthood or Druids to perform various religious rituals. Caesar also describes the pastoral economy of the various tribes that occupied the regions of Germania across the Danube. According to him, the *Germani* were only interested in warfare and raiding as this was how they earned their living. This made them a formidable enemy, unlike more civilized Celtic tribes. He further complained that the Celts were seduced by the luxury of Roman civilization and thus became weak.

Julius Caesar wasn't the only Roman who tried to describe the Germanic peoples. Another Roman aristocrat, born almost 150 years after Caesar, wrote a complete work named *Germania* in 98 CE. His name was Gaius Cornelius Tacitus, and he was born in Roman-ruled Gaul in the year 55 CE. He lived until 120 CE, becoming a politician, consul, senator, and even the governor of Roman provinces in Asia. In addition to his rich career, Tacitus found time to write and describe the peoples who intrigued him the most. Among them were the Germanic peoples, to whom he devoted an entire collection of writings. His intentions were also biased, but unlike Caesar, Tacitus wanted to prove that Romans had become a decadent society compared to brave and virtuous Germanic tribes. Modern scholars are not even sure if Tacitus spent any time on the Roman northern border or if he ever met with the *Germani*, but he did use sources such as Caesar's and Pliny's writings. He probably consulted the Roman merchants and soldiers who encountered the barbarian tribes of central Europe and used their stories to write an ethnographic account named *Germania*.

This work was discovered in the 19th century by German nationalists, who were inspired by Tacitus' description of Germanic valor and bravery. It was Tacitus who was the first to explain Germanic superiority by attributing it to racial purity. He described how Germanic people were untainted by intermarriage with other races and how they were the purest among all peoples known to Romans. However, today it is known that Germanic peoples indeed mixed with other races—for example, the Celts and the Slavs, their immediate neighbors. They also mixed among themselves, and often tribes shared nothing in common except the similarity of their language. Nevertheless, the Germans of the 19th century would start a new nationalistic movement after reading the words of ancient historian and politician Tacitus.

Tacitus' description of Germanic military habits seems more reliable. He wrote that various Germanic tribes, which often fought against each other, would unite on the battlefield when meeting their common enemy, the Romans. The Romans were baffled by this sudden cohesion of the *Germani*, and this was probably the reason they lost so many battles against these barbarians. The *Germani* would choose their common chieftain based on his previous experience and valor on the battlefield. The chieftain had power over his people only as long as he was able to lead them to victory. He would often be demoted after the lost battle and replaced with a more suitable individual. The aristocracy of the Germanic tribes was composed of the best warriors and their immediate families. But no title was hereditary, and each individual had to prove his worth in battle. Tacitus also noticed that, unlike Roman leaders, Germanic chieftains were at the front of the battle lines, not simply giving commands. They were the leaders, and they had to set an example for their followers.

Tacitus also explained the Germanic military success by how their society is structured. He emphasized that Germanic warbands were composed of family members and clan brethren. Unlike Romans, the Germanic peoples fought next to their kinsmen, which inspired them to show off as well as to watch each other's back. Because proving valor was so deeply engraved in their society, young warriors wanted to prove themselves to their kinsmen and peers, which made them especially dangerous enemies. The bravest warriors were rewarded by chieftains with sizable plunder. Tacitus also explains that they would bring their women and children to the battlefield and fought especially hard to win because they knew their families would be slaughtered or enslaved if they lost. Tacitus believed that the cry of the women and children inspired the Germanic men to fight with vigor and ferocity.

Tacitus also described the wider political and egalitarian nature of the Germanic tribes. He explained that the leaders of different tribes would gather at least once a year to discuss important matters such as warfare, famine, and even birthrates and the exchange of women. While the chieftains had the right to speak first, everyone also had the right to address the assembly and offer insight based on their own experience. The meeting was followed by a lavish feast, where they would all get drunk and celebrate the occasion. These feasts were often ritualistic, symbolizing good fortune and ensuring victory in future battles. But they also served a social function, as such gatherings strengthened the bonds of kinsmen, and many new families would form during the celebrations. According to Tacitus, the Germanic people valued marriage above all and were faithful to their spouses, unlike the decadent Romans of the empire. He insisted that adultery was harshly punished among the Germanic people and that monogamy was highly valued since marriage was considered the strongest bond between two people. Spouses would give gifts to each other on the day of the marriage ceremony, and these gifts included weapons and armor as a symbolic reminder of the primacy of warfare in the Germanic culture.

By the 9th century CE, Romans had conquered some of the territories they designated as Germania. To distinguish it from the area still ruled by the barbaric tribes, they would call the Roman provinces of central Europe *Germania Romana*, while the area beyond the Rhine was named *Germania Barbarica*. The Romans had tried to conquer *Germania Barbarica* continuously since the year 12 BCE but without much success. And when, in 9 CE, Arminius and his warriors ambushed the Roman legion at the Teutoburg Forest, his action was only one small part of the Germanic uprising against the Roman conquest. It was the uprising that convinced Augustus that Germania was not worth invading. The resulting frontier was established at the Rhine-Danube line, known as the Limes Germanicus, and it was held for centuries. However, the peace was uneasy, as the Germanic chieftains demanded payment in exchange for not raiding across the Roman borders. But this static border on the Rhine-Danube line was much more than just a border between the barbarians and the Roman Empire. It was a line that would forever divide the Germanic tribes west of the Rhine, who lived under the Roman rule, and the Germanic tribes in the east. The border also divided their culture, as western Germanic peoples assimilated with Romans and even started using only the Latin language, while the easterners continued their ancient tribal practices and preserved their Germanic language.

During the Roman Empire of Tacitus' time, most of the Germanic tribes settled along the banks of the Rhine and Danube, the territory of today's Germany. Here, the grounds were fertile, and the rivers provided them with life. The border became the site where merchants exchanged their goods and where culture was passed from Rome to Germany and vice versa. Romans founded garrisons along the border, which quickly turned into the towns and later into the culturally-rich German cities of the Middle Ages. Some of these cities exist even today and are known as Trier (Augusta Treverorum), Mainz (Moguntiacum), and Augsburg (Augusta Vindelicorum). Around the year 300 CE, when Rome was challenged by outside forces, many Germans saw the opportunity to invade, raid, and even to settle in Roman territory. They chose to serve in the Roman army in faraway lands. This service would bring them not only regular pay but also the right to own land within the Roman Empire. Slowly but surely, the Roman world was crumbling, and when the Gauls killed Emperor Valens (328-378) in Thracia, his successor Theodosius (347-395) agreed to cede even more land to keep the peace. But he also had another motive. These Gauls settled at the Rhine-Danube frontier would serve as a buffer from the upcoming Germanic invasion.

By the 5th century, Rome had weakened, and several Germanic tribes, pressured to unite by the constant increase of the population and by the Hunnic invaders, began migrating into the Roman heartland. Visigoths moved towards Greece as the Huns pushed them across the Danube. Their leader, Alaric (370-410), sacked Rome in 410. He then moved his people towards Spain. Another Germanic tribe, the Vandals, moved across Gaul into Spain in 406, and from there crossed to North Africa, which they wrestled from the Roman grip. During these turbulent times, many Germanic chieftains took the opportunity to seize territories that once belonged to the Roman Empire and turn them into their own kingdoms. They completely reorganized Roman administration and subjected the local population to Germanic rule. Germanic kings waged wars against each other, assimilating tribes and consolidating the hold over their new territories. In the 6th century, a new religion appeared among the Germanic tribes, and one by one, the Germanic kingdom succumbed to Arian Christianity. This heterodox sect denied the divinity of Jesus Christ and claimed he was only a human. Because of this, Arian Christianity was declared a sect by the Holy Roman Church at the council of Nicaea in 325.

The scholars of the 18th century thought that the rise of the Germanic tribes was the cause of the Romans' eclipse. However, modern scholars now think that the rise of Germanic tribes was a product of Rome's failing politics. If Rome hadn't weakened due to different influences, Germanic people would never have been able to enter its territories, let alone sack Rome itself. At this point, Germanic people were nothing to be afraid of, and Romans even used them as a force that would defend their outer provinces. They allowed Germanic tribes to inhabit the Roman territories, and more and more Germanic young people showed interest in serving the Roman army. Maybe the Germanic tribes were militarily superior to the Romans at the beginning of the Middle Ages, but Rome played it smart. The emperors, now in Constantinople, were removed from the birthplace of their empire and were even willing to sacrifice it to the incoming barbarians. But they never allowed the Latins to be assimilated. Instead, they managed to turn the Germanic tribes to Roman ideals. Instead of raiding for a living, Germanic kingdoms started growing their own food and producing their own goods. They settled, finally having a territory granted and land they could call their own. And, even though they remained fierce warriors who displayed outstanding bravery on the battlefield, they longed for peace and domesticity in their new homes, where their wives and children waited.

The 6th century saw the previous Western Roman Empire divided into various Germanic kingdoms, which dominated and eventually assimilated the Roman population. Even in Italy, the Germanic kings ruled. The first was Odoacer (433–493), who ruled as a client king of Zeno, Emperor in Constantinople. He was succeeded by Theodoric the Great, a king who is even today seen as one of the mightiest Germanic rulers.

The Franks

Distribution of the Frankish Tribes (green)
https://en.wikipedia.org/wiki/Franks#/media/File:Carte_des_peuple
s_francs_(IIIe_si%C3%A8cle).svg

During the late 5th century, another Germanic chieftain rose to power, united the tribes which lived between the flow of Lower Rhine and Ems River, and marched on the Roman territory of Gaul. His name was Chlodovocar (466–511), and his people were known as the Franks. Chlodovacar was the first to rule the united

Franks instead of numerous chieftains. He is remembered as Clovis, the first king of Franks, who defeated the Roman leader Syagrius in 486 at Soissons. Clovis settled his people in the Roman province of Gaul, absorbing the Roman and Celtic people who already inhabited the area. He married a Burgundian princess, Clotilda, and under her influence, he converted to Roman Catholicism. The baptism of this king remains a famous story, found in *The Chronicles of St. Denis*, where he is described as a pagan who, through a work of miracle and divine intervention, became a Christian.

Clovis turned to Catholicism in 496, and although *The Chronicle* tells a fantastical story of his wife's influence and the inspiration of God, the Frankish king probably had political motives, too. By renouncing paganism, he set an example for the Frankish people, who also accepted Christianity. This way, Clovis had no problem uniting the Franks with the Romans who previously lived in the territory that had become his kingdom. His kingdom now had a united people, bound by the same faith, creating cohesion among the subjects. Other Germanic kingdoms were still pagan and lacked this unity. If they were Christians, Germanic people chose heretical Arian Christianity, which only distanced them from their Roman subjects. Because of this, they were often regarded as foreign or pagan tyrants. Meanwhile, Clovis reaped the benefits of his united people. He quickly became a champion of the faith under the Catholic banner as he slowly started to dominate the other Germanic tribes. Among them were the Thuringians, his mother's tribe, and the dwellers of the Harz Mountains in what would be today's central Germany. He also fought against the Alemanni in 496, but this time his kingdom was invaded. Nevertheless, once he defeated them, he imprisoned their king, Chararic, and his son and took over their territories, which lay near Lake Constance in today's southern Germany.

Clovis was the founder of the Merovingian Dynasty, named after one of his ancestors, probably Merovich. This individual was a part of the Frankish legends, and the connection between the two cannot be confirmed. However, some of the historical sources dating at least a century after the period in which Clovis ruled claim that both Clovis and his Alemanni enemy King Chararic were grandsons of Merovich. Clovis died in 511 and was succeeded by his son Chlotar I. Under him, the Franks conquered even more Germanic tribes and became the rulers of the territory which we today call Germany. They even dared to raid northern lands, where the fierce Saxons lived. These were the territories near the modern region of Holstein.

The Merovingian dynasty started with only one tribe, the Salian Franks. But once they became ardent champions of the Roman Catholic faith, they spread their rule through northern Gaul (modern-day France) and entered central Europe, the territory known as Germania. There, they conquered the Bavarii, Saxons, and Alemanni, adding their territories to the kingdom. The Merovingians ruled until 751, but its kings started leaving the conquest to able military commanders. These commanders had the title Mayor of the Palace and were influential politicians as well as military geniuses. They managed to acquire the right for their sons to inherit the title and start their dynasties of dukes, lords, and princes. The founder of the dynasty which would inherit that position was Charles Martel. He was an illegitimate son of Pepin of Herstal, the Duke and the Prince of the Franks. Charles had to fight for his right to inherit his father's position, and he succeeded in 718. However, once he secured his position as the Mayor of the Palace, Martel became the acting king of the Franks as he controlled and kept Theuderic IV, the Merovingian king, in custody. It would be the son of Charles Martel, Pepin III (the Short), who would usurp the Merovingian throne and start a new dynasty in 751.

With the rise of the Franks and the territorial gains of Clovis, Germania ceased to be the land of the barbarians. The population accepted Christianity, and although in some parts the heretical

Arianism lingered, there was no more paganism. Germania became a Christian kingdom, and its kings gained the support of the pope in Rome and the patriarch in Constantinople. The Eastern Roman Empire, better known as the Byzantine Empire, slowly veined and couldn't assert its influence over the newly risen kingdom of the Franks. However, they maintained good relations or chose to simply ignore each other. Even though the kingdom of the Franks was secured, the conflicts never ceased. Internal struggles as well as new neighbors stirred the political situation of Medieval Europe and led it to the new era.

Chapter 2 – The Barbarian Leaders

The ancient history of Germania is complicated. The region was divided between many chieftains, and even though there is evidence they had yearly gatherings to discuss issues pertaining to all the Germanic tribes, they often warred with each other, and the territorial boundaries of their chiefdoms were very fluid. Some lesser tribes were absorbed into the greater ones, leaving little to no trail in history. However, each tribe remained distinctive while gaining a greater sense of belonging to something bigger. The Germani peoples, as Romans used to call them, had a collective awareness and recognized when a common enemy was a threat to their territories. In such cases, they would join forces, showing they were capable of displaying a sense of unity, of a nation, as early as the 2nd century BCE. Perhaps it was the barbaric way of life that divided them and pushed them into conflict with one other. The constant need to show off warrior skills and battle valor, to be recognized by their peers and earn the wealth of plunder, divided them into tribes. Each tribe had its chief, the best among the warriors, one capable of leading his warband into victory. Warfare was a necessity for Germanic tribes—without it, life wouldn't be possible. And warfare would start as soon as the opportunity presented itself.

But when facing an outside enemy, like Rome, the Germanic people would see past their previous quarrels and unite to bring down the threat. The foreign enemy was more than just an opportunity for valor. Romans were invaders who sought not only to add new territory to their enormous empire but also to convert the peoples who already lived there and spoil them with their lavish Roman lives. With their festivities, soft silky clothes, cushioned lives they spent in their marble palaces, the Roman people seemed weak to the barbarians. Romans were effeminate poets and philosophers who only sought to indulge in life's joys. The Germanic people didn't fight only to save their homeland but also to preserve their way of life. During these first conflicts between the Roman Empire and Germanic tribes, some of the greatest barbarian leaders were born. They lived, fought, and died trying to resist the civilized world which lay to the south. Some of them are celebrated even today as if the modern German people have a collective memory of their bravery, courage, and strength.

Arminius (18 BCE-19 CE)

Ancient Rome had a tradition of taking the male offspring of the rulers they defeated as hostages. They would grow up in Rome, directly under the supervision of the emperor. As hostages, these foreign boys weren't imprisoned. Instead, they were given an education, military training, and upbringing equal to that of highborn Romans. Sometimes, they would even study alongside Roman heirs to the throne. One such hostage of Rome was a son of Germanic chieftain Segimerus of the Cherusci tribe. His name is known only in the Latin form: Arminius. His Germanic given name is lost, but today he is known as Hermann throughout Germany.

Arminius was born around 18 or 17 BCE, but it is not known when exactly he was sent to Rome. Once in the capital of the Roman Empire, he received military training and stepped into the service of Rome. It is possible Arminius served alongside Tiberius, the heir of the first Roman emperor, Augustus. The crucial moment for Arminius occurred around the year 8 CE when he was transferred to the Rhine area to fight the Germanic tribes who still resisted becoming Roman provinces. Because of Arminius' Germanic ancestry, he was regarded as a valuable addition to the legions under the service of Publius Quinctilius Varus, who was in charge of pacifying the Germanic tribes in the region. Arminius was even given an auxiliary command, as with this rank he could negotiate with the nobles of the Germanic tribes. But Arminius took the opportunity to re-learn what it meant to be a Germanic man and even reconnected with his family. He met with his father, chieftain Segimer, and together, they planned to get rid of the Roman yoke.

At the time, their tribe, the Cherusci, were already pacified, but Arminius realized the Romans treated them as slaves instead of as part of the foederati (those bound to Rome by a peace treaty) as they were promised. Angered, he agreed to meet with the rest of the Germanic chieftains to make plans for the expulsion of Romans from central Germania. Since he already served the Roman army, he had all the tactical information they needed to devise a successful plan. They were aware that the local Roman garrison was well defended and that they could not attack it and expect victory. Instead, they opted for an ambush in the woods, far away from the fortified walls of the garrison. Arminius' experience in the Roman army won him the allegiance of the Germanic tribes, who united under his command.

The opportunity for the ambush came during the fall when the Roman army decided to move to another garrison on the Rhine for the winter. Arminius already had the support of Germanic tribes such as the Marsi and the Bructeri, but some stubbornly wanted to remain neutral. One such chieftain was Segestes, Armenius' uncle. However, seeing the might of the united armies and their will to fight the Romans, even Segestes joined the rebels, as did many other tribes who were neutral until this point. Of course, some chieftains remained loyal to Rome and even tried to warn Publius Quinctilius Varus, but he dismissed them, believing they were only jealous of Arminius' privileges since he had grown up in Rome. The attack of the barbarians was so sudden and unexpected that the three Roman legions led by Varus simply dispersed under the rain of arrows and stones which were being thrown at them. Varus tried to restore order, but to no avail. It is believed that Arminius, like a true Germanic leader, was in the middle of the battle, leading the attacks. However, Roman legions were still some of the best-trained armies in the world, and it wasn't an easy task to defeat them. The Romans managed to resist barbarian attacks for three days until, finally, the Germanic tribes overwhelmed them. Varus and the other high-ranking officers chose to commit suicide, as they knew all hope was lost.

The ambush led by Arminius wasn't the end of the Germanic troubles with the Romans. There was still much to do, and in fact, it was only the beginning of a greater uprising. The attacks continued, organized across all of central Germania. Arminius' next target was Aliso, the fort built by Romans on the River Lippe, in the northwestern Rhine area. But he was unable to take the fort until the legions occupying it decided to leave in the middle of the night. The uprising raged on, as the news traveled slowly in ancient times. Once Emperor Augustus received the news of Varus' defeat and the loss of his many legions, he decided the efforts to take Germania were simply not worth it. But the death of the emperor approached, and the conflict in Lower Rhine continued. Germanic tribes still wanted to expel Romans from their territory, and the perfect opportunity presented itself when the Roman legions stationed on the Rhine frontier rebelled against Tiberius' succession to their emperor Augustus.

One person responsible for managing the rebellion was Tiberius' nephew, Germanicus Julius Caesar, the commander of the Rhine frontier. He had to pay the rebellious legionaries to stand down, but sensing that they were still unsatisfied, he managed to channel their anger towards the Germanic tribes who continued attacking them. At one point, Germanicus and his legionaries confronted Arminius, but instead of defeating him, they only managed to capture his pregnant wife. This enraged the Germanic leader, and he once more called for the unification of the tribes to fight off the invading Romans. The renewed conflict dragged on for years. Some battles were won by the Germanic tribes, others by the Roman legions. It seems that the war against central Germania led to a stalemate, and Emperor Tiberius decided to call off Germanicus and his legions.

Arminius' plan to expel the Romans from central Germania finally succeeded, and he was the leader of the united tribes. He asserted his authority over the tribes, but they refused to name him a king. They still believed in their old system of government: each tribe choosing its own chieftain. Arminius' main challenger at this point was Maroboduus, chieftain of the Marcomanni, who managed to proclaim himself king. Because of this, Maroboduus was hated among his people, and many of them instead joined Arminius. The two Germanic leaders finally met in battle, and Arminius was victorious over the King of Marcomanni, who was forced to run for his life. Arminius now had full authority over the Germanic tribes, but many still denied him the title of king. In 19 CE, tribal warfare occurred, and Arminius was killed in one of the conflicts after his kinsmen betrayed him. The story of his deeds remains thanks to the ancient historian Tacitus, who wrote extensively about this Germanic hero.

Gaiseric (389–477)

In 406, another great migration of the Germanic peoples occurred. In history, it is remembered as the Crossing of the Rhine. Many Germanic tribes who lived in the eastern parts of Germania moved towards the west in search of a better life. The opportunity presented itself as the Western Roman Empire was already veining and the border on the Rhine was weakened. Among the moving tribes were Vandals, led by King Godigisel. But upon their arrival to southwestern Germania, the Vandals came into conflict with the Franks, who killed their king. Godigisel had an illegitimate son, Gaiseric, who proved his worth and became one of the most powerful men of his tribe. However, he was not their leader—at least not yet. The Vandals' origins are in Scandinavia, but during the 2nd century CE, they migrated to the territory of modern Poland. They continued their migration towards the southwest and eventually reached Spain. There, they were forced into an endless conflict with both the Romans and the Visigoths who occupied the Iberian Peninsula. Gunderic, the legitimate son of ex-king Godigisel, united the Vandals and Alanas and had a large army under his command. However, this army wasn't capable of wrestling Spain out of Roman and Visigoth arms. When Gunderic died in 428 CE, Gaiseric became the king. He was wise enough to see that his people would never prosper in a territory ravaged by eternal conflict. He decided to continue moving and searching for a land where he could establish his kingdom.

The opportunity to seize such land presented itself the same year Gaiseric became the king of Vandals—428. The intrigues of the Byzantine court complicated the situation in the empire. The ruler of the North African province, Boniface, felt threatened by Emperor Valentinian III and his mother, the regent Queen Galla Placidia. To protect himself from possible conflict, he invited the Visigoths to cross the Mediterranean Sea and be his allies against the Byzantine invasion. But this story is only one version of the events. Another story tells of Gaiseric being lame, having injured himself when he fell from a horse. Unable to lead the battle on the land, he wanted to conquer a country by sea, and North Africa was a perfect choice. There is no consensus among historians about how the events played out, but it is quite possible that Gaiseric accepted the invitation from Boniface while planning all along to wait for the opportunity to conquer Carthage.

Around 80,000 Vandals and Alans crossed from Spain into North Africa in 429, invading the Byzantine provinces. It took over fourteen months to take the first city in Africa, Hippo. But once it fell, the Vandals simply overran the rest of the North African territories, from modern-day Morocco to Algeria. Carthage finally fell in 439 CE, and Gaiseric led his army into victory, taking all the cities in North Africa one by one. The court intrigue back in Constantinople further weakened the political scene of the empire, and Emperor Valentinian III had no other choice but to recognize the Vandals as the new rulers of the African provinces. Finally, they had their kingdom. A Germanic tribe had reached the shores of Africa and established a kingdom, which they would rule for a whole century.

Once Gaiseric set his kingdom, the conflict with the Romans didn't simply disappear. It shifted from warfare to religious disagreement—and perhaps disagreement is not a strong enough word. Vandals, just as most Germanic tribes, were Arian Christians, while the Roman Catholics were Trinitarians (believing in the holy trinity of the Father, Son, and Holy Spirit). When Gaiseric took over North Africa, the people he now ruled were a mixture of Vandals and Romans. The hatred between the two was immense, and their king did nothing to prevent it. In fact, he encouraged it by prosecuting the Roman nobility of Africa and even confiscating their lands and possessions. The Roman Catholic populace of his kingdom was taxed heavily compared to the Arians, and he didn't allow Catholics to serve in the government.

Despite the religious conflict within the kingdom, the Vandals in North Africa flourished. They controlled the Mediterranean Sea and built a large fleet. In 442 CE, Gaiseric felt strong enough to lead his men in another conquest. This time, he had Italy in mind. His fleet landed in Ostia, which mounted no defense even though it was aware of the Vandals' approach. The road to Rome was completely opened, and Gaiseric threatened the holy city. Pope Leo I (who served from 440 to 461) negotiated with the Vandal king, and the two came to an agreement that Rome could be sacked if its inhabitants were unharmed and no buildings were destroyed. Gaiseric kept his promise to the pope, and the city was plundered. Among the treasures gathered, Gaiseric found the widow of the late Byzantian Emperor Valentinian III and took her and her two daughters back to North Africa. The three women remained there for twenty-five years. While Valentinian's wife and younger daughter returned to Constantinople eventually, his eldest daughter, Eudoxia, remained in Africa as the wife of Huneric, son and heir of Gaiseric.

Vandals continued to terrorize the cities of the Mediterranean world, and the Romans were aware they had to deal with them. Even though they never managed to defeat Gaiseric, they eventually managed to end the kingdom of the Vandals. Gaiseric warred openly against the Eastern Roman Empire (the Byzantine Empire) from 469 until 475, but each side had a significant number of victories and losses. Finally, when Zeno became emperor in Constantinople, he sued for peace with the Vandals. He recognized Gaiseric as the king of North Africa and asked in return that the king of the Vandals grant religious freedoms to the Roman people still living there and release all Roman prisoners. Gaiseric agreed to these terms and even promised he would no longer raid the shores of Anatolia and Egypt, which were still Roman provinces. The first Vandal king died of natural causes in 477 and was succeeded by his son, Huneric, who ruled until 484.

No Vandal king ever achieved the same greatness as Gaiseric, and although his kingdom prospered under the rulers who followed, it eventually started to wane. The last king of the Vandals was Gelimer (r. 530–534), who was defeated by Romans in the Battle of Ad Decimum (533). He was taken as a prisoner to Constantinople but was released and given estates in the Roman province of Galatia, where he died of old age. But the Vandals of North Africa ceased to be a nation, a cultural entity. They were absorbed into the Roman Empire and assimilated into the Roman way of life.

Odoacer (431-493)

As we saw in the example of Gaiseric, not all famous Germanic leaders ruled Germanic lands. Those who are remembered as heroes and great kings were usually conquerors, and they became famous for ruling foreign lands. Another stellar example of a Germanic leader is Odoacer, the first king of Italy. Although his ethnicity is disputed, the consensus among scholars is that he is of Germanic descent. Nothing is known of Odoacer's youth, and history can't pinpoint his birthplace, but it is possible he was the son of Edico (or Edeko) of the Germanic Sciri tribe. If this is true, Odoacer was the son of the great adviser of Attila the Hun. Unfortunately, there are three Edicos known to history, and they were all contemporaries. It is impossible to conclude which one was Odoacer's father.

The first mention of Odoacer in history is legendary. The *Life of Saint Severinus* by Eugippius, dated to the 5th century CE, tells the story of a soldier named Odoacer who found the saint in his home and asked for a blessing. Saint Severinus prophetically told him to go to Italy, as that is where he would find riches. Young Odoacer listened to the saint and stepped into the service of the Roman army. By 470, he rose to the rank of an officer and served under the military commander Orestes. Odoacer witnessed when Orestes overthrew the Western Roman Emperor Julius Nepos and placed his son on the throne. He might even have helped the commander, as Orestes had the full support of the Roman army. But then the army asked Orestes for payment in the form of a land they could settle and call home. They asked for a third of Italy's territory, and the new emperor and his father, Orestes, hesitated to answer—only because that territory was already settled. Expelling the Roman citizens from their homes would mean a certain rebellion and condemnation from the emperor of Constantinople, who was already against their rule.

Orestes didn't count on the ambitions of his officer of Germanic origin, Odoacer. He gathered the angry soldiers around him and promised that if they followed him into rebellion, they would be properly compensated. Together with what was left of the Roman army, Orestes fled to the city of Pavia to mount a defense, as he knew Odoacer was coming for him. But he didn't linger there, as it seemed that Odoacer would easily take Pavia. So, Orestes decided to reorganize his army at Piacenza, where the decisive battle occurred. Odoacer defeated Orestes and executed him. The soldiers elevated their new leader to the position of king. However, he yet had to deal with Emperor Romulus, son of Orestes. Another battle was fought at Ravenna on September 2, 476, in which the emperor was deposed. Orestes refused to kill Romulus; instead, he exiled him from Italy. From this point, all traces of Romulus Augustus disappear. Although Odoacer was proclaimed a king of Italy, he never strived for independence. Instead, he ruled as a subject of Emperor Zeno in Constantinople.

As a new king, Odoacer couldn't simply begin his rule. The old emperor, Nepos, still claimed the right to the throne of the Western Roman Empire, even though he was hiding in his villa in Dalmatia. Odoacer never moved directly against Nepos, but the old emperor was assassinated in his home in 480, which allowed Odoacer to annex Dalmatia. He also made a treaty with the Vandals and, through it, acquired Sicily. It is unknown how he solved the problem of the army that demanded one third of Italian territory as their property, but during his rule, he was admired by his soldiers, and they never showed anything but loyalty. The Roman senate still functioned throughout the reign of Odoacer, and it gave the new king its support. Because of this, or maybe influenced by the senate, Odoacer ruled as a Roman king, not a Barbarian. He even adopted the Roman name Flavius and added it to his birth name Odoacer. Even though he was an Aryan Christian just like other Germanic leaders, it seems that his kingdom was filled with religious tolerance, as there is no evidence of special taxes enforced on Roman Christians. The Roman Christian sources dating to the rule of Odoacer do not contain any complaints about his rule.

Odoacer's annexation of Dalmatia bothered Zeno, who saw it as the clear sign that the Italian king was trying to rule independently. The conflict between the king and the emperor in Constantinople deepened once Odoacer agreed to fight on the side of the anti-Zeno party in the Middle East. The emperor saw this as a direct threat to his own rule and made an agreement with Theodoric of the Goths, who was to dispose of Odoacer and rule Italy in Zeno's name. However, this proved to be a very difficult task. Theodoric was unable to defeat the Italian army, but his persistence in the conquest led to a joint rule. It was the Bishop of Ravenna who mediated the treaty between Odoacer and Theodoric until they both agreed to split the rule of Italy. However, during the celebration ceremony in honor of the treaty, Theodoric stabbed Odoacer to death and proclaimed himself sole ruler.

Odoacer was a very pious ruler, and he set it as his goal to preserve Roman nature, ideals, and culture throughout his reign. It is quite possible that if he decided to be as Barbarian as his contemporaries saw him, Italy would never transform into a medieval culture. Perhaps even the Renaissance would have been delayed. The Roman Empire was already entering its eclipse, and if not for people like Odoacer, who saw the value of its tradition, it would certainly have fallen much earlier. Even if only for one generation, Rome survived the hard times of early medieval history. But it would take another Germanic ruler to complete the transformation of the Italian peninsula, and he would create a kingdom of Italy completely independent of its Byzantine imprisonment. This Germanic ruler of Italy was greatly respected by his contemporaries and quickly became known as Theodoric the Great.

Clovis I (466–513)

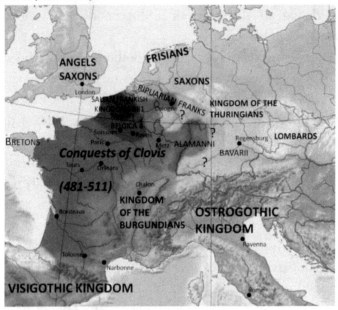

The Conquests of Clovis until 511
https://en.wikipedia.org/wiki/Clovis_I#/media/File:Conquests_of_Clovis.png

Clovis I was only fifteen years old when his father died and he assumed the throne of the Salian Franks. This tribe came to prominence as they fought against the invading Huns, on the side of the Romans. Even though he was so young, Clovis was well prepared for rule and quickly asserted his dominion over the other pretenders to the throne. By the age of twenty, he was already commanding an army large enough to oppose the governor of Roman Gaul, Syagrius. The Franks were not yet united under a single rule, but Clovis realized the importance of family alliances and asked his cousins Ragnachar and Chararic, petty kings of other Frankish tribes, for help against the Roman commander. While the first one accepted the alliance, the latter one refused. Chararic wanted to remain neutral during the conflict with Rome and decided later to join the winning side. But Clovis didn't want his cousin to be such an open threat, so, instead of marching against Rome, he turned against Chararic. Clovis managed to win the conflict and imprison his cousin. Later, Clovis had him executed and his petty kingdom annexed.

When he finally turned towards the Romans in 486, the Battle of Soissons occurred, and Clovis defeated Syagrius, who fled to Toulouse to seek shelter in the court of the Visigoth King Alaric II. Alaric refused to meddle in the conflict and refused Syagrius, allowing Clovis to capture and execute the Roman general. Clovis continued the conquest of Roman Gaul, and one by one, the cities of Reims, Rouen, and Paris fell under his command. He even killed Ragnachar, his cousin and ally, just so he could annex his petty kingdom, too. By 495, Clovis extended his dominion throughout western Gaul and finally conquered it entirely when he fought against the Alemani, pushing them across the Rhine River in 506. Almost the whole region of today's France was under the rule of Clovis I. Once he converted to Christianity, he found religious reasons to fight the Visigoths and push them across the Pyrenees into Spain. Christianity also brought recognition from the Eastern Roman Empire because, unlike other Germanic leaders, Clovis refused Arianism and converted to Catholicism. He shared the religion of the Byzantine Emperor Anastasius, who offered him an alliance.

The final battle with the Visigoths occurred in 507 when Clovis killed their king, Alaric II, at the Battle of Vouille. Even though the Visigoths had allied with the king of Italy, Theodoric the Great, it was the alliance between Clovis and the Byzantine Emperor Anastasius that prevailed. Since Constantinople had allowed Theodoric to rise to power in the first place, Anastasius vetoed him from meddling in the conflict between the Franks and the Visigoths. Alaric II was on his own against the might of the united Franks, and even though he fought vigorously, he didn't manage to save his kingdom. Once Clovis expelled the Visigoths from Frankia, he received the "royal purple" from Anastasius and chose Paris as his capital. But he didn't manage to take all the territories previously ruled by Alaric, as Theodoric the Great claimed

Provence for his grandson. Theodoric had married one of his daughters to Alaric II, and through their marriage and offspring, he asserted his right to this territory.

Clovis I died in November of either 511 or 513—historians can't seem to agree on the exact year. His kingdom was a mixture of Roman and Germanic culture and language as well as faith. While most of the Roman populace were Catholics, the Germanic part remained Aryan Christian even though their king renounced this religion. Nevertheless, the kingdom functioned as united peoples tolerated each other. With the death of Clovis I came the end of the Frankish expansion. The kingdom was already large, having taken the territories of Alemanni, Burgundians, Visigoths, and absorbing the smaller Frankish kingdoms which once occupied today's France. But all these territories were divided again between Clovis' four sons. While their father became regarded as the founder of modern-day France, their reigns were uneventful. Clovis was a Germanic name, but it was Latinized by early historians and changed to Louis, a name that would persist in the history of France. Eighteen kings named Louis would rule these territories for centuries to come.

Chapter 3 – The Merovingians and the Carolingians

After the death of Clovis, the kingdom was divided: first between his four sons and then again between his grandsons. The territory of Frankia continued to be partitioned with the passing of each of its subsequent kings. The throne pretenders often fought each other for supremacy, hoping to add their cousins' kingdoms to their own. For almost 150 years, the Merovingians ruled small kingdoms of Frankia without the desire to unite, expand, or better the lives of their subjects. They returned to their tribal instincts, with each family fighting for its own right to rule. This stage of unrest in Frankia lasted until 613, when Clotar II dared to dream of unification once more.

At first, Clothar ruled a very small kingdom called Neustria, located to the west of Frankia. Even though it was territorially small, Neustria was rich because it incorporated important trade centers and the cities of Paris and Orleans. But soon, it was reduced to the regions covering only Rouen, Beauvais, and Amiens. Clothar attempted to regain his kingdom on several occasions. The first was disastrous, but with each effort, he would take cities one by one. Realizing his worth, many of Clothar's cousins asked for his support in various dynastic conflicts that occurred after the death of the Merovingian kings of various territories. These were times of unusual instability in which families couldn't agree who should rule what. Court plots often resulted in the murder of children, potential wives of kings and their heirs, and even the kings themselves. The assassination of male children occurred so often that many ruling families resorted to raising them in secrecy. Clothar survived only because he was raised in a private villa, under the watchful eyes of loyal servants.

Clothar never shied away from plots and dynastic conflicts, which were regarded as normal at the time. Some historians see them as the barbarian heritage of the Franks from past times when, through conflict, various individuals had to prove they were worthy of rule. Clothar allied with his cousin Theuderic, ruler of Austrasia, but once Theuderic died in 613, he turned against his successor, Sigebert II. But it was the Austrasian nobles who abandoned Sigebert in favor of Clothar, and by deserting their rightful king, they handed Frankia to Clothar. With his previous conflicts against other cousins and kings, Clothar became the sole ruler of Frankia. The land was once more united, at least for some time. Unfortunately, history repeated itself after the death of Clothar's son Dagobert I, and the kingdom was again partitioned.

Dagobert is the last Merovingian king who was strong enough to hold the kingdom under one rule. It is believed that his successors had no real executive powers, as they allowed kingdoms to fall under the rule of palace mayors. Even though the internal conflict within Frankia was tearing the country apart, Merovingian kingdoms still fought some of the Germanic tribes of central Europe. At its prime, Frankia wasn't only modern-day France. It also incorporated the territories of modern Germany. In the north, it stretched almost to the banks of the Baltic Sea, but this was still the territory of the Saxons. The Upper Rhine, together with cities such as Cologne and Meinz (in modern Germany), was a part of the Frankish kingdom. Although the Saxons, Alemanni, and

Bavarians frequently warred with the Frankish kingdom, their territories were never annexed. Instead, they were turned into tributary states. During the 6th century, Frankia became the largest empire in Europe. But during the 7th and 8th centuries, the country saw more dynastic wars as the various mayors of the palace fought for supremacy. "King" became nothing more than a ceremonial title, while these mayors had all the real power. Through military conflict, they usurped each other's territories, and it wasn't unusual for close cousins to fight. With the rise of Charles Martel, a new era was dawning: the Carolingian Empire.

The Carolingian Dynasty

Carolingian Empire at its height
https://upload.wikimedia.org/wikipedia/commons/thumb/6/66/Fra
ncia_814.svg/1280px-Francia_814.svg.png

Charles Martel was never officially a king but acted as one beginning in 737 when King Theuderic IV of the Merovingian dynasty died. However, he worked aggressively to secure the Frankish throne for his sons. Since they were not of the Merovingian dynasty, Charles Martel had to gain the proper titles for himself and his children. Through various political and military accomplishments, he was awarded the title of prince, and as such, he ruled until he died in 741. At that point, no one was politically strong enough to deny his sons, Pepin and Carloman, the right to succeed the throne of the Frankish Empire. As tradition commanded, the empire was split once more. Carloman was proclaimed ruler of the eastern part, which included Alamannia, Bavaria, Thuringia, and Austrasia (most of today's Germany), while the western part of the empire, which included Burgundy, Provence, and Neustria (most of today's France), was ruled by Pepin.

The greatest member of the Carolingian dynasty and one of the early rulers was Charlemagne (742–814). The early Carolingians continued dividing the empire among their heirs, and the internal power struggles never stopped. However, once Pope Leo III crowned Charlemagne emperor in 800, the Frankish dynasty adopted a new view of their empire. Although the tradition of dividing it between heirs continued, the empire was now seen as a higher form of state, and as such, it needed to remain unified. Contradicting views on the Frankish Empire continued, and while its rulers made their offspring rulers of little kingdoms, they were still a part of the larger entity, the empire. In Germany, Charlemagne is known as Karl der Grosse, and he played a pivotal role in forming the Germanic Empire, which would rise under his successors.

Traditionally, the coronation of Charlemagne as emperor was seen as the birth of the Holy Roman Empire. But newer research suggests that the idea of the Holy Roman Empire was only being developed during his reign. He was simply seen as the Western emperor who opposed the Eastern emperor in Constantinople. Modern scholars now agree that the Holy Roman Empire is a creation of later times, but they do not dispute the significance of Charlemagne. He was, after all, the ruler who shaped the society of Europe and what would become the German Empire.

Charlemagne understood that his coronation as emperor was an attempt to continue the Western Roman Empire, which had fallen centuries ago. To honor the pope's wishes, he styled his empire as the ancient Roman emperors did before him, but he couldn't simply adopt new values and force them onto his subjects. Instead, he created a mixture of Roman administration, Christian piousness, and Germanic military power. These three elements of Charlemagne's empire would later be the foundation on which German society would be raised. But Charlemagne wasn't only a Roman emperor. He was also a devout Christian who pleased the pope. In the name of religion, as well as to expand the borders of his empire, Charlemagne fought the pagan people beyond his borders: Saxons, Slavs, and the Avars. Of all the tribes, Saxons were the thorn of Germanic-ruled Europe. They were a Germanic tribe, relatives of the Franks, and Charlemagne desperately wanted to integrate them into his empire. The main problem for the emperor was that Saxons were the last of the Germanic tribes to linger in their pagan religion, and although they promised they would convert and stop plundering the Frankish territories beyond the Rhine, they broke their promise as soon as Charlemagne's attention was elsewhere. It took a series of military expeditions from 772 to 804 (known as the Saxon Wars) for Charlemagne to defeat them, Christianize them, and integrate them into his empire.

The Roman influence on Charlemagne's empire can be seen in the appointment of governors, or consuls, who had the task of administering specific regions. The only difference was in the name of these administrators, as they were renamed counts. To keep the counts in check, Charlemagne employed imperial officials who would travel the vast empire to enforce the royal decrees. They were equal in power to the counts or even slightly above them, but their titles weren't hereditary, so they had no reason to gather power. Most of the royal officials serving the empire were monks and priests because they were the only literate social group within the empire. While nobles could afford tutors to teach them how to read and write, literacy was mostly confined to the church. Charlemagne himself usually spent his time on the battlefield, though he did hold courts in various cities around his empire. He never had a capital, but some of the cities were more significant than others. In Germania during the 800s, it was Aachen which became the center of Latin scholarship and culture. Charlemagne probably favored this city, as he founded its cathedral and spent most of the winters here. The city soon became the political center of the empire, and when Charlemagne died in 814, he was buried there.

The tradition of dynastical power struggles continued after the death of Charlemagne, and his successors, once again, turned to the partition of the empire. Because the Frankish rule was that all male successors inherited a part of the patrimony, Charlemagne made a decree in 806 by which his empire would be split among his three sons. Fortunately, only one son managed to outlive his father, Louis the Pious (774-840). In 814, he became emperor, and the Carolingian empire remained whole for another generation. But during Louis' reign, his own three sons warred among themselves, each wanting to secure his right to rule after the death of Emperor Louis the Pious. His sons were Charles the Bald (823-877), Louis the German (804-876), and Lothair (795-855). The three brothers made peace in 843 with the Treaty of Verdun. The empire was divided into the western part ruled by Charles the Bald (roughly modern France and Belgium), a middle part known as Lotharingia ruled by Lothair (central Europe from the North Sea to Italy), and an eastern part known as East Francia ruled by Louis the German (all the lands of the Carolingian Empire east of the Rhine).

When Lothair died, fifteen years of interregnum followed. Then, in 870, the two remaining brothers split Lotharingia between themselves. But only a decade later, after the death of Charles the Bald, Louis the German invaded his brother's part of Lotharingia and integrated it into East Frankia with a status of a dutchy. This territory would remain a disputed land and the cause of many wars between Francia and Germania over the next 1,000 years. But it is the death of Louis the Pious in 840 which marks the split of the Carolingian Empire into France and Germany. In the western part, people spoke medieval Latin, from which the French language would be born. But in the east, where people weren't as much under Roman influence, the spoken language was Germanic, which would later develop into modern German. Louis the German and his successors ruled as direct descendants of Charlemagne, and as such, they held the imperial title. The German-speaking continuation of the Carolingian Empire occupied central Europe and would soon develop into the Holy Roman Empire. With the first Holy Roman Emperor, Otto the Great, the basis for the German identity was born.

Chapter 4 – The Holy Roman Empire

The old Germanic territories started becoming a powerful central European kingdom in 936 with the coronation of Otto I as the king of the Germans. Throughout his reign, Otto established himself as a formidable ruler by defeating the Magyars, conquering territories that belonged to the Slavs beyond the Elbe river, and skillfully maneuvering his political allies and rivals. Otto's journey eventually led him to be crowned as the first Holy Roman Emperor in 962.

Otto's coronation took place in Rome, and thus began the millennia-long German ownership of the imperial title. The Holy Roman Empire is the anvil on which the German identity was forged. It united all the Germanic tribes in what we know today as Germany and was the foundation of a new major power in Europe.

The Ottonian Dynasty

The Dynasty Genealogy found in a 13ᵗʰ-century manuscript
https://en.wikipedia.org/wiki/Ottonian_dynasty#/media/File:Stamm
tafelOttonen0002.jpg

With the death of Charlemagne in 814, the Carolingian Empire began to slowly crumble. This signaled the end of Frankish dominion and launched the separate evolution of what we call Germany and France. Charlemagne's empire continued briefly under the control of his son, Louis the Pious, but after his death, the members of the dynasty fought a civil war lasting for three years. The empire finally broke apart at the end of the war with the signing of the Treaty of Verdun.

The Carolingian Empire was no more, and the states that rose from its ashes had to defend themselves on their own. One of these states was East Francia, a land ruled by several Germanic peoples, such as the Saxons, Bavarians, and the Franconians. They were the descendants of the ancient tribes and warbands that had dominated those territories from Roman times. But East Francia, broken away from the Carolingian Empire, was now being attacked from all sides by foreign invaders. The most notable ones were the Vikings who came from the north, raiding the border by sea, and the Magyars who attacked from the east.

The new Germanic kingdom was unstable. In 911, the remnants of the Carolingian dynasty faded out in East Francia, replaced by local noblemen. These new administrators proved to be highly ineffective and incompetent, so they requested help from the House of Saxony. Interestingly, just a century earlier, the Saxons were pagans and enemies of the Carolingians, but they were about to become a significant power and a driving force inside East Francia.

The Frankian dukes had elected Henry I, nicknamed "the Fowler," to be crowned in 919 as king of the Germans. This event marks the beginning of the Ottonian dynasty. Henry's first major act as king was to form a bond of vassalage with the Bavarian, Saxon, Swabian, and Franconian lords. This meant that the noblemen declared their allegiance to Henry but were still allowed to rule their tribes and peoples.

The German feudal alliance was first tested in 933 when Henry gathered an army composed of multiple Germanic tribes that were part of East Francia. The purpose of the army was to push against the Magyars who were consistently raiding the eastern borders. Henry emerged victorious and pressed on to vanquish the Danes who were invading Frisia. Henry proved to be a skilled military and political leader, having successfully gathered people from different tribes and marched them into battle against foreign invaders. His campaigns solidified his rule and the support he received from the noblemen.

Henry I forged the system that would govern the Holy Roman Empire over the next few centuries. He believed in a decentralized governing structure, thus allowing the lords of the five great Germanic houses—Franconia, Saxony, Bavaria, Swabia, and Lotharingia—to keep their autonomy and rule their own tribes. He even had plans to organize an expedition to Rome to receive the title of emperor from the pope. However, in 936, the king of the Germans died unexpectedly. But Henry's crown didn't automatically pass to his heir. After all, he was an elected figure. At the time, the king had to be elected by the dukes of the great houses. And so, they did. The dukes were pleased with Henry's rule and with the fact that he allowed them to govern and administer their lands and people, so they voted for Otto, Henry's son, to become the next king of the Germans.

Otto was crowned in 936 in Aachen, and documents from that period show that he was named "Otto I, Theutonicorum rex," which translates to "Otto the First, king of the Germans." He was an ambitious ruler that walked in his father's path, but he wanted to reach a further goal. Otto quickly demonstrated he was a capable leader on the battlefield by defeating the Magyar nomads and reinforcing the eastern borders. He didn't stop there, as he launched multiple military campaigns against the Slavic tribes that dominated between the Elbe and the Oder rivers. His conquest against the Slavs was successful, but he didn't stop at enforcing his rule over them. Otto assigned Christian bishops to convert the pagan Slavs to Christianity. He did the same once he conquered the Danes and the Bohemians, as well.

Otto used the Roman Catholic faith to unite the different tribes under his rule. The Ottonian dynasty now held a solid foothold by exerting control over not only the German dukes but also the non-Germanic tribes, and by investing in capable bishops. His campaigns brought new lands and peoples under Francian dominion.

Otto I reached the height of his power in 962 by doing what his father set out to do before his life was suddenly cut short: he traveled to Rome to help the pope end a dispute in Lombardy and, as a reward, claimed the title of emperor. There he was anointed in Saint Peter's Basilica as the Holy Roman Emperor. The title was finally renewed after being left unclaimed for almost forty years. This act reinforced the noble status of German rule by reminding people of Charlemagne and reconstructing the old Frankish alliance with Rome.

Otto's coronation would lead to the imperial tradition of all German rulers receiving the prestigious title in the centuries that followed. However, despite being coronated as emperor, Otto did not have the authority to directly control all the other Germanic tribes. Their dukes still held autonomy, even though they were bound to serve the emperor. But this didn't stop Otto from doing everything in his power to assert his royal dominion. Unfortunately, Germany as a unified state remained a dream. When Otto I died in 973, the German tribes were more united under the royal authority than ever before; however, that didn't last.

With Otto's death, his descendants had to pacify multiple rebellions organized by some of the noblemen, as well as foreign invaders. In the following decades, the Ottonian dynasty spent much of its power, influence, and resources on holding together everything that Henry and Otto had built. However, despite remarkable efforts and strong leadership, Otto's imperial lineage ended with Henry II in 1024 due to a lack of heirs.

The Salian Dynasty

The end of the Ottonian dynasty marked the beginning of a new chapter in Germanic history. Henry II's death caused a power vacuum and, with it, a significant amount of internal turmoil. However, the dukes of the Germanic tribes came to a solution by electing Conrad II as the new Holy Roman Emperor. He would be the first of Franconian noblemen to take the crown of overlordship. The Salian dynasty was born.

After Henry's death, a century of the Salian rule followed, marked by four emperors who would turn the newly built Holy Roman Empire into one of the most significant powers on the

European continent. The Salian dynasty continued many of the political and administrative policies instituted by the Ottonian rulers, but it also launched the process of centralization. Administration of the empire was centralized under imperial authority partially to subdue the dukes that had rebelled after Otto's death. To achieve this goal, the Salian emperors sought to use the alliance with the pope because it brought influence, power, and prestige.

Conrad II was crowned emperor in 1027, and a solid alliance was formed with the papacy. But that would later change when in 1075, the pope began a campaign of dominance over the ancient lands of the German tribes. During the time of the Ottonians, the relationship between the German administration and the Catholic Church was symbiotic. The two cooperated, and the Holy Roman Emperors acted as important leaders and protectors of Christendom. However, the papacy wanted to break the separation between state and church and therefore launched a campaign of reforms. One of the most significant events occurred when Pope Gregory VII issued an order for Emperor Henry IV of the Salian dynasty to give up his right to choose his bishops. At the same time, the papacy also issued a decree that banned any Catholic Church official from accepting a position appointed by a secular ruler.

This posed a major problem for the Salian dynasty—and the imperial rule, in general. The bishops weren't just representatives of the Church that spread Christianity throughout the land. They also acted as local administrators and owned land. But Henry IV refused to relinquish his right and sent a stern letter to the pope, accusing him of being hungry for power and trying to usurp what didn't belong to him. Henry's letter angered Pope Gregory. The conflict between the two figures escalated so much that the pope excommunicated Henry and forbade members of the church, as well as any vassals, from accepting appointments and orders from the emperor.

The pope's actions gave the German nobles the opportunity to rebel against the imperial crown once again. To stop that from happening, Henry arranged for an expedition in 1077 into the Italian Alps, where he spent several days waiting for Pope Gregory to grant him an audience. The emperor spent that time on his knees, despite the snow, forcing the pope's hand to receive him. His appearance as a humble man repenting for his crimes and begging for forgiveness from the church pushed the pope's hand to absolve him. As soon as Henry ended the conflict with Pope Gregory, he started appointing new bishops that would support him and even went as far as setting up a new papal election by supporting one of Gregory's rivals.

While Henry was successful in partially de-escalating his conflict with the pope, the situation back home didn't improve. In fact, during the next several decades, the noblemen led a long campaign against the emperor. It was the year 1122 when the rebellion ended, but no side emerged victoriously. An agreement called the Concordat of Worms was signed, giving the pope the power to name the bishops in the Holy Roman Empire. However, the emperor would retain veto power. But the conflict had also led to several changes that diminished the imperial crown's power. Further decentralization reduced the powers and rights of the emperor and thus diminished the direct control he held over the German peoples and their territories. This is a key factor that would continue to influence the Holy Roman Empire until its end.

The political and religious changes didn't affect just the papacy and the German nobility. The common people who lived during the 11th century, as well as the following century, felt the effects as well. The most revolutionary change was the rapid expansion of cities and the urbanization of many areas. This alone boosted the economy significantly. However, it was also promoted and funded thanks to the trade provided by the ongoing crusades during that time. Many new free cities were founded, while others claimed municipal liberty. These free cities were essentially free from serving the noblemen and the dukes, as they only had to swear loyalty to the emperor. Trade brought wealth, and many merchants and skilled traders moved to the free cities. They gradually formed guilds (associations), and as their economic power grew, so did their control over the markets and cities.

Guilds became the main force that drove the economy and pushed education further. Long-distance trading, whether by land or sea, increased greatly during the period between the 11th and 14th centuries. Some of the guilds from northern German cities banded together to form the Hanseatic League, a trade alliance that controlled most of the trade and shipping on the northern coast of Germany as well as the North Sea and Baltic Sea. At the same time, various German peoples expanded and settled in the regions that used to be dominated by the Slavs, such as Silesia and Bohemia.

The Hohenstaufen Dynasty

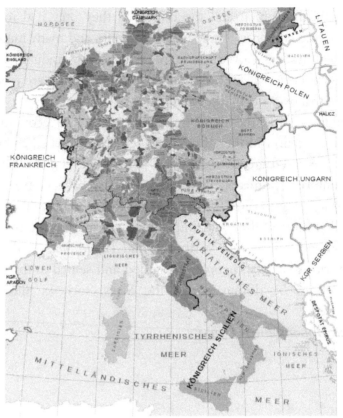

The Holy Roman Empire at its peak under the rule of the Hohenstaufen
https://en.wikipedia.org/wiki/Hohenstaufen#/media/File:Mitteleuro pa_zur_Zeit_der_Staufer.svg

The Salian imperial dynasty remained at the helm of the Holy Roman Empire until 1125, when the last Salian Emperor, Henry V, died from an illness. He had no heirs of his own. Henry named his nephew, Frederick II, as heir to his titles and possessions. With the death of the emperor, the nobles of the great German houses prepared for a new election. Frederick II of Hohenstaufen was the main candidate because he was the closest relation to Henry V. However, Frederick was arrogant and believed he could win the imperial title without compromising with the German princes. An election was held, but Frederick II was overconfident and refused to grant the princes the right to elect whether he would be emperor. The nobles did not want to return to an autocratic form of government that relied on familial succession, so they denied Frederick the title.

Several other candidates were available, but the elections did not continue smoothly. The imperial claimants were rivals and launched violent campaigns against each other. It took almost three decades after Henry V's death for stability to be reestablished when Frederick I of Swabia, a member of the Hohenstaufen lineage, victoriously navigated through the political conflicts. Also referred to as Frederick Barbarossa due to his ginger beard, he became the newly elected emperor of the Holy Roman Empire in 1152 (crowned by the Pope in 1155) and enjoyed a long reign until 1190.

Frederick I focused on restoring the rights and power of the crown as they were during Emperor Otto I's times. Due to the gradual decentralization that was supported by the great nobles, as well as the compromises made with the papacy during the Salian administration, the emperor had become almost powerless. The title was more of a symbol than actual authority. The heads of the noble houses ruled over their own lands, just like kings did. Besides, they no longer offered financial and military support to their emperor as they had during Ottonian dominance. This forced the emperor to use his own family's resources and whatever his territory could provide.

Frederick Barbarossa wanted to return power to the imperial crown. To achieve this, he organized multiple expeditions into Northern Italy, which was part of the empire, hoping to use some of its resources to improve his position in the German territories. During his first expedition in 1155, he helped the papacy quell a rebellion in Rome, thus improving the crown's relations with the pope, and was ceremonially crowned in Rome. However, his activity in Italy wasn't the only thing that occupied his time. He was also involved with the crusades.

In 1188, Jerusalem fell to Saladin's army. During that same year, the Diet of Mainz was held, where Frederick Barbarossa swore in front of the empire's Estates General to join the campaigns in the Holy Land. In 1189, the emperor joined Richard the Lionheart (the English) and Philip Augustus (the French) in a military campaign, known as the Third Crusade or King's Crusade, to retake control of Jerusalem. The combined forces were victorious against all odds, even though they were smaller in number than Saladin's army.

However, this victory didn't last long for Frederick because, on June 10, 1190, he drowned in the Saleph River during the campaign for Antioch. With the death of the emperor, the imperial troops lacked order and leadership and were easily defeated by the enemy. Only a small number of his forces survived and retreated to the crusader city of Acre. The military campaign ended as a disaster for the Holy Roman Empire. However, Frederick Barbarossa became a legendary figure as stories were told about him in the empire for generations. One of the most famous myths says that the emperor did not die in battle but lies asleep under the Kyffhäuser Mountains, located in the modern-day German state of Thuringia. There he waits for a time when the German people are in their hour of greatest need, to rise and lead them to greatness.

With the death of Frederick I, his son Henry IV took the imperial crown. His reign was short, lasting from 1190 to 1197. He focused on his father's affairs in Italy, and with his absence in Germany, the nobles began spreading their influence by ignoring the emperor's authority. Instability was once again present in the Holy Roman Empire, and it only worsened with the death of Henry IV. The internal struggle for dominance continued until 1215, when a new emperor rose to power, namely Frederick II. He took control over the empire, ruling for thirty-five years.

Just like the other Hohenstaufen emperors before him, Frederick II focused his attention on Italy, fighting against the papacy. And just like before, the German nobles were plotting to spread their control and dominance over imperial territories. But Frederick II was successful in bribing them by giving up some of his authority in exchange for stability and peace. The emperor gained support from the princes by offering them nearly complete autonomy over their states. Despite the brief respite, once the emperor's heir, Conrad IV, died, the nobles started producing new claimants for the imperial title. These actions led to another period of uncertainty and instability in the empire. During the following decades, the emperor lost most of his authority once again as the German noble families succeeded in taking full control over their lands.

The Black Death in the Holy Roman Empire

| 1346 | 1347 | 1348 | 1349 | 1350 | 1351 | 1352 | 1353 |

~·~ Approximate border between the Principality
of Kiev and the Golden Horde - passage
prohibited for Christians.

⤳□□□ Land trade routes

⤳ Maritime trade routes

The spread of the black plague in Europe
https://en.wikipedia.org/wiki/Black_Death#/media/File:1346-
1353_spread_of_the_Black_Death_in_Europe_map.svg

The Holy Roman Empire lacked a powerful central figure of authority until 1312 with the uncontested election of Henry VII. He, as well as his successors, invested a great deal of effort to return power and control to the imperial crown. The German princes continued to resist and make it difficult for the emperor to regain his authority; however, that wasn't the only challenge.

During the 14th century, the bubonic plague spread to the Holy Roman Empire. The source of the 1347 outbreak was Italy, and in just three years, it had spread throughout the German territories. A third of the European population died in the infamous Black Death. The cause was long-distance trade between merchants who traveled from the Italian coasts to the Middle East and Asia. The Silk Road had been opened to the Europeans by the Mongols who ruled over China, a land that had already been suffering from the plague since the 1330s. The merchants brought the plague with them to the Italian ports, from which it spread through the many trade routes that went from the Mediterranean across the entirety of mainland Europe, Scandinavia, and even Scotland.

The plague didn't just cause a massive number of deaths. With it came a massive economic crisis that led to famine throughout the continent. As poverty increased, more and more people became malnourished and too weak to fight disease. Consequently, a radical religious sect called the Flagellants emerged in Europe as well as the Holy Roman Empire. They were famous for owning no possessions and scourging themselves while traveling from one town to the next, seeking atonement. Due to poverty and death surrounding every town, the sect grew in influence and started blaming and persecuting the Jewish communities as well as other minorities.

During those times, the Jews were permitted to live in special areas and only in certain cities where the local administration or the clergy would benefit from them. In a way, they received special protection despite the persecution due to their financial and medical expertise. But, at the same time, they were hated by the common citizens who either despised them due to their religious practices or were envious of their wealth. The Flagellant sect contributed to spreading this hatred further throughout the empire. The Jews were now blamed for poisoning the wells and spreading the disease, even though they were suffering and dying from the plague the same as Christians. The hatred and fear led to a massacre, and many Jewish communities were destroyed. However, these dreadful events were not something that occurred only in German territory. Hatred towards the Jews had already existed for at least a few centuries. For example, during the 11th century, the crusaders that marched to fight the Muslims often stopped in several locations on their route to kill Jews. In fact, in some places—Germany included—the Jews were forced to dress in such a way to be easily identified. This included the display of the Star of David on their clothing.

The Flagellants continued to preach that God was punishing humanity for its corruption, pointing fingers specifically at the Vatican and the Catholic Church. As their word spread, the common people started blaming each other, whether they were Christian or Jewish, and trust in the secular administration plummeted as well. The papacy could not remain idle and immediately marked the Flagellants as a heretical organization. However, the clergy had suffered as well, both from the plague and the economic crisis, vastly diminishing their resources and influence.

In the Holy Roman Empire, the plague and conflicts between the nobles pushed the crown to launch a series of reforms to settle the problem of succession. Previous elections were repeatedly interrupted by conflicts and various political interests. Therefore, the idea of what the empire meant had to be clarified and changed. The first reform was made in 1356 with the signing of the Golden Bull, which defined all the procedures and protocols that had to take place during the election of the emperor.

From that point on, the emperor would be elected by the seven Kurfürsten (electors). Four of them were secular electors, namely the Duke of Saxony, the King of Bohemia, the Margrave of Brandenburg, and the Count Palatine of the Rhine. The other three were the Archbishops of Cologne, Mainz, and Trier. However, while these changes did bring some measure of order, the Holy Roman Empire was still politically unstable and unpredictable. The emperor lacked the centralized power and authority he needed to keep the princes under control. Thus, they frequently fought against each other for dominance, and the common people, as well as the economy, continued to suffer the consequences. The empire continued its descent until the Habsburgs took the throne and launched a campaign of massive reforms.

The First Habsburgs and the Beginning of Imperial Reformation

Frederick III of Habsburg was the first of his dynasty to take the imperial crown of the Holy Roman Empire. However, the country was still in chaos from the futile wars between the great houses. He made little progress in imperial reform, but he paved the way for his son, Maximilian I.

Maximilian succeeded in organizing a meeting with the electors and the German princes to debate the reformation of the empire. The historical Diet of Worms was held in 1495, wherein the nobles agreed to a series of changes.

One of the greatest reforms was the establishment of the Reichskammergericht, which was essentially an imperial court of justice tasked with settling the disputes and conflicts throughout the empire. Maximilian was also successful in creating an imperial court, known as the Reichshofrat, as a balancing measure that would give the emperor some authority and influence.

Progress was being made—but slowly—as discussions, debates, and negotiations resumed between the princes and the emperor. Another important reform was the creation of a regional administration system, known as the Imperial Circles (Reichskreise). There were six administrations implemented to manage the six major regions, and they officially started working in 1512. During the same year, the empire changed its official name, declaring itself the Holy Roman Empire of the German Nation. This move, together with the reforms, could be considered evidence of the rising of a unified German identity.

But the most important reform during this time of chaos was the declaration of the "Ewiger Landfriede," which translates to "eternal peace." Attempts to accomplish such a reform had been made since the 12th century, but with minor success. The concept behind it was to ban the German nobles' rights to armed conflict against other fellow noblemen. Until the Diet of Worms, any dispute or conflict between noblemen could be settled through armed conflict. This was the main cause of economic and social chaos and the lack of a unified identity. From 1495 onward, all disputes and conflicts would have to be settled at the court through a legal process and not on the battlefield.

Emperor Maximilian didn't dictate these reforms, and he was even against some of them. However, with their implementation, the Holy Roman Empire started enjoying a newly-found peace, which gradually boosted the economy and improved the lives of citizens throughout the empire.

Chapter 5 – The Reformation

The religious revolution known as the Reformation marked the beginning of a new era in the Holy Roman Empire. While its touch wasn't felt in society and politics until the 16th century, the Reformation started emerging two centuries earlier. The 14th century had gone through a series of massive transformations and crises, the most well-known of which were the Black Death of 1347 and the Papal Schism. These events made the German people, as well as other Europeans, think about their religion, church, and society itself.

The people experienced an internal crisis and, consequently, challenged the clergy's authority and the way they interpreted the Holy Scriptures. Various personalities, such as Jan Hus from Bohemia and John Wycliffe from England, emerged to criticize the church's privileges. However, during the 14th century, they lacked the ability to spread their opinions and views far and wide and were eventually executed. Both became precursors for the Reformation.

Hus was summoned to the Council of Constance, where he was condemned for heresy. Even though he went under imperial protection, he was executed. This event led to a rebellion in Bohemia that lasted for fourteen years. The church silenced Hus and Wycliffe, but after the spiritual crisis during the days of the

Black Death, they could no longer silence the people's desire for reform. In the following century, the church authorities would become overwhelmed by the need for an inner religious experience.

Technology Paves the Way

Until the beginning of the 15th century, ideas and opinions were being spread painstakingly slowly by word of mouth and handwritten works. Pamphlets and books were written and copied entirely by hand, taking months before they were ready to be sent to other corners of the realm. This process also involved many mistakes, errors, and the occasional reinterpretation of the text. Printing did exist to some degree, but even that was entirely manual. Craftsmen had to carve the pages they wanted to copy into wooden blocks and then use them to print one page at a time by stamping. This process yielded better results than the handwritten copies; however, it was expensive, and printed works were only sent to rich monasteries, noblemen, and wealthy merchants.

All of that would change in the German city of Mainz, where Johannes Gutenberg would invent the printing press in the 1440s, an invention that played a key role in launching a revolution throughout Europe.

Gutenberg worked with metal, mainly crafting highly polished metal mirrors. But he wasn't well known before his famous invention. History took note of him in 1439 when he was sued by an investor who partnered with him to create the printing press. The court took an inventory of every item in his workshop, where various metals and printing types were noted.

As a skilled metalworker, Gutenberg first invented a special alloy by combining antimony with lead and tin. This resulted in a strong material perfect for molding durable printing types that would last a long time without deforming. Also, he invented a new oil-based ink so that his printed works could last much longer than those written in traditional ink. Finally, in the coming years, he created the first printing press model, using wine presses for inspiration for the mechanical parts. At first, printing was still expensive because his first model was still inefficient. However, he made improvements during the time he printed presumably 200 copies of the Bible, known today as the Gutenberg Bibles.

After he improved the design of the printing press, Gutenberg's revolutionary invention started spreading throughout Europe. The written word started becoming available to almost everyone. Before that, a skilled scribe could produce only a few pages per workday, and a wooden block printing press could produce a few dozen. Gutenberg's press was capable of printing more than 3,000 pages per day. But more importantly, printing became affordable, and periodical texts could be produced in mass. Before the printing press, only important works, such as religious and scholarly texts, were being copied or printed.

A few decades after the invention of the printing press, ideas started spreading like wildfire throughout the Holy Roman Empire, as well as most of Europe. With hundreds of books, religious materials, and intellectual works being produced every year, the Reformation was underway, as well as the humanist movement.

Humanism

Gutenberg's printing press is one of the main reasons the humanism movement spread throughout the German territories. Its driving goal was to find and restore many of the ancient texts from the classical age to recover the lost knowledge and wisdom. These texts were copied and widely spread, leading to a better and more diverse education in Europe. The humanists began challenging the authority of the Catholic Church and the way they interpreted the holy texts.

Initially, humanism started spreading from Italy. The movement was secular for the most part, focusing on social problems and civic values. Italian humanism was pushed and sponsored by the nobility and the wealthy merchant class. On the other hand, in the Holy Roman Empire, humanism became a movement focused on the spiritual aspect of society. In German cities, the movement was spreading from the universities, which, during those times, were attached to the church.

Furthermore, German humanism was less elitist than its Italian counterpart, and it contained a populist element. In other words, it was primarily aimed towards the masses instead of the intellectual and wealthy classes. The printing press allowed humanistic ideas to spread to the public, and new humanist schools were being raised to educate a new Christian generation. While the Italian scholars focused on the famous classical philosophers, politicians, and orators such as Cicero and Plato, the Germans preferred to study and interpret religious texts. They began researching the earliest biblical sources that were written in Hebrew, Latin, and Greek, seeking out the original Christian practices to reform the church.

One of the most famous humanists north of the Alps was Erasmus of Rotterdam, who lived from 1466 to 1536. He and other humanists were deeply embedded in the church, but they desired to reform the institution and its practices. During these pre-Reformation decades, the humanists gathered thousands of books written in the aforementioned languages to translate and study. Consequently, some of them rediscovered the philosophical and religious concept of Hermeticism.

Hermeticism dates to the first century CE, according to Plutarch. Its doctrine claims that there is one God and that he is present in every religion. The scholars sent out to scour the monasteries for ancient texts found numerous volumes discussing this religion. These sacred texts formed what is known as the Corpus Hermeticum, and they shared information about topics such as magic, alchemy, and astrology. These discoveries during the Renaissance period led the humanist scientists and scholars to explore the concept of magic. The Catholic Church did not appreciate their pursuit of cabbalistic mysticism and the occult. The church condemned their actions, even though some of the hermeticists were monastery abbots and bishops.

The rediscovery of ancient knowledge led to a desire to research the original biblical sources of the Christian faith. The humanists sought a purer translation, and they printed new versions of the Penitential Psalms and other Scriptures to spread the new teachings. These actions, led by the most revered humanist in the north, Desiderius Erasmus, would trigger the Protestant Reformation.

Erasmus of Rotterdam was a pious Christian, and despite his critique of the Catholic clergy, he did not abandon Catholicism. He was a firm believer in a personal relationship with God instead of signs and rituals. However, his writings, especially the printing of the Greek New Testament, laid the groundwork for the Reformation. He became one of the earliest celebrities in the print world, and his works that called for the reformation of the Christian way of life resonated with many scholars and common folk on the continent. But his intention wasn't to break the church apart. He was loyal to the Vatican and the papacy. His goal was to clean the clergy of corruption and bad practices. However, his main work, the Greek New Testament, fueled the beginning of the Reformation in the Holy Roman Empire and thus did damage to the Catholic Church.

Martin Luther and the Protestant Reformation

During the Renaissance period, the papacy did not focus entirely on religious activity and moral guidance. It was one of the most important benefactors contributing to the emergence of artists and scholars. The popes also acted as secular rulers over their domains, the Papal States. The most famous pope during those times was Alexander VI, and he wasn't widely known for his piety and Catholic resolve. His goal was to amass wealth and dominate over the Papal States with the help of his warlord son, Cesare Borgia, who was depicted as a ruthless character in Niccolò Machiavelli's famous work titled *The Prince*. Pope Julius II is another such example: he was known as the warrior pope for waging several wars during his papal appointment. These Renaissance popes may have been important patrons of the artists that sparked a cultural revolution, but their focus on power sunk the Catholic Church in scandal.

The clergy's corruption continued to deepen while the people were seeking an honest spiritual experience and religious guidance. The anti-papal sentiment reached its height when the church started selling indulgences. These certificates were either bought or received as a reward, relieving the bearer of any guilt, sin, and punishment. The clergy went as far as specifying the amount of time that would be spent in purgatory for certain sins and reducing that time by selling an indulgence. This became a popular scheme that brought the clergy ample revenue. The masses were quite content for a while. On the other hand, Christian scholars and humanists like Erasmus condemned the practice and mocked the greed and decadence of bishops and priests.

But not all clerics and priests agreed with the indulgence practice. Martin Luther was one of them. He was a priest and theology professor who would soon become the main figure of the German Reformation. He and other humanists watched the situation develop with great concern until it reached its high point in 1515. Two years before that, Pope Leo X ascended to the papal seat. He belonged to the famous and powerful Medici family from Florence, and he wanted to be seen and remembered differently from all the popes who came before him.

Pope Leo X was an important patron of the arts, investing enormous amounts of wealth in talented artists, humanist scholars, and especially into the project to rebuild Saint Peter's Basilica. However, the papacy's treasure wasn't bottomless, and he needed a new source of wealth. In 1515, Pope Leo declared a new type of indulgence that could be sold by the clergy: the plenary indulgence. By purchasing this document from the church, a relative would be able to release the soul of a loved one from purgatory. This type of indulgence was also being sold in the Holy Roman Empire under the authority of the Archbishop of Mainz and Magdeburg because he needed funds to settle the large debt he'd amassed to win his election. Half of the profits made by selling the plenary indulgences in the territory he administered would go into his own pockets.

Martin Luther, who was a professor of theology at the University of Wittenberg, became increasingly concerned with this practice. He was also outraged when he learned that the archbishop was convincing the buyers that the certificate would instantly free them of all sins and any requirements of penance and confession. In 1517, Luther was so worried about innocent Christians following a path to damnation that he wrote a letter to the archbishop, officially noting his objections against this practice. But his warning was ignored, so Luther started writing a set of theological theses on the subject (this was a common way to stir up debate within the church).

Luther's collection is known as the Ninety-five Theses, and they were sent to the archbishop and posted on the walls of the university. He challenged the indulgence sellers to a debate, but he did not go directly against the indulgences themselves. Luther was careful because it was the pope who allowed these certificates to be sold, and he couldn't go against him at the time. He disputed the corrupt sales method only in the German territories.

However, despite Luther's caution, the printing press spread the word about his attack on the church. His theses were meant for internal debate between theologians and scholars, but the press made his works available in every tavern and workshop in the Holy Roman Empire and beyond. Martin Luther quickly went from a simple priest and professor to one of the most famous people in all the lands of Germany. His theses were being discussed even in Rome.

The pope decided to silence Luther through internal authority by asking the order of Augustinian monks to which Luther belonged to show him the errors of his ways. However, during the order's convocation, Luther presented his case in such an impressive manner that he drew the other monks to his side. Consequently, the Dominican order went against the Augustinians to silence Luther. They were famous inquisitors who already had a rivalry with the Augustinian order, so they readily defended the archbishop.

Since the matter wasn't resolved, the pope demanded Luther's presence in Rome within two months. Luther knew that this meant excommunication or perhaps even execution. The same thing happened to predecessors like Jan Hus. So, he sought the protection of Frederick of Saxony, the patron of Wittenberg University. Frederick, an elector, immediately sided with Luther as the famous professor who had placed his university on the European map and could be used for other ambitions against the papacy and the emperor.

Pope Leo couldn't act severely because his authority in the Holy Roman Empire wasn't as solid as before. The German citizens and nobles were gradually pulling away from the Catholic Church, complaining that too much money went to Rome and the papacy wasn't investing nearly enough. Nationalist sentiment was spreading. Furthermore, the election for the new emperor was approaching, and the pope hoped to push his candidate on the throne because he was worried about the Habsburgs taking over. He needed the German princes and electors, including Frederick, to be on his side so that they could cast a favorable vote.

Luther continued publishing new works that fueled the debate against Catholic clergy and the sale of indulgences. In the following years, he grew in popularity: historians estimate that over 10,000 of his pamphlets were printed throughout the Holy Roman Empire, both in German and Latin. These works marked the beginning of the Protestant Reformation. In 1520, Pope Leo issued a decree demanding Luther to retract more than forty of his works due to certain errors that didn't fit with the church's views. Luther refused and burned the decree the day he gathered a congregation at the university. This act declared that the pope no longer had authority. As a reply, Pope Leo issued a new decree the following year in which he excommunicated Luther and ordered the clergy to find and destroy his works. Luther's followers gathered in his defense, making it clear to everyone that the Germans were breaking away from the Catholic Church.

In 1521, Luther's presence was demanded at the Diet of Worms, where the new Holy Roman Emperor Charles V, the ruler of Spain and a Habsburg, convened with the nobles. The new emperor was powerful and feared due to the vastness of wealth and power he had gathered thanks to the lucrative Spanish colonies. Even the German noble houses feared him because he had enough power to make them submit to a central authority: himself. Furthermore, Charles was a pious Catholic, which made the Protestants anxious. But Luther was under Frederick of Saxony's protection, so he traveled to Worms. The emperor was determined to bring order to his lands, so he condemned Luther and his works. Charles didn't arrest him, but Luther did become an outlaw. However, this act didn't stop the Protestant Reformation.

Frederick arranged to have Luther taken to the Wartburg Castle, where he would be protected to continue his work. From there, Luther began translating the original Scriptures to build a German Bible. He succeeded in creating the German New Testament by seeking inspiration from Erasmus' work, the Greek New Testament. The new Bible went to print in 1530, and it's estimated that, by 1546 (the year of Luther's death), over half a million copies were printed. Furthermore, the publishing of the German Bible had a secondary but equally important effect. It served to standardize the German language throughout the German lands. Up to that point, there were many different dialects throughout the empire.

The emperor couldn't do anything against Luther despite the edict he issued at Worms. The German people supported the Protestant Reformation, and Luther was being protected by a few German princes, such as Frederick of Saxony. However, Charles banned Luther's works in the lands over which he had direct control and even executed several Protestants that he judged as heretics. The Reformation was about to become violent.

In the following years, several followers of Lutheran teaching began spreading their new ideas throughout the German territories. Their preaching against the church, the emperor, and feudalism sparked a series of revolts among the imperial knights and clergy, as well as the peasantry. The rebellions were violent. At first, Luther supported them, feeling their anguish, but he tried to resolve everything peacefully by mediating between the church and the rebels. However, he was unsuccessful, and the violence continued. Luther feared that these rebellions were endangering his theological revolution, so he printed a new work in which he sided with the imperial authorities and supported violent action against the rising peasantry. Consequently, both Protestant and Catholic German noblemen raised arms against the rebels and vanquished them. It is estimated that the professional military killed more than

100,000 peasants, together with their leaders, some of whom were Luther's close students and followers, such as Thomas Muntzer.

In 1525, the Protestant peasants' rebellion officially ended, but the Reformation continued with what we now call the Princes' Reformation. Backed by the Saxon prince, Luther started building the new Lutheran Church that would confiscate the properties of the Catholic Church and replace all their rituals. In the following years, the wealth that was taken from the German Catholics was enough to fund the state-supported Lutheran administration. Luther also directly contributed to a new manual that would guide the Protestant pastors on their responsibilities and religious duties.

While Luther was leading the Protestant Reformation in Saxony, he wasn't the only reformer. In Switzerland, Huldrych Zwingli was leading his own reformation beginning in 1522. His view of Protestantism was more liberal than Luther's, and they didn't agree on multiple points. This posed a problem to Luther's dream of a Protestant Germany because Zwingli's reformation quickly started spreading to the southern German cities. The Reformation was in danger because, if divided, the Catholic Church could easily go against each group separately. Seeking common ground, the two reformers met in 1529 to discuss the issue. However, the meeting failed because Luther and Zwingli could not agree on all points, and no compromise was made.

Despite the divide, the German princes continued supporting the Saxon model of Protestantism under Luther. The emperor's edict was ignored for the most part, but Charles grew increasingly worried about having two different religious views and institutions in his empire. Furthermore, he feared that he might lose support from the princes who were converting from Catholicism. In 1526, he allowed the German nobles to decide how to deal with the Protestant movement in their states. However, in 1529, he reversed his decision, going against the Protestant Reformation once more and, in 1531, demanded them to restore the Catholic Church's properties.

Fearing the wrath of the emperor and the Catholic Church, the Protestant princes began forging mutual defense alliances with each other and their neighbors. The divide between the two religions was creating a rift in German society, and it was becoming wider with each passing year. In the hope of healing this rift, the Diet of Regensburg was organized in 1541. Theology experts from both sides met to discuss the issues and seek a compromise. The meeting was another disaster, and it greatly angered Charles. The emperor launched a campaign of negotiation with the French, as well as the Turks—who, until then, had been his most hated enemies. His goal was to war against the Protestants, and so he did.

With Luther's death in 1546, the emperor marched against the Protestant princes and defeated them. Two years later, he issued a new decree declaring the restoration of the Catholic faith throughout the empire. However, Charles was betrayed by the prince of Saxony, Maurice, who allied with the French dynasty of Valois. The Valois were the enemies of the Habsburg dynasty, and with their help and support from the remaining Protestant princes, a new war commenced between the two sides. In 1552, the Princes' War wreaked havoc on the emperor's military. Charles lost in this conflict and was forced to later abdicate in 1555. The emperor accepted his defeat, retiring to a Spanish monastery, and peace was declared at Augsburg.

After decades of conflict in the name of the Reformation, the princes were given the right to choose between Catholicism and Protestantism in the lands or cities they governed. The people were obligated to respect their decision and to follow the faith of their prince. Any other religion was forbidden, including Zwingli's version of the Protestant Reformation. Peace between the two sides would hold over the next six decades until the rise of a new wave of Catholicism and a new form of Protestantism known as Calvinism.

Chapter 6 – The Thirty Years' War

When Charles V abdicated, he recognized that the empire was too great to be managed by one Habsburg emperor, so he divided the territories. The eastern corner of the empire, mainly Austria and Bohemia, was given to the Austrian branch of his family, who we refer to as the Austrian Habsburgs. This family would dominate that area for the next three centuries. As for the Holy Roman Empire, Charles pushed for his brother Ferdinand I to be elected, and so he was in 1558.

The situation was complicated, as the Protestant princes had started to officially solidify their position. But Ferdinand, just like his brother, was a pious Catholic. He supported the diminishing power of the Catholic Church and invested in its reformation. While the Catholic Reformation began at the same time as the Protestant Reformation under the influence of Catholic humanists like Erasmus, it didn't become drastic until 1545, when the Council of Trent was held. In the following two decades, the pope met there on occasion with the high clergy to discuss the corruption and decisions that affected the religious life of the German people. Among his goals was to end the schism that was happening and refute Luther's teaching. But by labeling the Protestants as heretics and forcing the church to become more rigid and inflexible, the Council of Trent had the opposite effect: the rift between the two faiths widened. However, the pope managed to slow down the spread of Lutheranism and even stopped it completely in some parts of Europe.

Calvinism Emerges

Jean Calvin
*https://en.wikipedia.org/wiki/Calvinism#/media/File:Portrait_of_Jo
hn_Calvin,_French_School.jpg*

While Luther's Protestant wave was slowing down, Calvinism started spreading and reinforcing the movement. Named after Jean (John) Calvin, a French Protestant reformer accused of heresy, Calvinism took hold in Geneva between the 1530s and 1540s. Calvin fled to the Swiss city to avoid the French authorities and shaped it into his vision of a Protestant theocracy. The main difference between Calvinism and Lutheranism at the time was the fact that Calvin focused more on conservative ideals and discipline, and his main goal was to spread his theology everywhere on the European continent.

Protestants flocked to Geneva, craving a so-called heavenly city in the middle of a corrupt world full of sin. Scholars, merchants, and crafters moved to the city, thus sparking an economic boom. The Swiss city became a beacon of Protestantism that allowed Calvin to print his theological works and spread them throughout Europe with the help of his missionaries.

Calvin's missionaries risked their lives to spread his teachings, especially in France and the Holy Roman Empire. In France, Protestantism was entirely forbidden, but in the empire, it depended on each prince (per the Augsburg peace treaty, the princes could determine the faith that would be followed throughout their territories). Calvinism and Protestantism, in general, were particularly successful with nobles who desired a decentralized authority.

The first German prince to adopt the new faith was Frederick the Pious, the elector of the Rhineland-Palatinate. Initially, he was a Lutheran, but he gradually moved on to Calvinism by allowing Calvin's missionaries to teach at Heidelberg University and to take positions within the Palatine Church. From Heidelberg, Calvinism would gradually spread throughout the empire, although Louis VI, Frederick's successor, tried to restore the Lutheran faith.

Catholicism was undergoing its own reformation, and it was strengthening while Calvinism continued to spread. The two faiths were causing tension among the Germans, and they were about to clash. The rise of Calvinism played a significant role in causing the destruction and chaos of the Thirty Years' War, during which religious conflict led to violence, but it cannot be solely blamed. During the same period, the European noble houses were competing against each other. Eventually, the Spanish and Austrian Habsburgs confronted their French, Danish, and Swedish adversaries. Ultimately, the war was ignited from both political and religious pressure.

Conflicts began erupting as soon as the early 1600s. In 1607, Maximilian I of Bavaria invaded and took control of Donauworth. The city was occupied to defend the Catholic population, which was the minority. The duke acted with the support of the emperor and began the process of restoring the Catholic faith.

As a response to Maximilian's actions, in 1608, the Protestant princes forged an alliance that became known as the Protestant Union, under the command of Frederick IV, Elector Palatine. But in the Holy Roman Empire, the Catholic Church still enjoyed a great deal of support, so they formed their own military alliance called the Catholic League just one year later, with Maximilian as its chief representative and commander. Maximilian represented the Catholic faith and Frederick the Protestant faith, even though they were related—both were part of the Wittelsbach dynasty. The two sides were originally supposed to be alliances to guarantee security and good diplomatic relationships. However, it didn't take long for both sides to turn into little more than military factions eager to go to war against each other.

The Thirty Years' War Begins

The year 1618 marks the beginning of the Thirty Years' War, and it all started with an uprising in Bohemia. The people rebelled when Ferdinand II of the Habsburg dynasty began enforcing the Catholic faith in Bohemia. Prague, then the capital of Bohemia and the city of reformer Jan Hus, did not support the emperor and was against the Catholic reformation. The city was dominated by Calvinists. However, in 1617, Ferdinand II became the king of Bohemia, and one of his goals was to restore Catholicism. His first act was to reorganize the Catholic mass at the same church where Jan Hus preached. This action angered the Protestants, and in 1618 they rose and apprehended the three royal representatives of the Habsburg Crown, throwing them out the window of the government palace in Prague. This revolt is now known as the

"Defenestration of Prague." However, the royal officials survived the fall.

In 1619, Ferdinand II officially became the Holy Roman Emperor, and the conflict escalated. Protestant nobles in Prague issued a proclamation that declared Bohemia an elective monarchy. They disposed of Ferdinand and chose a new king. Frederick V, a Calvinist who ruled the Rhineland-Palatinate and was also the leader of the Protestant League, was the perfect candidate, and he ruled as king of Bohemia for one year. Because of the shortness of his rule, he remains known to history as the "winter king." Ferdinand was angered by the coronation of Frederick. He was elected Holy Roman Empire only three months earlier, and he viewed the coronation of a Protestant as a direct attack on his imperial rule. To challenge Frederick, he needed to raise an army, and nearby Bavaria offered the perfect ground to do so. Bavaria was under the rule of Duke Maximilian I, Ferdinand's ally. As it bordered Bohemia, it was a natural choice from which to launch an invasion. At the Battle of White Mountain on November 8, 1620, imperial forces crushed the army of King Frederick, as none of his Protestant allies showed up. Frederick was exiled to Holland, and his rule in Bohemia ended.

Ferdinand took over the Palatinate and reestablished his authority in Bohemia. Catholicism was restored by force, and many Bohemians were punished for being Protestants. Consequently, thousands of Protestants abandoned their homeland and emigrated to different parts of the empire. Ferdinand appointed a governor of Bohemia, through which he could control the kingdom and extract revenues. Czech nobleman Albrecht von Wallenstein was the first governor and military leader. As soon as he came to the position, he started gathering a mercenary army that would serve the imperial needs. This army had the first chance to show its might in 1525, when the Danish king, Christian IV (1577–1648), invaded Germany. He was a Lutheran, so one of the reasons for the invasion was religion— but it wasn't the only one. He also had an interest in the Baltic region and hoped he could claim the territories of northern Germany for Denmark. But the army of the Danish king was no match for the imperial army under the two brilliant commanders, Johann Tserclaes, Count of Tilly, and Albrecht von Wallenstein, governor of Bohemia. The two Catholic commanders easily beat Christian IV in a series of battles. The Danish were forced back to Denmark, and Ferdinand was now unopposed in his rule.

The height of Ferdinand's power came when the emperor issued the Edict of Restitution in March 1629. With the edict, he demanded all the Catholic lands confiscated by Protestants since the Peace of Augsburg (1555) to be returned to Catholic rulers. The Augsburg settlement had a clause named "Ecclesiastical Reservation," which guaranteed that no further Catholic lands were to be conquered by the Protestants. However, this clause was not enforced for eighty years, and Ferdinand sought to retroactively enforce it with the use of the imperial army. Furthermore, Ferdinand's edict sought to forcefully re-Catholicize not only the territories but also the people.

In 1630, Ferdinand dismissed Wallenstein. The military commander was unpopular with both Protestants and Catholics, who put pressure on their emperor. Since Ferdinand needed supporters for the election of his son, Ferdinand III, as king of Romans, he complied with the people. But this decision proved to be very costly, as in July of the same year, Germany was invaded by Swedish King Gustavus Adolphus Vasa, simply known as Gustav II (1594-1632). He was a very pious Lutheran, and he came to help fellow Protestants against the Edict of Restitution. As with the Danish king, he had an interest in the Baltics, which he had already taken from the Poles through wars (1626-1629). Gustav II had the full support of the Protestant rulers of Germany, and in 1631, the imperial and Swedish armies clashed in the Battle of Breitenfeld. Gustav II was a great and innovative tactician, and he deployed more nimble, linear formations of his army. The imperial force, commanded by the Count of Tilly, still used the old Spanish formation, which was slow to move but hard to break. But the Swedish king had no trouble crushing his enemies' lines with the innovative use of firepower and mobility. By March 1632, he invaded Bavaria, having crushed the count on the battlefield. At another battle, near Rain on the River Lech, Gustav II crushed the Catholic League with skillful usage of artillery and cavalry. The Count of Tilly died in this battle, and his troops, having no commander, scattered across the battlefield in panic. Bavaria was conquered by the Swedes, and from it, they launched attacks on the Habsburg heartland—Austria.

In May of 1632, when Gustav II entered Munich (the capital of Bavaria), Ferdinand II was forced to recall Albrecht von Wallenstein as fear from the Protestants rose. The brilliant military leader was quick to organize a new imperial army and, with it, successfully confronted the Swedes. In November of 1632, Wallenstein met Gustav II at the Battle of Lützen. The imperial force didn't fare well at the beginning of the conflict, but Swedish King Gustav II was shot during the battle as he led the cavalry charge. Swedes did not abandon their mission in Germany when their king died, but fortune turned her back to the Protestants. Without their charismatic and brilliant leader, they couldn't keep up with the Catholics. The conflict came to a stalemate for the next two years.

In 1634, Ferdinand II realized Wallenstein was too ambitious, so he plotted to get rid of him. Soon, he employed several lieutenants of the imperial army to assassinate the general. The leader of the imperial forces was murdered in his bed in Eger, but Ferdinand II won his greatest victory at this time, proving he didn't need Wallenstein to end the war. In September 1634, at the Battle of Nördlingen, the imperial army was joined with the Spanish infantry, and together, they managed to crush the Saxon-Swedish alliance. This battle ended Swedish dominance in Germany, and the Protestants suffered their greatest defeat of the Thirty Years'

War. The German Protestants were forced to seek a separate peace with Ferdinand, which was signed in 1635 under the name Peace of Prague. The emperor granted a major concession to the Protestants to secure peace within the empire. Unfortunately, the hostilities didn't end because the foreign rulers involved would not let the German Protestants enjoy their peace.

The Spanish warred with the Dutch, and even though they were involved with their German cousins in the Thirty Years' War, the Peace of Prague didn't concern them. The Swedes weren't involved in the peace, either, and they continued their fight against the imperial forces. The French, the longtime enemies of the Habsburgs, supplied the Swedes for the war with the Holy Roman Empire, as it was against their interests to allow Ferdinand to consolidate his position as an emperor. French statesman and ardent Catholic Cardinal Richelieu allied with Protestant Swedes and the Dutch. To keep the war with the empire certain, he also started a conflict with the Spanish and Austrian Habsburgs. Europe entered the final and most devastating stage of the Thirty Years' War.

The last decade of the conflict brought agony to the empire's civilians. The battles themselves were few and far apart, but the mercenary armies employed by both sides were ravaging the countryside to destroy the provisions for their enemies. Besides destroying fertile land and cattle, the armies enjoyed torturing the civilians, raping the women, and burning the homes of common people. Thousands of starving villagers were forced to abandon their land and seek fortune in another area, leaving whole German territories completely depopulated. Aside from poverty and hunger, peasants were hit hard by diseases, and tens of thousands of them died in agony. Today, the estimation is that, at the end of the Thirty Years' War, Germany lost at least one third of its population. Aside from the war, Germany was engulfed in the great European witch hunt, which only added to depopulation. There was no central authority to overlook the trials in which thousands of suspected witches lost their lives. Territorial princes and magistrates were free to punish the women accused of witchery as they saw fit, and most sentenced them to death. Confessions were forced out of the frightened and powerless women, and torture was considered a valid means of extorting a confession.

The war, which had strictly taken place within the borders of the Holy Roman Empire, finally spilled out, taking over much of the continent. Conflicts occurred in the Netherlands, Bohemia, Denmark, and Italy. France sent its troops to Germany, but they fared very poorly, and the Spanish forces easily pushed them back to France. Having financed both Sweden and their army, the French realized that their involvement was proving too costly. The successor of Cardinal Richelieu, Cardinal Mazarin, was eager to end the conflict. In fact, by 1643, all major forces involved in the war wanted to end it. Peace negotiations started in the Westphalian cities of Osnabrück and Münster, but that doesn't mean the war ended. The conflict continued parallel to the peace talks. By 1645, Ferdinand III, the successor of the Holy Roman Emperor Ferdinand II, suffered a series of defeats that forced him to seek peace. In 1648, the Peace of Westphalia was finally concluded. More than 150 delegates signed the treaty as the representatives of the Holy Roman Emperor and the rulers of Spain, France, Netherlands, and German principalities. The thirty years of warfare finally ended, and a new political order was brought to the empire.

With the Peace of Westphalia, Sweden got an important part of the Baltic territories, but it was France that profited the most. The emperor was willing to grant most of Alsace and Lorraine to the French. The Dutch won the recognition of their independence by Spain, and the Rhine Palatinate was given to the Calvinist Wittelsbach line of Frederick V. In Germany, territories were restored to the provisions established in 1555 by the Peace of Augsburg. However, the rulers of German territories were now free to choose the religion of their domain, and even then, the people could practice whichever religion they chose. The Peace of

Westphalia fundamentally changed the political scene within the empire. The emperor's authority was significantly diminished, as the 300 princes of the empire had formal sovereignty over their territories. They were also allowed to conduct foreign policies without imperial restrictions. By allowing this to happen, Ferdinand III forever ended the Habsburg dream of converting the Holy Roman Empire into a centralized empire, such as Sweden or France.

Chapter 7 – The Age of Enlightenment

In 17th and 18th-century Europe, it was uncommon for a kingdom to be ruled by a female. But the Austrian Hamburg Emperor Charles VI (1685-1740) had no sons, and he had to ensure that his eldest daughter, Maria Theresa, inherited his throne. He not only issued an edict that legitimized female succession in Austria but also actively worked on persuading the other European rulers to accept Maria Theresa as his heir. Charles' Pragmatic Sanction, a decree which ensured Maria's succession, was accepted by almost all neighboring kingdoms. However, some rulers hoped they could profit from the dynastic instability in Habsburg Austria and declined to accept the Pragmatic Sanction. One of these was the ambitious king of Prussia, Friedrich Wilhelm I (r.1713-1740).

Maria Theresa (1717-1780) was only twenty-three years old when her father died in 1740, leaving her the throne of Austria. But when she tried to establish herself as the empress, she was denied this privilege by the Prussian ruler who contested her claim to the throne. He invaded Austria in December of the same year and occupied Silesia, a strategically important part of Austria. Inspired by the Prussian defection, other rulers who had previously accepted

Pragmatic Sanction now declined the young empress her crown. Among them were France, Spain, Saxony, and Bavaria. Facing such mighty enemies, Maria had few options. However, Hungary accepted her and crowned her their queen, which allowed her to use the Hungarian army as a defense against her attackers. Austria was already invaded by the Bavarians who occupied Vienna and by the French who entered Bohemia when Maria Theresa personally traveled to Hungary to appeal to the nobles. Their queen had just given birth to her first son, and holding the newborn tightly in her arms, she addressed the Hungarians. Her famous appeal and her persona of a queen mother in danger were enough to buy her the loyalty of the Hungarian nobles. Soon, the army was marching in defense of Austria.

Eight years of succession war followed, but Maria managed to secure the crown of an empress. She lost Silesia to Prussia, but the Austrian throne was hers. Salic law still denied her the right to bear imperial titles, but she found a loophole and crowned her husband, Francis I, instead. Thus, Maria Theresa became the de facto empress of the Holy Roman Empire and, ultimately, one of the greatest rulers of the Habsburg dynasty.

Prussia

But the question must be asked: how did Prussia, a principality (duchy) that fared poorly during the Thirty Years' War, rise to power with which it could veto the emperor's decree? Prussia had ambitious rulers, the Hohenzollern dynasty, which used the period of war to gain power. The lands owned by Hohenzollern were small and scattered all over northern Germany. However, the family united and formed Brandenburg-Prussia, which included Pomerania. The territories were known under the common name Prussia, but Brandenburg belonged to the Holy Roman Empire while Prussia was outside its borders. During the conflict with the Swedes in the 17th century, the leader of the Hohenzollern dynasty, Georg Wilhelm (r.1619–1640), had to flee his own country and seek refuge in Konigsberg, today's Kaliningrad (a

Russian city and province on the Baltic Sea between Poland and Lithuania). It was George's successor, Friedrich Wilhelm (r.1640-1688), who reorganized the Prussian army and transformed it from a feeble military power to a juggernaut.

Friedrich's military reformation helped him change the political image of his duchy, too. Prussia was under the fiefdom of Polish rulers, but Friedrich helped the king of Poland to fend off the Swedes during the Second Northern War (1655-1660), and as a reward, Prussia was released from its feudal obligations to the Polish Crown. As the sovereign of Prussia, Friedrich ruled as an absolutist, holding all the political power in his own hands. His title was the Great Elector, and he continued to militarize the state. After all, a powerful army already helped him realize some of his ambitions, and it was key to further political influence on Europe. His son, Friedrich III (1657-1713), continued the success of Prussia by building upon his father's ambitions. In January of 1701, he crowned himself King of Prussia. The duchy became a kingdom, while he assumed the name Friedrich I of Prussia. Because Brandenburg was still within the borders of the Holy Roman Empire, Friedrich I convinced Emperor Leopold I to elevate him to the position of a king in exchange for military help against the French during the War of the Spanish Succession (1701-1714). By agreeing to elevate the ambitious Prussian duke to a royal title, Emperor Leopold I admitted his decline in power.

Prussian rulers continued to rely on military power, and the successor of Friedrich I, Friedrich Wilhelm I, was known as the "Soldier King." He converted the Prussian army into one of the most feared in Europe. However, Friedrich Wilhelm I invested in education and farming, too, raising Prussia above all other German principalities. His father made military service mandatory for the middle class, but Wilhelm decided to allow people to pay a tax if they chose not to serve. He used this money to open new schools and hospitals and to buy and store grain, which he later sold to other principalities for a much higher price. Unlike his father,

Wilhelm I never treated the royal treasury as his personal funds. Instead, he lived modestly and sold all his father's crown jewels, leaving the treasury filled with money. Wilhelm I also never started a war, even though he managed to expand his kingdom greatly. He joined the Great Northern War (1700-1721) on the side of Russia and managed to gain some of the territories in Sweden. In the east, he moved the borders of Prussia to the Memel River and invited Protestants from all over Germany to come and settle there. The rest of Germany was Catholic, and Protestants were never welcomed there, but Prussia was a Protestant state that over 20,000 people agreed to inhabit.

Friedrich Wilhelm I was succeeded by his son, Friedrich II, also known as Friedrich the Great (1712-1786). Unlike his father, Friedrich II was a philosopher and a lover of arts. Nevertheless, he proved to be a worthy successor to the Prussian throne. Only a year after his coronation, Friedrich II moved his army to Silesia, a possession of Habsburg Austria. There, he campaigned in three different wars between 1740 and 1763, in which he triumphed and took Silesia from the combined forces of Austria, France, and Russia. In 1748, Austria moved against Prussia with the hopes of gaining its territory back. While Prussia had the support of Britain only, Austria allied with France, Spain, Russia, and Saxony. The king of Prussia displayed his military genius by launching a preemptive strike on Saxony in 1756. The Austrians and their allies were confused and allowed Prussia to dominate the early years of the war. The military power of Prussia reached its full potential, and Friedrich II beat the Austrians and French in two different battles during 1757 and then the Russians a year later. Scared by the military might of its neighbors, Sweden joined the war at this point. Sweden joined Austria, and Prussia began losing territories. The Russians took its eastern parts, together with Berlin, the capital of the kingdom. However, Britain defeated France in the battles led in their overseas colonies, and this changed the course of the war in Europe. Luck seemed to be on the Prussian side as Russian

Empress Elizabeth died in 1762, leaving her empire to the incompetent Peter III (1728-1762), who pulled Russia out of the conflict. Sweden followed, and soon, Austria was alone. The Battle of Burkersdorf—the decisive battle between Prussia and Austria—occurred on July 21, 1762. Prussia won and negotiated the prewar boundaries of its kingdom, including the conquered Silesia. With the conclusion of the Seven Years War, Prussia emerged as one of the greatest powers in Europe, capable of humiliating even the great Austria.

In the following two decades, Prussia allied itself with Russia and Austria and took part in the partitioning of Poland. The province of Royal Prussia, which was a fiefdom of the Polish monarchy, was annexed during the first partitioning and renamed West Prussia. This linked East Prussia (which was part of the Holy Roman Empire) and Pomerania, and the territories ruled by Hohenzollerns were not scattered anymore. Finally, for the first time in history, they were contiguous. Two more partitionings of Poland followed, and Prussia took part in those, too—this time under the rule of Friedrich Wilhelm II (1744–1797), nephew of Friedrich II, who died without a son to succeed him. During the second partitioning of Poland, the whole western part of this monarchy was annexed by Prussia, while in the third, Prussia gained Polish territories south of East Prussia. This area was rearranged by Friedrich Wilhelm II and divided into the provinces of New Silesia, New East Prussia, and South Prussia.

Die Aufklärung (Enlightenment)

Prussia wasn't the only principality that tried to place itself on the political scene together with the greatest European powers. However, other German provinces were less successful. They realized the Holy Roman Empire's grasp on them was weakening, and the territory of Germany had suddenly become divided into hundreds of little kingdoms. However, only Prussia and Austria became relevant enough to play the game of power struggle, while the rest of the provinces were either swallowed by the bigger players or existed in irrelevancy. Foreign powers took advantage of the situation in Germany and tried to occupy some of its territories. Louis XIV of France gained Alsace between 1678 and 1681, while some smaller kingdoms tried to assert their influence through art and culture. Saxony and Bavaria became the lead examples of richness with their newly-built castles in Dresden and Munich (their respective capitals). But no matter how efficient their bureaucracy or how much personal wealth their rulers gained, the political scene of the 18th century was dominated by two European powers: Austria and Prussia, the Hohenzollerns and the Habsburgs. Their rivalry would mark the event for the next century.

But something else happened amid Prussia's efforts to dominate the European political scene. The cultural and intellectual life of Germany was going through a change. Influenced by the Enlightenment of France and Britain, the social reforms grasped by the principalities were known as the German Enlightenment, or Aufklärung. In Germany, the Enlightenment started with two great intellectuals of the 17th and 18th centuries, Christian Thomasius (1655-1728) and Gottfried Wilhelm von Leibniz (1646-1716). Christian was a professor of law at Leipzig University and, throughout his academic years, he insisted on the idea that human reason was capable of moving society to new heights. Using his principles, he ended the persecution of witches in Germany by using the rational mind to expose witchcraft as a product of human fantasy. Gottfried, on the other hand, was a philosopher and mathematician who left his mark on German science. Together with Newton, he is credited for the invention of infinitesimal calculus (known today as calculus).

The Aufklärung continued in the 18th century and brought forth great intellectuals such as Moses Mendelssohn and Immanuel Kant. They were both philosophers who worked at the same time, playing with similar ideas. In 1763, the two even competed against each other for the Berlin Prize, a literary competition. Mendelssohn won with his essay "On Evidence in the Metaphysical

Sciences" and earned the status of a "protected Jew" within Prussia. Immanuel Kant came in second with his work "Inquiry Concerning the Distinctness of the Principles of Natural Theology and Morality," but he was already a renowned philosopher with many praised publications behind him. Today, Mendelssohn remains popular because of his then-controversial ideas of religious tolerance. When he was challenged by the Swiss theologian Johann Kaspar Lavater to either dispute Christian morals or convert to Christianity, he simply replied that it is possible to admire someone's morality without converting to his faith. He admitted to his friends that he admired Jesus as a historical person and believed that his moral teachings were in place. The great German philosophers supported Mendelssohn, but the controversy itself and the publicity it received took a toll on his health. Nevertheless, he started using his influence to help the position of Jews in Germany who were suffering singular, religion-based restrictions and taxes.

Immanuel Kant was probably the most influential mind of the German Enlightenment. His work, *The Critique of Pure Reason,* remains one of the most influential works of philosophy. It challenges the traditional perception of knowledge and investigates the limits of human reason itself. He claimed that both experience and reason are essential for gaining valid and objective knowledge. The German philosophers of the day admired Kant and continued to work on his ideas, but it is our modern perception of his philosophy that best illustrates his greatness. Immanuel Kant is still teaching us valuable lessons, even today.

The Aufklärung in Germany would never occur if the bourgeoisie of the empire had not grown in power. They were the educated class of society, the civil servants, the businessmen, and the jurists, and they prepared the rest of society for acceptance of the new, revolutionary ideas of philosophers such as Kant or Thomasius. During the 18th century, the middle class began to rise in power and wealth and started asserting its own influence on society. But society wasn't their only target. They also demanded the reform of the empire's institutions that were outdated and obsolete. In the end, it was this enlightened middle class that pressured their leaders to start social reform. Subsequently, enlightened absolutism (or despotism) emerged in Germany.

Responding to the public demands, German rulers started reforms and, with them, changed the nature of politics in the Holy Roman Empire. Under the influence of the Aufklärung, rulers started granting religious freedoms and religious tolerance, as well as freedom of the press and freedom of speech. Enlightened leaders of central Europe started supporting philosophers and artists through patronage, and they would offer a place at their courts to the enlightened thinkers of the 18th century. No matter how enlightened these rulers became, they were still despots who ruled with the iron fist of autocrats. Because they strongly believed in their divine right to rule over the masses, they refused to grant constitutions to their subjects. A constitution would mean the end of the absolutistic power of German princes, and they wouldn't allow it to happen. The monarchs of Germany saw themselves as divine tools placed in their positions so they could improve the lives of their subjects. Thus, they were (and are) called the enlightened absolutists. All their efforts to improve society met resentment from both nobility and commoners. The reforms proposed by the Austrian monarchs, for example, contained an absolutist nature and lacked an understanding of the traditions and customs of society.

The most well-known enlightened absolutist is king Friedrich the Great of Prussia. In his youth, he practiced the arts and was absorbed in the Aufklärung movement. He used his knowledge of the movement during his rule to reform education, making it a state-sponsored institution. He banned torture as a practice of justice and implemented religious tolerance throughout his kingdom. He was also a patron of famous French philosopher

Voltaire, as well as many other writers and artists. Nevertheless, his rule was completely autocratic and marked by strict militarism. Society had the image of an ideal enlightened ruler in their minds, but Friedrich the Great was very far from it. Rulers who came somewhat closer to those ideals were Austrian monarchs Maria Theresa (1717–1780) and her eldest son Joseph II (1741–1790).

Maria Theresa successfully defended her right to be crowned queen of the Austrians and Hungarians, but as a woman, she couldn't take the title of Empress of the Holy Roman Empire. Nevertheless, she fought for the title and granted it to her husband, becoming the power behind the throne. Modern history is certain it was Maria Theresa who was the true ruler. As a de facto empress, she brought forth a variety of enlightened social reforms in areas that included education, the economy, agriculture, and the military. Once her husband died in 1765, her power didn't diminish. She continued ruling as a Dowager Empress behind her son, Holy Roman Emperor Joseph II. Through her influence, Joseph II became one of the most enlightened rulers of Europe. He modernized the administration of the Habsburg lands, extended religious tolerance throughout the empire, reduced the influence of the church on the state, and promoted free trade and free thinking. Although enlightened, Maria Theresa was more conservative than her son, and her opposition stopped Joseph from implementing all the social reforms he intended. However, when she died in 1780, the emperor was free to implement his program. In fact, he was so eager to change the world around him that he issued thousands of new edicts. But with all those edicts, he proved his autocratic grasp over the empire. He reformed the legal system and the financial system of the empire, abolished serfdom, and secularized some of the church's numerous properties. He also established compulsory elementary education for all citizens, abolished capital punishment, and guaranteed religious freedoms to everyone. However, all his reforms were short-lived and didn't last long after his death.

In Germany, during the mid-18th century, the Enlightenment movement was questioned and critiqued. Events in Europe such as the Seven Years War and the partition of Poland, as well as the American Revolution in North America, led to people abandoning the rationality of Enlightenment for emotionality. Reason was no longer valued, and passion took its place. Philosophers and artists such as Johann Georg Hamann and Johann Wolfgang von Goethe started exploring human emotions. Their goal was to capture their audience by evoking strong feelings such as terror or passion, even if it meant using violence. In such a manner, Goethe's novel *The Sorrows of Young Werther*, first published in 1774, describes the tortures of an unrequited love that eventually leads to suicide.

The Enlightenment failed due to the absolutistic power of the German rulers, but if nothing else, it opened the path for the radical change that was coming from the west: the French Revolution and Napoleon Bonaparte. At the end of the 18th century, Germany was divided into a myriad of small kingdoms that swore allegiance to either Austria or Prussia. There was never a chance for Germany to recover from the Thirty Years' War because the dynastic struggle between the Hohenzollerns and the Habsburgs took hold. The Holy Roman Empire pulled itself apart by proving to the German rulers it offered no protection from outside or inside conflicts. The empire's medieval institutions became obsolete as each ruler set up the administration of his own principality. Germany wasn't prepared for the events of the next century, and the revolution that followed brought dramatic changes.

Chapter 8 – Napoleon and the Revolution in Germany

Portrait of Napoleon Bonaparte
https://en.wikipedia.org/wiki/Napoleon#/media/File:Jacques-
Louis_David_-
_The_Emperor_Napoleon_in_His_Study_at_the_Tuileries_-
_Google_Art_Project.jpg

In 1848, Europe was shaken by a series of revolutions that flooded the continent like a wave. In February, the revolutions started in France, with the intention of setting up the Second Republic. By springtime, all the major powers experienced political upheaval. The revolution occurred spontaneously in each country rather than as a coordinated effort among the people. The simple spread of the news was enough to influence over fifty countries to successfully bring down monarchical rule in Europe. In Germany, the revolution started in March 1848 when radical liberals and nationalists organized mass demonstrations to bring down their absolutist rulers. German cities transformed from centers of trade, art, and culture to battlefields where street violence held sway.

But the origin of the revolutions of 1848 goes back to the French Revolution of 1792. The Enlightenment inspired people to bring down the monarchy, but consequences that no one could foresee shook Europe's political and social system. The Napoleonic Wars revived nationalism in Germany, especially after the dissolution of the Holy Roman Empire in 1806. After Napoleon's defeat in 1815, the people's efforts and dreams of a republic were smashed when the great powers of the world met in Vienna and formed an alliance to balance the continent's political scene. The monarchs proved they still held all the power and suppressed liberal political agitations around their kingdoms. However, the people continued to dream, and their anger culminated in the spring of 1848. Revolts spontaneously broke out across Europe, and the streets of all the main cities were flooded with people who demanded social and political reforms.

Revolution in France and Its Influence on Germany

The French Revolution lasted from 1789 until 1799. It brought the monarchy down and changed the lives of citizens of France forever. The French people and their fight for freedom from the outdated feudal system inspired the whole of Europe. Revolution spread around the continent like a wildfire, but nowhere did it make an impact like it did in Germany. There, the revolution not only ended the monarchic rule but also brought down the political system that was in place for over 1,000 years—the Holy Roman Empire. While the French Revolution was still in its early years, the Holy Roman Emperor Leopold II decided not to meddle but to observe the situation. He was hoping to turn the revolution to his advantage by using the unrest in neighboring France to solve the age-old struggle between the Habsburg dynasty and the French Crown.

Prussia, another French neighbor, also failed to react to the revolution, as it was busy prospering from yet another partition of Poland. However, it became obvious to the German rulers that if they sat idle, they could lose their thrones, too. Emperor Leopold also had a personal interest in the French Revolution since Queen Marie Antoinette was his sister, and he was afraid something terrible would happen to her. This prompted him to make an alliance with Prussian King Friedrich Wilhelm II, and together, the two German rulers issued the Declaration of Pillnitz. In it, they warned the French revolutionaries that if any harm was done to the French royal family, they would suffer the consequences. But this decree was received as an open threat, and the French did not respond well. The tensions between Austria and the revolutionaries culminated in 1792. The French Revolutionary Assembly declared war on Austria, but at that point, the army of France was in disarray. The revolutionaries had gotten rid of the aristocracy, and there were no capable officers left to lead the army. During their first attack on the Austrian Netherlands, the French soldiers deserted, and the attack itself was a disaster. Before the revolutionaries could retreat and reorganize, the Prussian army invaded France in June of 1792.

But the Prussian general, the Duke of Brunswick, didn't even attempt to appease the situation in France. After taking some of the major fortresses, he issued a decree that turned out to be yet another threat. He repeated the words of Leopold II and demanded that the French king be restored to the throne.

Brunswick failed to break the will of the revolutionaries. He only deepened their anger. Prussian support for the monarchy only pushed them to embrace revolutionary ideals, which resulted in the execution of French King Louis XVI and his wife Marie Antoinette in 1793. The execution was certainly provoked by threats made by the German rulers, but it didn't solve anything. In fact, Spain and Portugal realized the dangers of the French Revolution and its influence on Europe and joined Austria and Prussia against France. Since Britain and the Dutch Republic failed to respond to the revolutionaries' pleas, France declared war on them. Cataclysmic struggle was about to break out in Europe, and it would transform the continent through the series of conflicts known as the French Revolutionary Wars.

Many recruits joined the French army as the revolutionary government gained the support of the people, but it still wasn't enough to pose a serious threat to the allied monarchies. During the early campaigns, France suffered heavy losses, and the people who once supported the revolution started rethinking their choices. In truth, all the French army lacked was experience. They had no capable leadership, and all the soldiers recruited had never seen the battlefield before. But after a year of conflict, the French army started winning and even expelling the Allied forces from their territory. By 1794, the French army was ready to go into the offensive and invaded Italy and Spain. Soon, Belgium was overrun, and the Rhineland lost some of its territories, too. In less than a year, the Netherlands was conquered, and the French established the Batavian Republic in its territories. The French victory was sudden and dramatic, and it prompted Prussia and Portugal to retreat from the conflict and the alliance.

Austria was now weakened and an easy target for France. In 1796, the assault was launched when two French armies crossed the Rhine while a third came from the south, where a young military officer named Napoleon Bonaparte led his soldiers through Italy. The goal of the three armies was to meet in Austria and together take Vienna. Austrian military commander and son of Emperor Leopold II, Archduke Charles managed to defeat the French who were invading from the Rhine. But Napoleon continued his efforts in Italy, where he took the city Mantua. There, he accepted the surrender of the Austrian armies, and the path across the Alps was now open to him. Instead of allowing him to cross, the Austrians sued for peace and accepted humiliating terms. The Treaty of Campo Formio (1797) forced the Austrians to surrender Belgium and Northern Italy, while the Republic of Venice was divided between France and Austria. However, this treaty failed to provide peace, and the conflict was soon renewed.

In the meantime, Napoleon displayed his ambitions to seize power, and the revolutionary French Government was happy to see him gone on his exotic Egyptian campaign. His absence allowed France to make political decisions that would reshape Europe. In Switzerland, the French established another puppet government and named it the Helvetic Republic. In Italy, the French turned their attention to Rome. They deposed Pope Pius VI and established a pro-revolutionary republic in the Eternal City. As a response to these French movements, a second alliance was established between Austria, Britain, and Russia. In 1799, they launched their attack on France. The alliance was doing well in the early conflicts, with Russia taking French possessions in Italy and Austria fighting off the French army and driving it back across the Rhine. But it was the internal conflict among the members of the alliance that determined the end of the war. The Russians retreated because they couldn't reach an agreement with Austria about the conquered territories. Napoleon returned from Egypt and realized his ambitions by proclaiming himself the First Consul, head of the French government. Angered by the political development in Europe, he wanted to retaliate for the second coalition's meddling. Napoleon led an offensive.

The Napoleonic Wars and the End of the Holy Roman Empire

The French Empire at its height in 1812 and its allies (red)
https://upload.wikimedia.org/wikipedia/commons/thumb/f/f5/Euro
pe_1812_map_en.png/1920px-Europe_1812_map_en.png

Napoleon renewed his campaigns in Italy in 1800. He was successful and changed the course of the war with the victory at the Battle of Marengo when he drove the Austrian army across the Alps. After the victory at the Battle of Hohenlinden in Germany, Napoleon took his army to seize Vienna. Napoleon's victories cause the second coalition to shatter and the Habsburgs to capitulate. With the Treaty of Luneville, signed in 1801, the Austrians were forced to cede the German territories across the Rhine to the French. They also recognized the French client republics in the Netherlands and Italy. After the victory, Napoleon changed his politics, turning from a revolutionary commander into an absolutist. He crowned himself emperor in December of 1804 and revealed his ambitions to conquer Europe. The violent Napoleonic Wars (1803–1815) would devastate the continent in the next decade.

Since the Treaty of Luneville granted German territories to France, the Holy Roman Emperor Francis II (1768–1835) had to come up with a way to compensate the German princes who were forced to cede their lands. To do this, the emperor issued the Principal Resolution of the Imperial Deputation, by which imperial and ecclesiastical lands were granted to the princes who lost their land in Rhineland. The result was the loss of forty-two imperial cities, which became private possessions of the German princes. But along with the transfer of territory, other effects of the Imperial Deputation were also massive shifts of allegiance. Several German states independently made an alliance with France, which only sped up the dissolution of the Holy Roman Empire.

This shift of alliances made Austria nervous, and the third coalition against France was formed in 1805. The signing parties were Austria, Portugal, Britain, and Russia. However, Napoleon's experience as a military leader proved to be crucial. Although outnumbered, his armies managed to inflict a series of defeats on the coalition. Britain was the only signing party that had some success against the French, mainly because of its dominance in naval battles. At Trafalgar, the French navy suffered a defeat, but in Germany, the French army proved their might on the battlefields. After the victory at the southern German city of Ulm, Napoleon led his army against the allied Austrians and Russians. In December 1805, in the Battle at Austerlitz, the French army won such a decisive victory that the Austrians were forced to back out of the war entirely and sign a treaty. The Treaty of Pressburg detailed the land Austria was to cede to Napoleon's German allies, as well as the war reparations they should pay. The Habsburg Monarchy was ruined by this treaty: it was the last nail in the 1,000-year governance of the Holy Roman Empire over Germany.

By 1806, Napoleon had already signed an official alliance with sixteen German principalities, including Baden, Hesse-Darmstadt, and Saxony. These principalities officially left the Holy Roman Empire and formed what is known as the Confederation of the

Rhine (Rheinbund). The territories of the German principalities that signed the alliance were to serve as the buffer zone between France and the Habsburg Monarchy and its coalition. In time, major principalities such as Saxony, Bavaria, and Württemberg were granted the status of kingdoms by the French emperor. Considering these events and the threat that Napoleon posed to the Holy Roman Empire, Francis II officially abdicated as emperor on August 6, 1806. The formal dissolution of the Holy Roman Empire took place on the same day. The rest of the German principalities felt abandoned, and needing protection, they felt pressured to join France and the Confederation of the Rhine. King Francis II continued to rule Austria. Together with Prussia, Swedish Pomerania, and Danish Holstein, he continued to defy Napoleon's ambitions to conquer Europe.

A new coalition was formed in 1806 between Prussia, Britain, Russia, Sweden, and Saxony, which, in the meantime, had left the Confederation of the Rhine. But over the next two years, the coalition was unable to thwart Napoleon's plan to rule Europe. The French emperor inflicted a series of defeats on his enemies. In October 1806, he took Berlin and occupied East Prussia, making a base there which would be later used to launch an attack on Russia. In June 1807, the Russians capitulated and signed the Treaty of Tilsit. France got half of Prussia, which was to become Napoleon's Kingdom of Westphalia.

The division among the German states was best depicted in 1809 during the conflict between Napoleon's armies and those of the fifth coalition. The Confederation of the Rhine was still effective, but the only support Napoleon received during this conflict with Austria and Britain came from Bavaria. The rest of the states tried to remain neutral. However, Napoleon once again displayed his dominion on the battlefield. The decisive battle occurred at Wagram, just outside of Vienna, where around 300,000 soldiers clashed. Austria capitulated, and the Treaty of Schönbrunn was signed, by which the Habsburg Monarchy ceded its Adriatic ports—Galicia, as well as Carinthia and Carniola. Francis II was also forced to agree he would implement an embargo on British goods and recognize Napoleon's brother, Jérôme Bonaparte, as the king of Spain.

The Napoleonic Wars divided Germany, as each state independently gave allegiance to whomever they wanted. However, this situation had an unexpected consequence among the people of Prussia, Austria, and Bavaria: they realized they were all one people, and the sense of German nationalism started growing. The newly-acquired territories of France were populated by German people who resented their new status. The citizens of the Kingdom of Westphalia raised rebellions in their attempt to rejoin their Prussian relatives, and other German territories showed unity against the French overlordship. By the time the sixth coalition was formed in 1812, German people everywhere were united against Napoleon's rule. At that time, Napoleon was in Russia, where he suffered a disastrous defeat. On his way back, with his armies heavily decimated, Napoleon was forced to confront the sixth coalition, made up of Austria, Britain, Russia, Sweden, and Prussia.

The largest battle in Europe before World War I happened in October of 1813. It involved over half a million troops, and it is remembered by the title the Battle of Nations or the Battle of Leipzig. The late 19th-century nationalists grasped the opportunity to celebrate this battle as the romanticized struggle of the German people to expel their French oppressors. But in their celebration, the nationalists decided to remain silent about the fact that Napoleon's troops were aided by his German allies from the Confederation of the Rhine. Nevertheless, the sixth confederation's army won the decisive Battle of Leipzig and pushed the French back over the Rhine. Bavaria, Saxony, and Württemberg switched sides and helped the coalition invade France, where Napoleon was overthrown and the royal Bourbon family was restored. The Confederation of the Rhine collapsed once Russia invaded East

Prussia, or the Kingdom of Westphalia. After the battle, most of the confederation members joined the coalition and took part in the Congress of Vienna, during which the borders of European countries were redrawn. In 1815, the German Confederation was born, replacing Napoleon's Confederation of the Rhine. This was not yet Germany as a single state, but the time of its unification was approaching.

The German Confederation was composed of thirty-eight sovereign states and four free cities, all the wreckage that was left after the dissolution of the Holy Roman Empire. They were governed by the Austrian emperor who, in the case of Germany, served in the role of president. Still, each state had a level of individuality, and its representatives met only once a year in Frankfurt. The Austrian representative would also attend the meeting to discuss any major problems the confederation might have. The German Confederation was a very conservative environment that tried to expel all the French revolutionary influences and liberal ideas. The German Confederation issued several very oppressive pieces of legislation with the intention of preventing the rise of the populace. The press was censored, leaving the people of Germany largely unaware of the liberal tides that were sweeping through Europe. In 1820, Austria, Prussia, and Russia formed the Holy Alliance to preserve autocracy within the German Confederation and allow the monarch to have tight control over these lands.

The Revolution of 1848 in Germany

Since the Congress of Vienna in 1815, the German Confederation had been stable and prosperous under its conservative rule. However, by 1830, the people realized that stability was an illusion, and tension grew once more in Central Europe. Threatened by revolutions, the monarchs of Austria, Prussia, and Russia met in secrecy to form yet another Holy Alliance. The meeting took place in Berlin in 1833, and the alliance's goals of preserving the monarchic rule were reaffirmed.

France and Belgium had already deposed their monarchs in 1830, and Poland was on the verge of rebellion. The Holy Alliance managed to subdue the revolutionary sentiment that was rising in its member's countries, but this was only a temporary solution. When, in 1848, the revolutionary current from France reached Germany, the alliance was unable to prevent the uprising. The nationalism and liberal ideas from the rest of Europe reached the German populace, and they expressed revolt against the conservative government that ruled them. The first signs of the revolution happened in March of 1848 when riots broke out in several German cities. The people demanded political and social reforms, but they, too, were divided between the radicals, influenced by French revolutionaries, and the liberals, who were mostly educated individuals.

The era before the revolution of 1848 was known as the Vormärz era, the German romanticism which brought forth nationalism. The pan-German anthem "Das Lied der Deutschen" (The Song of the Germans) was written in 1841, and it evoked a nationalistic spirit and ideas among the people. Famous German poet Heinrich Heine wrote lyric poetry filled with images that stirred national passion, although the Nazis later found his persona to be inadequate, as he was originally Jewish. These nationalistic ideas inspired the youth of Germany, who formed clubs that gathered people of the same opinions. Youth clubs sprouted all over Germany, rising from both sports clubs and university fraternities (known as Burschenschaften in Germany), and they promoted liberal and nationalistic ideas. The government tried to prohibit the activities of youth clubs by issuing repressive edicts and decrees to limit the spread of nationalistic and liberal thinking. Membership in Burschenschaften was made illegal, and universities had to employ inspectors who would monitor the activities of students and professors.

The first mass protest organized to call for a unified Germany took place in 1832. It is known today as the Hambacher Fest, an event that gathered around 30,000 students, professors, politicians, and workers demanding a unified government and freedom for citizens. This protest didn't achieve much, but it was a symbol of the growing influence of liberalism and nationalism and a prelude to the March Revolution of 1848, wherein the spirit of Hambacher Fest grasped the whole of Germany. The citizens' discontent grew with each passing year, so when the revolutionary wave came from France, the German populace was already on the verge, ready to take up the streets and fight for the new order. The German middle class formed mobs all over the German cities, demanding freedom of the press, the unification of the state, and the formation of a parliament. They were quickly joined by factory workers and farmers, who were hit hard by the rapid industrialization taking place.

Amid the revolution, which spread throughout Europe, the working class was exposed to the writings of radical left socialists such as Karl Heinrich Marx (1818–1883), who had just published *The Communist Manifesto*. Marx was trained as a philosopher and a journalist, and his masterworks were written as a call to the working class to pick up arms and fight for their rights. His ideas set the foundation on which modern Communism was raised. He believed that human history could be observed as an ongoing economic and social struggle. His vision of the future was one in which production and development are controlled by the workers themselves, who would, in time, build a stateless and classless society. Marx's *Manifesto* and his persona remained obscure during the revolution of 1848, but after his death, his ideas would shape the future of Germany. Karl Marx would have a tremendous influence on the whole world, for good or for bad.

When the revolution in France turned into a coup that removed King Louis-Philippe, the German people saw the change that the masses can bring. By February, they had already issued a resolution that demanded a constitution. The stage was set for the March Revolution, and smaller protests occurred early in Baden, the

Duchy of Hesse, the Duchy of Nassau, and the Kingdom of Württemberg. The rulers of the German Confederation were caught off guard by the spontaneous protests that were popping up in their territories. To appease the people, they made various concessions, but in Baden, violence erupted. The ducal army attacked the republican demonstrators, and this violence would soon spread throughout Germany. The revolutionaries prepared, raising a republican militia led by Friedrich Hecker (1811-1881). They were ready to confront the soldiers of Baden and Hesse, and the first conflict came on April 20, 1848, in the Black Forest. The aristocratic army defeated the revolutionaries, but with heavy losses. Disappointed, Hecker emigrated to America, where he later became the commander of a Union regiment during the American Civil War.

In Berlin, the capital of Prussia, which was a conservatively autocratic kingdom, the protesters dared to take to the streets. They demanded concession from King Friedrich Wilhelm IV (1795-1861), who responded that he would give them a constitution, parliament, and the freedom of speech and press. But he didn't stop there. Inspired by the revolution, the Prussian king promised he would help his people unite Germany into one nation and state. But the people believed their king's promises were empty and continued with protests. The situation in Berlin culminated when one of the anxious Prussian soldiers guarding the barricades fired at the angry mob. By March 18, the Prussian capital became a war zone. The conflict lasted for three days, and hundreds of protestors were killed by Prussian soldiers. In the end, King Friedrich Wilhelm went out on the streets of Berlin to appease the situation. He reaffirmed his intentions of concessions and visited the graves of the fallen protestors who had died during the conflict.

In Austria, Emperor Ferdinand I was shocked by the situation in Germany. Austria was the leader of the German Confederation, and the protests there were aiming at the Habsburg emperor. But it wasn't only Germany that was worrying him—the situation in Austria wasn't good, either. By March, the revolution took to the streets of Vienna, where it raged until July of 1849. The revolution in Austria was sparked by various nationalities that were part of the Habsburg Monarchy and sought autonomy: Slovaks, Serbs, Croats, Hungarians, Poles, Czechs, Italians, and Romanians. The threat to the Habsburg emperor came from two sides: the German Confederation and his empire. Pressured, Ferdinand I reluctantly exiled his favorite politician and chancellor, Klemens von Metternich, who had kept the conservative spirit in both Austria and the German Confederation and led the politics of central Europe for three decades. However, the resignation and exile of the Austrian chancellor to England weren't enough for the people. Soon, the emperor was forced to abdicate and name his nephew, Franz Joseph (1830-1916), as his successor.

In Frankfurt, a new National Assembly emerged and replaced the German Confederation, taking over its duties. The National Assembly met in Frankfurt and was accordingly named the Frankfurt Parliament. Elections followed, and the parliament swelled up to 586 delegates, all chosen from the rows of liberal intellectuals. The chair of the parliament was taken up by the Hessian statesman, Heinrich von Gagern, and the parliament immediately started working on the constitution. The constitution intended to establish the foundations for a unified nation-state of Germany with a single parliament. But the first difficulty emerged almost immediately as the delegates argued whether to include Austria in the new, united Germany or leave it out. The problem arose when some of the delegates pointed out that Austria was a multinational empire, filled with Slavs, Italians, and Romanians, and as such, it wouldn't fit into a new state that was based on cultural, lingual, and national unity. The argument lasted for months until they reached the resolution that Austria should not be admitted into the new state but should be bound to it by a special treaty. When even after a year the Frankfurt Parliament failed to yield a constitution, it started losing prestige among the German populace. France, Russia, and other European forces didn't even recognize the legitimacy of this parliament, while Austria and Prussia completely ignored it. When the parliament finally released its constitution in March 1849, it barely passed the vote and was recognized only by some of the minor states of the German Confederation. The major European powers refused to do so.

When the revolution was only starting in Prussia, King Friedrich Wilhelm IV was on the side of the people and even promised them a constitution. However, he soon realized, by the example of the German Confederation, that the political tide in Europe was very much against the radical ideas of the revolutionists. Therefore, when the people offered him the crown (as they were proud to have a king who would give them a constitution), Friedrich declined it, calling it a crown made of mud and clay. The Prussian king turned to autocracy once more. In Frankfurt, the parliament fell apart, and the revolution dissolved into separate movements across the Confederation. The most radical leftists continued to meet and eventually tried to organize their parliament in Stuttgart, but they were soon chased away by the Royal Dragoons of the Kingdom of Württemberg. The fragmented revolution allowed German princes to assert their dominion once more, and the demonstrations were often stifled by ruthless violence. In Stuttgart, where the leftovers of the National Assembly exiled the Duke of Baden, the Prussian army stormed the demonstrators acting on behalf of the German Confederation. In Saxony, the conflict culminated in remarkable proportions when the military, called by King Friedrich Augustus, joined the protesters. The king was forced to call on the Prussian army to quell the uprising, and tensions escalated. The crowd was angry and grew more violent with each passing day, finally forcing Friedrich Augustus into the fortified armory. The protesters tried to enter the armory, but the royal guard fired at them, and the City of Dresden became a war zone. The revolutionary protesters barricaded themselves in the city, expecting the Prussian army. They even organized a provisional government that would manage the conflict and eventually force their monarch to accept the liberal reforms guaranteed by the Frankfurt constitution. The Prussian and Saxon troops united against the protesters, and the street fighting that followed was ruthless and brutal. By May 9, no revolutionary forces remained in the city. The majority were slaughtered, but some managed to escape the country and find refuge in neighboring countries, as well as America. Among them was famous composer Richard Wagner, who fled to Switzerland. The conflict in Saxony is remembered as the May Uprising.

By June 1849, the revolution was over. The monarch managed to tighten the conservative yolk on the population of Germany. The leaders of the revolution were either dead or imprisoned, the German Confederation was back, and the assembly returned to the conservative vision of the exiled chancellor Metternich. The disappointed liberals and nationalists who survived the revolutionary year were now mockingly called the Forty-Eighters, and they collectively emigrated to the United States. The failure of the March Revolution changed the course of Germany's history. Instead of unifying the nation, the powerful states of Austria and Prussia resumed their struggle for dominion over the German Confederation. The peace and the prospect of unity were doomed, and the nation-state, the dream of the revolutionaries, would be born out of future bloodshed.

Chapter 9 – The Many Wars and the Unification

In 1850, after the revolution, Prussian King Friedrich Wilhelm IV finally issued a constitution. However, it was a conservative document supporting his autocracy. He did give some liberal freedoms to the citizens and formed a Prussian Parliament consisting of the lower house (the Landtag) and the upper house (the Herrenhaus). The delegates of the Landtag were to be elected, but the voters were not equal. The members who paid higher taxes held higher voting powers. The members of the Herrenhaus were appointed by the king himself. The king also had complete authority over the cabinets of the ministers and the civil service and army. But the king suffered a stroke in 1857, and Prussia fell under the regency of his younger brother, Wilhelm. By 1861, Wilhelm took the throne as King Wilhelm I.

The German statesman Otto von Bismarck (1815–1898) was appointed as Prussian minister-president and was tasked with unifying Germany under Prussian rule. He served under Wilhelm I (1797–1888), who had succeeded to the Prussian crown a year earlier. A decade before, there was almost war between Prussia and Austria in the autumn crisis of 1850, but Prussia withdrew and suffered a diplomatic defeat. Bismarck tried to correct the past failure. Prussia had weakened greatly, and the only way it could join the major European powers on the political scene was at the head of a unified Germany. Bismarck was no idealist—he understood very well that the new nation-state would have to be born out of major conflict, a war of enormous proportions.

However, the Prussian kingdom had formed a budget commission to lift the state out of the economic crisis that emerged after its defeat by the Austrians. This commission was in Bismarck's way, as it was opposed to waging another expensive war. The army needed to be reorganized, and this endeavor would be extremely costly. Instead, the budget commission thought it would be much wiser to implement liberal social reforms. Bismarck confronted the commission and, in his speech, stressed the need for Prussia's military power to unite Germany. He planned to exclude Austria from unification, and the only possible way to do it was through major conflict. In the next few decades, this Prussian politician would repeatedly demonstrate his will to wage war to achieve his ambitions. Parliamentary delegates refused to vote in favor of war, but Bismarck managed to inspire the people and awaken the nationalism and patriotism among them. The people wanted unification with the German Confederation and expressed their single-minded determination. Bismarck further managed to raise the funds for military reforms without the consent of parliament. He ignored their votes and evaded their authority just so he could have his war and unite Germany under Prussia.

But while the budget commission was against the war and military reforms because of their cost, many conservative officers, civil servants, and aristocracy opposed the unification of Germany because they feared that the status of their beloved Prussia would diminish with the union. They also expressed their fears that the Prussian king would be forced to accept liberal reforms under a unified Germany. Bismarck agreed that the destiny of Prussia was a concern, but he argued that if Germany was unified under their ruler, Prussia would emerge as the greatest European power. During the 1850s, Prussia was marginalized by other European powers such as France and Britain, who had dominated the Crimean War (1854–1855) against Russia. Bismarck pointed this out and argued that Prussia had to return to the political scene of Europe immediately if it wished to continue existing. Otherwise, it represented a very attractive war prey with its rich coal mines and iron industry.

The war between Prussia and Austria erupted in 1866, two years after the Second Schleswig War fought between Denmark and the united forces of Prussia and Austria. The reason behind the conflict in 1866 was that the Austrian Empire disputed with the German Confederation about the Danish territories conquered during the earlier war. The Prussians accused Austria of breaking the settlement that followed the Second Schleswig War and then invaded Holstein. In response to the Prussian accusations, the German Confederation authorized the mobilization of troops to counter the invasion. Bismarck was not intimidated; he even wished for war and declared the Confederation dissolved. Most of the German states joined the Austrian side in the conflict, while Prussia had the support of minor northern German states and the Kingdom of Italy. Italy had its reasons for stepping into the conflict with Austria. It hoped for territorial gains—specifically, the Veneto (the area surrounding today's Venice), which was under Austrian control. Europe's major powers stayed out of the conflict.

The Prussians prepared for war even before it was declared, and they had the advantage. While Austria was still mobilizing its troops, the Prussians invaded Saxony and Bohemia. The modernization of the army served Bismarck well, as the new breech-loading rifles overwhelmed the Austrian soldiers. The Austrians suffered their first defeat at Königgrätz, on July 3, 1866, and immediately sued for peace. But Prussia turned against the Austrian allies since Bismarck understood German states wouldn't accept Prussia's dominance easily. By the end of the month, the

Hanoverian army was defeated, and the Bavarians were pushed back to the River Main. The Peace of Prague, which ended the conflict between Prussia and Austria, was signed on August 23rd. The war lasted only for seven weeks, but Austria ended up excluded from the future unification of Germany. Prussia emerged as the leading state in the German Confederation, which was immediately dissolved so the Prussians could form a new one. The new alliance, known as the North German Confederation, included twenty-one of the German states, all occupying the territories north of the River Main. The German nationalists welcomed the new Confederation, and Prussia became their only hope of a unified state that would exclude multinational Austria. Prussia annexed Austrian allies such as Nassau, Hesse-Kessel, and Hanover, and forced several other states to join the Northern German Confederation. The position of Prussia changed on the larger European scale, and the kingdom was back in the political game of central Europe. Bismarck remained the minister-president and, as such, dominated not only Prussian but also the politics of the new Confederation.

The Franco-Prussian War

Prussia's return to the political scene of Europe alarmed France. France felt threatened not only by the fact that the Hohenzollerns had gained control over all of Germany but also by their military power. Napoleon III (1808–1873) understood very well that French influence on the southern German states was the cause of Bismarck's turn towards them. To integrate these southern territories into his new Confederation, Bismarck would have to wage war against Germany's centuries-old enemy, France. But first, the Prussian minister-president ensured that other European powers wouldn't meddle in the conflict. His diplomatic skills proved to be great, as he managed to persuade Russia and Great Britain to stay out of the war. But he needed a reason to declare the war on France, and the opportunity presented itself in Spain. The Spanish throne had been vacant since the revolution in 1868 and was now being offered to the cousin of the Prussian king, Prince Leopold of the Hohenzollern-Sigmaringen dynasty. If he accepted the Spanish crown, France would be surrounded by territories controlled by Prussia, and it had to act immediately. Napoleon III first tried diplomacy, sending his trusted ambassador Vincente Benedetti to meet with Wilhelm I to demand the refusal of the Spanish crown. The Prussian king agreed to the French demands, as he wasn't willing to participate in yet another military conflict. However, France wasn't satisfied. Napoleon III insisted that Wilhelm I should promise that no Hohenzollern would ever occupy the Spanish throne. He even asked that an official apology be issued by the Prussian king, but he only managed to insult Wilhelm I, who rejected all of France's demands. This situation was the perfect opportunity Bismark needed to proclaim war on France. Indulging in shrewd politics, he issued Ems Dispatch, a document that described the French-Prussian correspondence. Bismarck's version of the correspondence was much different than the original. He changed several sentences to insult France and inspire anti-French sentiment among Germans. The reaction was immediate, as France declared war on Prussia on July 19, 1870.

Prussia had the full support of the whole north German Confederation as well as the south German states, who allied with Prussia against France. Just as in the previous war with Austria, Prussia mobilized its army quickly, while France took its time. The result was the invasion of France under the supreme command of King Wilhelm I. But it wasn't easy to breach the French border, and it took several weeks for Prussia to gain the upper hand. On August 2nd, the French army was overwhelmed and defeated on several fronts. The following weeks saw Prussian victories at Weissenburg, Wörth, and Spichern, forcing Napoleon III to change the commanding officer in the middle of the conflict. The newly-appointed Marshal François-Achille Bazaine couldn't break the Prussian advance and was forced to retreat to the City of Metz, a fortified stronghold close to the French-German border.

Prussians besieged the city, but Napoleon III personally led the newly-built army to relieve the city and his commanding officer Bazaine. Hearing of the approaching French army, the Prussians split. While one part of their forces kept Metz under pressure, the second part ambushed Napoleon at Beaumont on August 30th. The defeat the French suffered made them retreat and regroup so they could mount a defense for the upcoming decisive battle.

Outside the French town Sedan, on September 1, 1870, the German and French forces clashed in battle. The exhausted French forces were desperate and tried to break out of Sedan so they wouldn't get trapped and besieged, just like at Metz. They moved towards the city of La Moncelle, which was in a strategically better position for defense. Saxon and Prussian troops approached the city and found it easy to enter. The fighting continued on the city streets. Feeling overwhelmed, the French general ordered a retreat, but one of his officers, Emmanuel de Wimpffen, decided to disregard the order and launch an offensive. He was successful against the Saxon troops, but his rally was short-lived, as the Prussian and Bavarian troops came to help their allies. The situation was hopeless for France, and when Napoleon arrived at the battle scene on the evening of September 1, he called off the French attempts at a counterattack. The French suffered heavy losses—around 17,000 soldiers were killed, almost double the German losses. The next day, the French emperor surrendered and was taken into custody. The German victory at La Moncelle caused the collapse of France's Second Empire. However, the provisional government in Paris continued to wage war with Prussia for another five months. In turn, the Prussians continued towards Paris and besieged it. Parisians endured constant shelling as well as bombardment and finally surrendered on January 19, 1871.

Germany Unified

Europe after the war
*https://upload.wikimedia.org/wikipedia/commons/d/dd/Europe_18
71_map_en.png*

In Germany, the nationalism spirit sparked by Bismarck's politics grasped the populace even stronger as they celebrated the glorious victory of King Wilhelm I. But the biggest event in history for Germany occurred on French soil: Wilhelm I was crowned emperor of unified Germany on January 18th, in the Versailles' Hall of Mirrors in Paris. The new empire, or the so-called Second Reich, came into existence just as Otto von Bismarck predicted—from bloodshed. Baden, Württemberg, and Bavaria joined the North German Confederation, and Germany was finally unified, but it was ruled by the iron fist of Prussia. The new monarchical empire Wilhelm I created included all the German states of the previous German Confederation, excluding Austria as well as the tiny states of Luxembourg and Liechtenstein, which decided to remain neutral.

The newly-formed German Empire, or the Kaiserreich, was an autocratic state with a constitution issued in 1871 that ensured Prussian domination. Bismarck, who took up the role of chancellor, granted some democratic concessions to keep the liberals at peace. The bicameral parliament was founded with a lower house (Reichstag) whose delegates had to be elected. He also allowed the formation of political parties, but he was careful to preserve the conservative spirit of the North German Confederation. If the political parties wanted to propose legislation, they had to be approved by the Bundesrat, a federal council under the control of German princes, who could block all liberal reforms. But Prussia, as the dominant force of the empire, was the only state with veto powers within Bundesrat. The constitution guaranteed that only fourteen votes were enough to block a constitutional change, and Prussia alone had seventeen delegates. The emperor had all the executive power, and Bismarck, his chancellor, had it, too. According to the new constitution, the chancellor was obliged to oversee all the aspects of the government, and the authority to enact legislation lay with him. Bismarck made sure that he created an imperial structure with a constitution to safeguard these institutions and Prussian dominion. Although the imperial constitution had traces of democratic ideals, it completely supported and ensured the authoritarian nature of united Germany.

France's Third Republic signed a settlement with the German Empire on May 10, 1871, in Frankfurt. The hostilities officially ended, and France was forced to cede the territories of Alsace and Lorraine. It also had to agree to stay under German occupation until it paid the war indemnity of approximately five billion francs. While united Germany celebrated its victory over France, these events paved the road for future European conflicts, from which it would emerge as the global power. Germany's and Prussia's astonishing climb to power was a warning for the rest of Europe, which finally realized the consequences of allowing Prussia to pursue its militaristic ambitions.

Imperial Germany wasn't only among the greatest European powers in military terms. It also managed to surpass Britain in industrial and economic development. Iron and coal were mined to produce machines, which were transported easily all over the empire with the newly-built railroad system. French Alsace and Lorraine were also industrial centers, and now they added to Germany's already mighty industry. With economic gains came the prosperity of the people. The populace of the empire increased, transforming towns into cities and cities into metropolitan areas. Britain had dominated the industrial scene of Europe since the early 18th century, and now Germany became a worthy rival. The German exports of goods tripled in the decades that followed the unification. At the turn of the century, Germany was quickly rising to become a global economic power, second only to the United States.

Bismarck succeeded in bringing about the German Empire, but he continued to work tirelessly to ensure his vision of a nation-state was completely fulfilled. The people still needed to be unified, and the empire needed to be firmly centralized, with Prussia at its helm. He needed to maintain the conservative nature of the state, and to do this, he needed to stop religious activism, which had spread through the German Catholic minority. His efforts in the field of religion are known as the Kulturkampf. It all started in 1864 when Pope Pius IX (1792–1878) called on the Catholics of Europe to fight against the secular nature of society. The pope opposed state-sponsored education and civil marriages, and in 1871, he issued a declaration that claimed the pope was always right when it came to religious matters. This angered Bismarck, and in 1872, he expelled the Jesuits from Prussia. The May Law he issued the same year gave the state the right to train and appoint all the clergy in Germany. He closed Catholic seminaries and arrested those who either openly opposed him or broke the new law. Furthermore, he confiscated all the church properties and heavily regulated the activities of the Catholic clergy. Pope Pius proclaimed Bismarck's May Law invalid and called on the German Catholics to oppose the official religious persecution. The result of the May Law was the formation of the Catholic Center Party in the south of Germany. But Catholics from all over the empire joined this political party to support it and officially voice their opposition to the law. Bismarck thought of Catholicism as an obstacle to Germany's prosperity. Catholics were extremely loyal to the church instead of to the united nation-state, and the chancellor wouldn't allow it.

But the repression measures he implemented only served to strengthen the resolve of his enemies. Pressed by other matters of the state, Bismarck abandoned his Kulturkampf. He joined the Catholic Center Party so they could more effectively fight the growing socialism within Germany. The first workers' party in Germany was founded in 1863 by Ferdinand Lassalle, a Forty-Eighter who had just been released from prison, where he had served time for his involvement in the revolution. The name of the party was the General German Workers' Association (or ADAV, shortened from its original German name). But this party wasn't the only one. Marxists Wilhelm Liebknecht and August Bebel founded the Social Democratic Workers' Party of Germany (SDAP) in 1869. Although ADAV and SDAP started as bitter enemies with different socialist ideas and programs, they agreed to convene in the meeting organized in May of 1875 to discuss the possibility of unification. This would greatly help plan the future of the workers in Germany. The newly founded party was named the Socialist Workers' Party of Germany (SAPD). It grew rapidly, and with the new members came new ideas and plans. The party was forced to change its name to the Social Democratic Party of Germany (SDP) when its ideology changed and its members started demanding a republican government.

In 1878, there were a few attempts to assassinate Emperor Wilhelm, and while the Socialists took no part in them, Bismarck took the opportunity to accuse them and eventually crush their influence in Germany. He issued a set of laws, named Anti-Socialist Laws, to eradicate socialism. The first law forbade the organizations which, through their activities, sought to overthrow the established state and social order. He even pointed out that this included Social Democratic, Socialist, or Communist political parties. He also employed state militia to break up any workers' assembly or political gatherings of the said parties. The radical newspapers were also shut down to suppress the spread of Socialist ideology.

But just as with the Catholics, Bismarck's ideas to stop German socialism failed. The leaders of various organizations went into hiding, and the Socialist Party continued to grow, with new members joining each day. Seeing that it was impossible to suppress socialism, the chancellor changed the tactic. He issued a series of progressive social programs with which he tried to anticipate the Socialist demands. The first such program came in 1881, and it intended to prevent accidents in the workplace for miners and industrial workers. In 1883, a national healthcare system was introduced in Germany, as well as a program to help disabled people. In 1887, a retirement pension system was set up, and with it, Germany emerged as a state with the most progressive social system in the entire world. Even though Bismarck tried to suppress socialism in his country, the welfare programs he introduced ended up being by far more progressive than the ones in France or Britain.

Aside from fighting against religious activism and socialism, Bismarck had his ideology to promote. He still felt the need to unite the people into one single nation and to prevent the old principalities from demanding autonomy. He had yet to create one German national spirit which would inspire the people to fight for the common goals of the state. To do this, Bismarck came up with the idea of unique policies that would foster national unity, commonly known as Germanization. He was keen to eradicate multiculturalism in Germany by opening various national institutions. To manage these new institutions, Germany needed a new set of laws. They came in 1900 in the shape of a civil code, known as the Bürgerliches Gesetzbuch. Many new national institutions were there to promote cultural nationalism, and they required the use of the German language in all aspects of life. Education and government also demanded strict use of German, and consequently, the ethnic minorities of Germany were assimilated. Bismarck even went so far as to organize a forced relocation of Poles. In 1885, he wanted to colonize the areas previously conquered from Poland with ethnic Germans. In total, 20,000 individuals of Polish descent were exiled to Russia. The Poles' resistance and soon pro-Polish political party were organized to oppose Bismarck. As with the Catholics and Socialists, governmental efforts to suppress ideology only resulted in disobedience and defiance.

Bismarck's domestic politics brought many changes to Germany, but they all eventually failed. However, he was more successful in foreign politics. He was aware that France still held a grudge for the loss of territories during the Franco-Prussian War, and he formed international alliances with other European powers as a safeguard. The first such alliance came to be in 1872, and it was called the League of the Three Emperors because it gathered the emperors of Russia, Germany, and Austria under the same military alliance. But this alliance broke up during the Russo-Turkish War (1877–1878), and the German chancellor joined the Austro-Hungarian Empire in a dual alliance against Russia. In 1882, Italy joined the alliance, and through this country, Austria and Germany were linked with Britain and Spain due to the Mediterranean Agreement of 1887.

Chapter 10 – World War I

Scenes from the Great War
https://upload.wikimedia.org/wikipedia/commons/2/20/WWImont age.jpg

World War I, a military conflict that destroyed the German Empire, was a demonstration of the horrors various nations could unleash upon each other. It started on July 28, 1914, when Germany was under the rule of Wilhelm II (1859-1941), an authoritarian and bellicose ruler. While he was still a crown prince, Wilhelm fell under Bismarck's influence and, once he succeeded to the throne in 1888, abandoned the progressive politics of his father, Emperor Friedrich III, who ruled for only ninety-nine days and died of throat cancer. Wilhelm II idolized Wilhelm I and wanted to return Germany to the state it was in during the early rule of his grandfather. The young monarch was impatient, and he demanded the war, while Bismarck tried to maintain peace. The clash between Wilhelm II and the Germans' great politician led to a domestic disaster.

Wilhelm wanted to take up a more active role in the politics of Germany and would often clash with Bismarck just to prove his capability to lead the country. He even tried to gain the support of Germany's working class by arguing against Bismarck's Anti-Socialist Laws, but he only managed to anger the aging politician. After another heated argument with his emperor, Bismarck—nicknamed the Iron Chancellor of Germany—resigned in 1890. Kaiser Wilhelm II was resolved to rule the German Empire more personally, and he employed a puppet chancellor. But the emperor's meddling in domestic and foreign politics resulted in a series of crises, the first in 1896. Wilhelm hated the British and rushed to send a telegraph to the president of Transvaal Republic (an internationally recognized republic in South Africa from 1852-1902, settled by the Dutch), congratulating him on the victory against the British. Once the telegram became public, the British were outraged, and the debacle of Wilhelm's politics was known to all European forces.

But Wilhelm resented the policy of avoiding the conflict with Britain implemented earlier by Bismarck, and he started building a fleet—one that would overpower the naval might of King Edward

VII of England. The German population didn't object to building a fleet, as they saw it necessary to protect German colonies and trade interests across the sea. The British were alarmed by Germany's sudden interest in the navy, and the competition began. Both powers were building battleships tirelessly just to keep with each other's pace. The naval race resulted in Britain and France establishing the Entente Cordiale in 1904, an agreement that ended their centuries-old animosity and united them to protect their colonies. As France already had an alliance with Russia, the third power was automatically added to the agreement. The focus of the new alliance was to counter Germany and restore the power balance within Europe.

In 1905, the German emperor created another debacle while visiting Morocco: he held a series of speeches in which he insinuated that he supported Moroccan independence. As this African state was a French protectorate, naturally France had to react and started gearing up for war. However, Germany proposed a conference to resolve the issue, and persuaded by Britain, France agreed to attend. The Algeciras Conference was held in Spain in 1906, and it proved to be a disaster for Germany. France had the support of Britain, Italy, Spain, Russia, and the United States, while Germany had only the Austro-Hungarian Empire by its side. The conference decided to grant control of Morocco to France, and Germany had to suffer an embarrassing political fiasco.

The following year, Britain and Russia signed a convention in St. Petersburg, ending the rivalry between the British Crown and the imperial Romanov Dynasty. Germany was now surrounded by the three greatest allied European powers: France, Britain, and Russia. When the Second Moroccan Crisis came in 1911 and the rebellion against the sultan broke out, Wilhelm seized the opportunity to intervene and challenge Anglo-French control in Africa. He sent a gunboat, the SMS Panther, to help the rebelling Moroccans against the French and the British who came to quell the rebellion. However, the Germans were not powerful enough to fight both armies and had to sue for the end of the crisis. Germany offered recognition of French dominion over Morocco in return for territorial concessions in Congo. With the Treaty of Fes signed on November 4, 1911, the Second Moroccan crisis ended. But the result was not what Wilhelm wanted it to be. Instead of breaking the Anglo-French alliance, his actions managed only to strengthen their opposition to Germany. Although Wilhelm's actions didn't start the global conflict known as World War I, his attempts to meddle in European politics set the stage for it. Alliances were formed, and the relations between the states were so tense that it took just one spark to ignite the war. That spark came from an unexpected place: the Balkan, the silent giant of Europe.

The Start of the War

The rival factions at the start of the war
https://en.wikipedia.org/wiki/World_War_I#/media/File:Map_Eur
ope_alliances_1914-en.svg

After centuries of Turkish rule and the struggle to end it, the Balkan region was like a keg of powder waiting to explode. It was populated by ethnic groups that felt extreme hostility towards one another: Slovenes, Croats, Serbs, Romanians, Bulgarians, and Albanians. Europe was entering its era of ardent nationalism and was influenced by great forces, and these ethnic groups wanted to form their own nation-states. But after Ottoman rule, the Balkan was Austro-Hungarian territory, and the signs of individuality coming from the small ethnic groups of the region were a threat to the empire. After Turkey retreated from the Balkans in 1878, Austria-Hungary occupied the province of Bosnia-Herzegovina in hopes that it would prevent a nationalistic uprising. Austria wanted to annex this territory, but Russia, a champion of Slavic spirit, prevented it. However, in 1908, Russia had a change of heart and agreed to the Austrian annex of Bosnia-Herzegovina in exchange for territories in the Mediterranean. But Austria jumped forward and proclaimed the annexation without signing the treaty with Russia. Another ethnic group opposed the annexation, as it believed it had territorial rights within Bosnia, too: the Serbs. The war was about to break, but Germany stood up with its ally, Austria, forcing the Russians and the Serbs to calm their passions.

By 1912, the Ottoman Empire was dying, and to share its former territories, a Balkan league was formed among Bulgaria, Macedonia, Serbia, and Greece. During the First Balkan War (1912-1913), the League of Balkans forced the Turks out of the Balkan region, and with them gone, a dangerous power vacuum formed in the region. European major forces— France, Austria, and Russia—met in London to arrange the post-war settlement. The result was the creation of a new nation, Albania. But this didn't resolve the problem in the Balkans. It only elevated the hostile situation and, to this day, the Balkan Peninsula remains the problematic region of Europe. Bulgaria asked for part of Macedonia, but its meddling in the settlement only sparked another war. The Second Balkan War started in 1913, and Bulgaria lost to allied Serbia, Romania, Greece, and even Turkey. Serbia and Greece divided Macedonia between themselves, and some of the Bulgarian territories near the Black Sea were ceded to Romania. But matters were not settled, as this conflict only stirred the various Balkan ethnic groups to aspire to nationalism.

The event which plunged Europe into conflict occurred on June 28, 1914, in Sarajevo (today's capital of Bosnia and Herzegovina).

Gavrilo Princip, a Bosnian nationalist, assassinated the Habsburg Archduke Franz Ferdinand (1863–1914). He was angry that Austria annexed Bosnia and Herzegovina and thought that killing the next in line to the Austro-Hungarian throne would shake the world enough to free his country from the imperial grasp. However, the outcome was much more violent and bloody. A war ensued, one that would, for the first time in human history, be fought between all major political world powers. At the time, the war was simply called "The Great War." The name World War I was given to it only after World War II proved that the world was still not safe from such large-scale conflicts.

Franz Ferdinand wasn't the only victim of the assassination. His wife, Sophie Chotek Ferdinand, was shot too. They were the guests of the provincial governor of Sarajevo, who had invited them to attend a military parade in the city. Gavrilo Princip also wasn't the only assassin. His companions had failed in previous attempts to kill the archduke by bombing his car. But the same day, when Franz Ferdinand was on his way to the hospital to visit those who were hurt in the bombing attempt, his driver made a wrong turn, and Gavrilo approached the car and shot two shots from his pistol. Gavrilo Princip was immediately apprehended, and during the later questioning, he revealed he was a member of the Bosnian nationalistic youth organization "Young Bosnia," which was trained and financed by the Serbian nationalistic group known as "the Black Hand." Even though the Serbian government learned about the assassination plans and made the leaders of the organization call it off, Gavrilo Princip and his co-conspirators continued with the plan. The assassination was supposed to trigger conflict between Austria and Serbia, and the plotters hoped Russia would join and help their Slavic relatives. But the outcome was much worse. The tensions between the Anglo-French alliance and Germany, created by Emperor Wilhelm II, was just waiting for a spark like this to enter into open conflict. Gavrilo Princip and the assassination of Franz Ferdinand were just the sparks the great European forces needed.

Austrians were outraged by the events of June 28th and called for revenge upon the Serbian people, counting on the support of Wilhelm II and their alliance with Germany. Russia was expected to side with Serbia in the conflict, but instead, it consulted with France. Together, they tried to find a peaceful solution to the problem. But, on July 23rd, the Austrians issued an ultimatum to Serbia. This infamous July Ultimatum was filled with humiliating demands the Serbians would surely decline, even if it meant war. The whole world accused Austria of deliberately pushing for war, but they were aware Austria's ally, Germany, was a very powerful military force that they were not prepared to fight at the time. Austria was permitted to send an ultimatum to Serbia. Crown Prince Alexander of Serbia asked Russia for support, but the only thing he managed to get was moral support. The Russians advised him to accept the ultimatum and not risk war. In the end, it seems Serbia accepted all the points of the July Ultimatum except Clause 6, which demanded Austro-Hungarian police operate on Serbian soil. At first, the Austrians were disappointed Serbia accepted the ultimatum, but they saw the rejection of Clause 6 as reason enough to attack. A conference was proposed to solve the issue further, as Europe saw the Serbian's willingness to adhere to the ultimatum, but Austria declined, wishing for war. On July 28th, war was officially declared, and Germany sought a way to back out of the conflict. Wilhelm II reached out to Britain, trying to make a treaty that would bind them to stay neutral, but it was too late. His previous actions had angered Britain, and the proposal was refused.

The Fighting

Early in August of 1914, all the European countries started recruiting for the upcoming war. Romanticized nationalistic pride took over as the people joined the army to fight for their king and country. From Moscow to Paris, millions of young men were joining the army, and everyone expected the conflict to be brief and to end before Christmas. In Germany, people were enthusiastic about the war, thinking they would surely be the absolute winners. Their goal was to display Germany's military dominance over Europe. Even the Social Democrats abandoned their pacifist endeavors once they were persuaded that Russia was the aggressor. Oddly enough, the Jews who were openly oppressed not so long before during the reign of Wilhelm I and his grandson Wilhelm II, were enthusiastically joining the German army to help in the fight for the fatherland.

In the 1890s, Germany devised a secret strategy known as the Schlieffen Plan, which would allow for quick mobilization of the troops in the case of conflict on two fronts. The plan included a quick occupation of France by dispatching forces through neutral Belgium and Luxembourg. Paris would fall before Russia even started mobilizing its army (due to the lack of infrastructure throughout the vast Russian regions). After taking France, Germany would easily turn its attention towards the east and help Austria fight Russia. While Germany occupied France, Austria planned to invade Serbia and later confront Russia. The plan was detailed, and it also relied on Italian help. But Italy declared it would stay neutral during the war. Without Italy, Germany and Austria were surrounded by their enemies and were known as the Central Powers. They had the promise of the Turkish sultan that he would join their alliance, but they could not rely on his word. Nevertheless, Germany continued with its plans and mobilized over 1.5 million soldiers.

During their crossing of Belgium, the German army immediately encountered a problem. They didn't think Belgium would organize resistance, but their passage through the neutral country was halted for a time when Belgian resistance caused them significant losses. The Germans had violated Belgian neutrality guaranteed by the treaty of 1837, and Britain reacted by joining the war on the side of France and Russia in the alliance known as the Triple Entente. The British army hurried to France to help slow the German occupation. The French army was stationed near the German border, as it hoped it could be faster and invade Germany. However, the French now had to move their army south to Paris, and mobilization was very slow. The first conflict between France and Germany occurred in September at the Battle of Marne, where the French managed to halt the German advance. Unfortunately, they too suffered great losses, and the conflict bogged down to a stalemate. Pushed by their officers, the young soldiers of both sides lost their lives in a fruitless offensive on enemy positions. Suffering trench fires and brutal assaults, the western front yielded no results for over four years. Millions of lives were lost in the suicide mission to advance towards the enemy territory, but neither side could make a decisive breakthrough. The Schlieffen Plan failed, and Germany was forced to divide its army and fight on two fronts.

The Russians surprised everyone by proving that the bad infrastructure of their empire, with its lack of railroads, was not a problem when it came to the mobilization of their army. Russians invaded East Prussia quickly. But a pair of brilliant German generals, Paul von Hindenburg and Erich Ludendorff, smashed their further advance. Back in Germany, they were celebrated as national heroes, and their victory over Russia helped lift the nationalistic spirit of the people even more. New recruits were pouring into the army and, very quickly, Germany was ready to invade Russia's Polish territories. But the campaigns in the east, although very successful, were short-lived, and Germany soon had to assume a defensive stance once again.

Austria managed to take Belgrade (the capital of Serbia) early during the conflict, but it also suffered great casualties. Because of this, Serbs managed to expel the Austrians in early 1915, and the Habsburg forces spent the rest of the year trying to invade Italy. To quickly deal with Serbia, Germany and Austria persuaded Bulgaria to join the war and invade Serbian territories. Pressured from the east by Bulgaria and from the west by Austria-Hungary, the Serbian army was crushed and forced to retreat through Albania. Through the snowy mountain ranges of Albania, the Serbian army suffered frost, hunger, and disease. More than 240,000 soldiers died in this endeavor, promptly named the "Albanian Golgotha" (the place where Jesus was crucified). Germany considered this a victory and, on November 29, 1915, issued a proclamation stating that the Serbian army was destroyed and that the Balkan front was closed. The Russian tsar had to intervene and threatened he would pull his army out of the war if allies France, Britain, and Italy didn't rush to rescue the Serbian army from Albania. The French president promised their transport ships would halt all transportations of goods and military equipment until the remnants of the Serbian army were delivered to safety. Around 5,000 soldiers died during the transportation, and they were buried at sea, near the small island of Vido (part of Greece). In their honor, Greek fishermen refused to catch fish in the area for the next fifty years.

The horrors of modern warfare took victims on all fronts. The similar destiny of suffering soldiers occurred throughout the continent. The industrial age had produced modern guns and rifles, and war became even more brutal, with millions of victims on both sides. The main tactic of World War I was to break the enemy's resolve through mass infantry attacks on their bases and trenches. The soldiers of both sides were constantly exposed to machine-gun fire and artillery bombardment, but the bloodiest battles of this conflict were waged in France. Verdun and the Somme were the scenes of the bloodiest carnage in Europe in 1916. The stalemate at Somme lasted for years, and more than a million soldiers lost their lives in futile attempts to overpower their opposers. Desperate to break the stalemate, Germans unleashed the horrors of chemical warfare, using poisonous mustard gas against French soldiers and leaving them to die in agony. The British army introduced innovative primitive tanks designed to crush enemy troops. Even with the use of such modern weaponry and chemicals, after three years of constant fighting, the western front barely managed to move ten miles (16 km).

Wilhelm II lost his faith in German military power as victory slipped out of his hands. But aside from its inability to move the western front forward, Germany also replaced its civilian leadership for a military government. Due to the prolonged war, the country's economy suffered, and all that kept the people from revolting against their government were the victories on the eastern front. Russians were pushed to a retreat, and in Moscow, both soldiers and workers rioted. The imperialistic government was toppled, and Tzar Nicholas II was forced to abdicate. In November 1917, the Bolsheviks took over Russia, and Germany helped install Communist leader Vladimir Lenin (1870–1924) in Russia. In turn, Lenin sued for peace with Germany, taking Russia out of the war. By the Treaty of Brest-Litovsk signed between Germany and Russia, Germany gained control over the Polish territories as well as the Baltic States, Finland, and Ukraine. The Allies saw through the punitive nature of this treaty and used it as propaganda to deal harshly with the Germans during the rest of the war. Back home, German radical Socialists realized the imperialistic intentions behind Germany's involvement in the war and started their own propaganda, which helped turn the workers against the war. Germany was on the verge of failing in its war efforts. However, the government managed to deal with the workers' strikes and continue the war.

By 1918, the United States joined the war and sent troops to the western front to help relieve the French and British army. As the Germans could no longer bear the stalemate at Somme, they planned a final, massive assault along the whole western front, which ranged from Belgium to northeastern France, Switzerland, and the German territories in the northwest. In March, the Germans managed to push the front seventy-five miles from Paris and started shelling the French capital. In Berlin, celebrations had already started, as everyone believed victory was near. But the Allies refused to surrender, and they managed to hold the position for months. German soldiers were already at the end of their strength by July when the Allies managed to push them back to their previous trench position on the Belgian border. Germans sacrificed more than 250,000 soldiers during this last offensive, and they gained nothing. This costly defeat was a final straw for the civilians of Germany. Soon, anti-war demonstrations swept the whole country as people wondered why they had allowed more than six million German soldiers to die.

At the same time, Austria, Turkey, and Bulgaria started losing the war on the eastern front. Bulgaria and Turkey were the first to drop out of the war in early 1918, and Austria-Hungary sued for peace on November 3, 1918. The nationalist uprisings throughout the Habsburg Empire shook Austria, and it could no longer support the war. Germany suddenly found itself completely alone against the Allied powers, and it anxiously accepted defeat. It was the new liberal chancellor from Baden, Prince Maximilian (1867–1929), who carried the full authority to negotiate peace. He approached the Americans, first offering to accept their proposal of a post-war settlement based on national self-determination. But American President Woodrow Wilson refused to negotiate with Germany due to its imperialistic nature and intentions during the war. The situation back in Germany reached dangerous levels as the people continued to protest the war. Even the navy mutinied and caused such chaos in Germany that the Kaiser's advisors started pressing Wilhelm II to abdicate. Wilhelm didn't want to part with the crown, so he offered to abandon his imperial titles and remain king of Prussia. But it was too late for compromises. On November 9, 1918, Prince Maximilian of Baden proclaimed to the public that Emperor Wilhelm II had abdicated. Germany fragmented into a series of ethnic enclaves, and all the ex-emperor could do was sit back and watch his empire crumble.

Fearing that the Communists would take control over Germany after the emperor stepped down, a Socialist politician, Philipp Scheidemann, declared the rise of the German Republic. He had no authority to act, and the radical leaders responded by announcing the start of a Communist regime. Prince Maximilian resigned as chancellor out of the fear of the approaching Communist revolution, and power was handed to Socialist leader Friedrich Ebert. On November 10, Ebert managed to establish a provisional government comprised of Social Democratic Party members. Their first task was to replace the old imperial constitution with a new one more suitable for the German Republic. The Republic was organized with an elected president and a chancellor appointed by the Reichtag. But before any of this could be done, the provisional government had to officially end the war. On the 11th hour, of the 11th day, of the 11th month, Germany finally accepted defeat and capitulated to the Triple Entente. Almost ten million lives lost later, World War I ended.

The Weimar Republic

At the end of World War I, the Treaty of Versailles was signed, by which Germany lost many of its territories gained before and during the war. Alsace-Lorraine France had to be returned to France, and the territories gained with the Treaty of Brest-Litovsk were lost. The treaty also disarmed Germany, obliging it to have an army limited to only 100,000 men and no fleet, submarines, or airplanes. Germans also had to accept responsibility for the whole war and pay an indemnity of more than thirty-two billion US dollars. French troops occupied the Rhineland until the full amount of money was paid. The Treaty of Versailles left the citizens of Germany in shock. They had a hard time accepting responsibility for the war since they had no part in the Austrian provocations of Serbia. Furthermore, German propaganda insisted that Germany didn't lose the war since its territories were never occupied. Germans held to the fact that their forces retreated from the war in goodwill, and they felt that they were harshly punished without reason. The people felt that the provisional government had betrayed them by allowing such a draconic punishment to happen. But the truth was that the German provisional government had no other choice but to agree to the terms of the victorious Allied Powers.

The situation in Germany only escalated. Inspired by the Russian Bolsheviks, a Communist group known as the Spartacists arose. Their leaders, Rosa Luxemburg and Karl Liebknecht, organized a massive rebellion in Berlin. Still, the post-war elections continued, and the new government emerged while the army was dealing with the rebellion in Berlin. Even though Rosa Luxemburg and Karl Liebknecht were killed during the brutal crackdown of the uprising, the Communists continued their violent revolution. The government, mostly made up out of SDP members but also consisting of Radical Socialists and Catholic Centre, had to retreat to Weimar so it could work on the constitution. The violence on the streets of Berlin continued, and it started spreading to other cities in Germany. But the country elected a new president, SDP statesman Friedrich Ebert. He ratified the new constitution, which was a remarkably progressive document guaranteeing democratic rights and participation for all citizens. The German president would serve for seven years, while the members of the National Assembly (Reichstag) served for four years. The national elections would determine how many seats each political party would occupy during the four-year mandates. The president's duty was to elect a chancellor who would form a cabinet and, with its help, govern the state. Even though the government formed in this way was liberal and a true representative of the republic and its people, many resented it for accepting the terms of the Treaty of Versailles. They also saw the problem in Article 48 of the new constitution, which gave the president the right to dismiss the constitution and the Reichstag in times of crisis. This would allow the president to wield absolutist power in the case of a new war, something the German populace dreaded.

From the beginning, the Weimar Republic was unstable and suffered the attacks of radical political groups. In 1920, these attacks turned into an uprising when Wolfgang Kapp, an ardent nationalist, led Freikorps (a volunteer military unit) soldiers to occupy Berlin and overthrow the government. But his attempt was unsuccessful, mainly because he had no support from the people. In Bavaria, right-wing extremists were more successful. Munich was turned into the main hub for radical nationalists. Communists were on the move, too. In Ruhr, they started a workers' uprising that required the intervention of militia. Soon, the French got involved, and to pacify the Ruhr region, they occupied it in 1923. But the result was the opposite of what they hoped to achieve. The occupation only inflamed radical nationalism, and although passive, resistance continued. All these uprisings and attempts to overthrow the government didn't bring anything good to Germany. Its economic recovery after the war was slowed down by the political instability within the country. The German national currency became nearly worthless, and people found themselves unable to afford a loaf of bread. The Weimar government printed new bills, trying to keep pace with inflation, but this only made things worse. It was this economic crisis that sparked further political unrest, and another failed coup occurred in 1923 at the Munich Beer Hall. However, this putsch was led by an ambitious military veteran and politician, Adolf Hitler.

The Weimar government managed to prevent the total collapse of the German economy by issuing a new currency, and the economy slowly recovered. With a better standard of living, the violent uprisings started calming down. But the improvement of the situation in Germany was only an illusion. The state entered a new phase: the calm before the storm. In the second half of the 1920s, Germany saw economic, cultural, and political renewal, and its post-war diplomatic isolation ended. Relations with Britain, France, and the United States were repaired, and the Allied forces even decided to soften the sanctions against Germany. The Dawes Plan, signed in 1924, convinced Britain and France to lower the war reparations Germany still owed. By 1926, foreign relations were so good that Germany was even invited to join the League of Nations.

Berlin's abundant nightlife and cultural ascent gave the impression of a better life—but the storm clouds were gathering above Germany once again. Socialist statesmen Ebert died in 1925, and a new president was elected, the aging war hero Paul von Hindenburg. The new president still held a grudge over the humiliating Treaty of Versailles, and he made a deal with the Soviet Union in 1926 by which the German army was permitted to train in Soviet territory. This way, the German military defied the post-war limitation to maintain a small army. Behind the back of the Allied forces, Germany was preparing for a new war.

In 1929, the world was shaken by another economic crisis known to history as the Great Depression. The US stock market crashed, and the loans it was giving to Germany had to cease. Without these loans, Germany's economy faltered, as it was once again drowning in the debts of the war indemnity. The very next year, the consequences of the Great Depression were very severe in Germany. Businesses were shut down, factories had to stop producing, and the unemployment rates skyrocketed. German society was in the clutches of fear and desperation, while its government proved unable to fight the new crisis. The spreading anxiety was a perfect breeding ground for the rise of radical nationalism, and in the new elections held in 1930, the radical political parties won. The SDP managed to hold the most chairs in the National Assembly (24%), but the National Socialist Party, better known as the Nazi Party, won an unbelievable 18% of the chairs. The radical Communists also had a very high number, at 13%. The Reichstag was often in conflict as the dramatically different political parties argued about new legislation. But the fighting wasn't kept within the Reichstag, soon pouring onto the streets of Berlin and other major cities of Germany. Fights between the Nazis and the Communists, who were unable to maintain a democratic parliament, resulted in bloodshed in the streets. The situation quickly escalated, and President Hindenburg felt forced to invoke Article 48 of the constitution, which granted him the power to make all the decisions in the case of a state emergency. The Weimar Republic was destroyed by the economic crisis and by the radical political parties which won the elections.

Chapter 11 – World War II

Warsaw, the capital of Poland, in ruins
https://en.wikipedia.org/wiki/World_War_II#/media/File:Warsaw_Old_Town_1945.jpg

Hitler's Rise and Nazism in Germany

Adolf Hitler at a political rally in 1933
https://upload.wikimedia.org/wikipedia/commons/6/66/N%C3%B
Crnberg_Reichsparteitag_Hitler_retouched.jpg

In 1932, Adolf Hitler almost won the new presidential elections but was defeated by the old Hindenburg, who somehow managed to get 53% of the votes. Adolf Hitler was an obscure Austrian who migrated to Bavaria right before World War I. He enlisted in the German army, where he found a sense of belonging after his failed career as an artist. Even after the war, he continued working for the German army as a spy, monitoring the radical political parties emerging in Germany after the war. He also held resentment for the Treaty of Versailles and Germany's loss of the war. But instead of accepting defeat, he found scapegoats to blame: the Socialists and the Jews. Even though Jews massively joined the German army during the war, Hitler convinced the people that Jews were nothing more than foreign traitors who backstabbed Germany, sabotaging its war efforts. To bolster his political career, Hitler joined the German Workers' Party in 1919 and quickly climbed to leadership of the organization. Soon he changed the name of the party to the National Socialist German Workers' Party (NSDAP), shortened to the Nazi Party. He often spoke against the Weimar Republic, and his passion quickly attracted people to him. During the Beer Hall Putsch in Munich (1923), he was jailed for nine months. He took that time to write his manifesto, known as *Mein Kampf*. In it, he carefully chronicled his twisted delusions about the superiority of the German race and described how Jews and previous Socialist Party stood in the way of German greatness. By 1932, Hitler's Nazi Party became a massive political force that continued to grow, fueled by people's resentment towards the Treaty of Versailles and the inability of the current government to deal with the economic crisis of the Great Depression.

In the Reichstag elections of 1932, the Nazi party won 38% of the votes, surpassing the previously popular SDP, which won only 21%. The Communist Party was far behind, with only 14% of the votes. Despite the obvious win, President Hindenburg refused to make Adolf Hitler his chancellor. Instead, he chose military officer Franz von Papen, who soon proved to be unpopular among the delegates of the Reichstag and the people. The elections had to be repeated, and the Nazis' growing popularity won them over 200 seats in the National Assembly. Hitler's growing popularity was a concern, but Hindenburg saw replacing von Papen as an opportunity to get back on Germany's political scene. He formed a coalition between the German National People's Party (DNVP) and the Nazis. When von Papen promised Hindenburg he could control the Nazis, the president finally agreed to make Hitler his chancellor. On January 30, 1933, Adolf Hitler officially became Germany's chancellor, with von Papen as his vice-chancellor. Only a year later, Hitler assumed the title "führer" (leader), ending the Weimar democracy.

Since 1926, the Nazi Party had held annual meetings in Nuremberg, providing Hitler with a great opportunity to spread his propaganda. In 1934, the meeting gathered more than one million

Germans, and the famous young filmmaker and photographer, Leni Riefenstahl, was tasked with bringing Hitler's vision of Aryan superiority to life. Her movie, the *Triumph of the Will,* was proclaimed one of the most successful and dangerous propaganda movies in the world. The film shows Hitler delivering one of his maniacal speeches to the assembled masses. Through careful choreography of the masses and innovative shots, Leni delivered a message of German purity to those who couldn't attend the meeting in person. But what she failed to convey through her movie was the Nazis' real intention—to purify Germany of non-Aryan elements through war and extermination. For Hitler, the biggest danger to national unity and greatness were the Jews, Communists, and both physically and mentally impaired people. Only with these dangers out of sight could Germany conquer other nations and climb to sit on top of the world's order.

Hitler's speeches were filled with crude and violent rhetoric. This appealed to a population that already resented the Jews and feared the Communists. No matter what classes they came from, supporters flocked around their new führer. Traumatized by the Great Depression, middle-class citizens and workers of Germany, as well as old war veterans and young members of the Freikorps, all supported the Nazis and their charismatic leader. Students and intellectuals weren't spared—the mass media used to spread Nazi propaganda appealed to them, too. Attracted by the technology the party used, as well as by its efficiency and racial pseudoscience, universities succumbed to Hitler's propaganda.

In 1933, Hitler also invoked Article 48 of the Weimar Republic constitution and took emergency power into his hands. He used it to outlaw the SDP and thus eliminate the only remaining opposition to his political ideals. Thousands of leftists were arrested, but he did not stop there. He also persecuted the right-wing politicians who dared to challenge him. By summer, the Nazi Party was the only political entity within Germany. To completely unify the state under his ideology, Hitler gradually outlawed independent trade unions as well as the country's state governments. In 1933, the Jews of Germany started feeling the first signs of oppression caused by the rabid anti-Semitism of the Nazis. Jewish civil servants, teachers, and jurists were the first to be removed from their posts. In the end, Hitler took control of all German media, and opposition newspapers and radio stations were banned. He chose a propaganda minister, Joseph Goebbels, whose task was to not only convey the Nazi ideology to the masses but also control all the media people were consuming.

June 30, 1934, is remembered as the "Night of the Long Knives," when, under the command of Heinrich Himmler, Nazis murdered their own party members who were considered unfit. Among them were members of the Sturmabteilung (Storm Detachment), the most radical Nazi paramilitary wing. Their leader, Ernst Röhm, died that night, too. Hitler justified this purge of the party by claiming their radicalism could eventually lead to separation. Only through murder could he consolidate his dominion over the whole Nazi Party. The publicity approved of Hitler's authority, and as soon as President Hindenburg died on August 2, 1934, Hitler proclaimed himself führer, the leader of Germany, putting an end to any possible individual claims on leadership.

Once Hitler consolidated his power, he started working to repair the German economy and army. He established his inner circle, made of Minister of Propaganda Goebbels, Reichsführer Himmler, and the military leader Hermann Göring, and together they worked to make Germany a powerhouse of Europe. Göring used the industrial factories that had succumbed to the Great Depression to start military production. Consequently, Germany's unemployment rates decreased, while its manufacturing production increased. The workers and the industrialists were so delighted with the economic rise of Germany that they were ready to forgive their lack of democratic freedoms. However, even though Hitler enjoyed widespread support, he also had to rely on terror and violence. As early as 1933, he formed a secret police force, the Gestapo, and outlined plans for a system of concentration camps where Jews and political and criminal prisoners labored and died in horrible conditions. In 1935, the appearance of the Nuremberg Laws excluded Jews from German citizenship. This set of laws strictly defined how to classify Jews and non-Aryans and forbade marriage and intercourse between Jews and Germans. Only those who were of pure German blood and their relatives were eligible for Reich citizenship. The rest had no rights and were considered only to be the Reich's subjects. Jews were strictly forbidden from employing German females younger than forty-five to prevent the accidental mix of blood. By 1938, cities across Germany constructed ghettos, where the Jews were to live in confinement.

The night of November 9, 1938, is remembered as the Kristallnacht (the Night of the Broken Glass), when Goebbels' anti-Semitic propaganda fueled the German population into a violent rage. Thousands of Jewish homes, businesses, and temples were destroyed, and countless Jews were beaten, killed, or taken to the concentration camps. To avoid further oppression, more than half of Germany's Jews escaped the country. Those who stayed did so willingly to take care of aging family members or protect family businesses built over the generations. Many even stayed in hopes that the madness would soon pass because they believed it couldn't last for long. While his accomplices continued anti-Semitic pogroms across the country, Hitler focused on rebuilding the army with which he would conquer Europe and provide living space for the superior Aryans. His first move was to withdraw Germany from the League of Nations and take back the industrial heartland of Germany, the Saarland, which had been under French occupation since the end of the war. In 1935, the League of Nations organized a plebiscite in Saarland, and 90% of its citizens chose to join Germany rather than stay under French rule. Inspired by this non-aggressive victory, Hitler declared he was pulling Germany out of the restrictions imposed by the Treaty of Versailles and that he was building the army. The European powers were alarmed, and Britain, France, and Italy met to discuss how they would react. But, since they could not come up with a unanimous resolution, Hitler continued with his activities unopposed.

In 1936, the Spanish Civil War raged, and Hitler took the opportunity of Europe in dismay to make another threat. He declared that Germany would no longer respect the territorial boundaries imposed on her after World War I and that it would seek to expand towards the west. This was a direct threat to France, but Britain was unwilling to risk the war and voted against new sanctions on Germany during the meeting of the League of Nations. This divide between the European allies was proof enough for Hitler that he had no strong opposition. He moved his troops to the Rhineland, violating the Treaty of Versailles. However, France and its allies decided not to respond, and the opportunity to deal with the Nazis early on was lost. Through its inaction, Europe allowed Hitler to rejuvenate the German military and sway the whole of Germany into his megalomania.

Hitler planned for war, and to successfully lead one, he needed allies. First, in July of 1936, he turned to his native Austria, which he already planned to absorb into Nazi Germany. By October, he signed an agreement with Italy's fascist leader, Benito Mussolini. He also sent troops to Spain to help their fascist leader, General Franco, to overthrow the republican government. Japan joined last, at the end of 1936, and concluded the formation of the aggressive coalition known as the Axis Powers. To stop the outbreak of war, European powers started caving to Hitler's demands in hopes of appeasing him. First in the series of demands was to bring all the Germans living in the neighboring countries under the rule of the Third Reich. Nazi leaders called their country the "Third Reich," as it followed the Second (the German Empire ruled by Wilhelm I and Wilhelm II). The First Reich was considered to be the Holy Roman Empire started by Emperor Otto in 962.

To unify Austria and Germany, Hitler moved his troops on March 9, 1938, and they entered Vienna. Hitler followed four days later and was cheered by the pro-Nazi masses, which called for Austria's absorption into the Third Reich. All the European powers could do while watching Hitler's rise to power was complain, and they remained inactive even when Austria was taken. Hitler's next target was the multiethnic republic of Czechoslovakia. There, Hitler became a hero and representative of ethnic Germans living within the republic's Sudetenland, an industrial region on the border with Germany. Supported by their native country, the Germans of Sudetenland started holding demonstrations, demanding the autonomy of the region. To support the cause in Czechoslovakia, German troops started gathering on the border. Britain tried to resolve the situation and sent Prime Minister Neville Chamberlain to talk some sense into the German leader. But Hitler threatened open warfare over Sudetenland, and the Europeans backed down again. France and Britain allowed Hitler to annex this region, but they promised to defend the rest of Czechoslovakia if the need arose. Seeing the perfect opportunity to start the war he desperately wanted, Hitler claimed all of Czechoslovakia, but, in the end, agreed to negotiate. On September 29, 1938, he met with the leaders of Britain, France, and Italy, and they settled on the Munich Agreement, by which all regions of Czechoslovakia inhabited by Germans would vote whether they wanted to join the Third Reich. What was left of the republic would be protected by Britain and France. While the British celebrated avoiding war, Hitler moved his troops through Czechoslovakia. In March of 1939, the German army overran the republic, and Hitler led his victorious soldiers through Prague. Britain and France did nothing to stop him, even though they promised the safeguard of Czechoslovakia.

Britain and France made similar promises of safeguard to Poland in case of German aggression, but Czechoslovakia proved to Hitler that they wouldn't do anything. By April of 1939, he planned a full-scale invasion of Poland and started negotiating with Soviet leader Joseph Stalin. In August of 1939, they made a non-aggression pact, which they used to peacefully divide Poland between themselves. In the meantime, the Nazi Party financed the Germans of Danzig (Gdansk in modern-day Poland) to demand autonomy and create a pretext for invasion. Confident that the Soviet Union wouldn't meddle, Hitler started the invasion of Poland on September 1, 1939. However, he was wrong about France and Britain, as they declared war on Germany only two days later. World War II had started.

The Course of the War

London after the Blitz
https://upload.wikimedia.org/wikipedia/commons/5/5d/View_from_St_Paul%27s_Cathedral_after_the_Blitz.jpg

Germany started the war with new tactics, which involved an easily-movable force consisting of speedy tanks that were supported by air attacks. The goal was a quick victory and conquest of territories before the enemy realized what had hit them. The tactic was conveniently named blitzkrieg, the "lightning war." Although the blitzkrieg strategy was first used in 1936 during the Spanish

Civil War, now Hitler was attacking Poland. The mechanized infantry and tank divisions attacked violently and quickly, while dedicated special units interrupted Polish communication and supply lines, creating confusion and fear. Poland didn't even have time to mobilize its army before the blitzkrieg was over. But German victory wasn't only due to these new, innovative tactics. Hitler's earlier deal with Stalin put Poland between two enemies. While more than two million German troops invaded from the west and raced towards Warsaw, the Russian army attacked from the east. The Poles weren't prepared for two fronts, and there was nothing they could do to stop the invasions. Warsaw fell on September 27, 1939, and Poland was divided between the Germans and the Russian dictator.

Blitzkrieg surprised not only Poland but also the British and the French. Even though the two powers promised they would safeguard this country, they were unable to mobilize in time to mount a defense. They could only stand idly by and watch while Poland was being divided between the Nazis and the Soviets. Seeing how slow European powers were to react, Hitler set off to execute his big plan, "The Final Solution," with which he would exterminate all Jews. Even though the realization of the plan started in Europe, it was by no means constricted to this continent alone. Nazis dared to dream about world conquest and the spread of the Aryan race over all continents. Poland was just a starting point. The Jews were forced to wear a yellow Star of David so they could be easily recognized. Soon, their businesses and all their possessions were confiscated, and they were confined in the ghettos. Once in the ghettos, the Polish population of Jews started succumbing to hunger and disease. Over three million Jews were registered in Poland, and that number halved before the western Allies could react.

Hitler's move towards Poland gave Russia an excuse to invade the Baltic states of Latvia, Lithuania, and Estonia. The Soviets also had their eye on Finland, but they found this country to be much more resilient. The Germans conquered Denmark and Norway in March of 1940, while Britain and France still gathered their army. After their swift victories, the Germans installed puppet governments in the conquered areas, led by native Nazi sympathizers. In the spring of 1940, the Netherlands, Belgium, and Luxembourg were also conquered in preparation for the invasion of France. Once more, Hitler employed blitzkrieg tactics, and the Germans moved towards Paris with remarkable speed. There was no one to stop them. The British tried to help, sending their forces across the North Sea, but heavy German airplane bombardment had them stranded on the beach at Dunkirk, unable to move forward. The remaining British vessels tried to save their soldiers, and even local fishermen and pleasure yacht captains joined the rescue operation. In late May of 1940, more than 300,000 British and French soldiers managed to escape to England. But tens of thousands of them were killed during the German blitzkrieg. France was defeated, and it officially surrendered on June 22nd. Southern France was turned over to a puppet government under the leadership of collaborator Henri Philippe Pétain. In history, it remains known as Vichy France, the name of the resort town where the new government was headquartered.

It took Hitler only two weeks to conquer France, and his next goal was England. But the major challenge he faced was defeating the Royal Air Force that guarded the sky over the English Channel. The German Luftwaffe (Air Force) was commanded by Hitler's personal friend, Hermann Göring. The Battle of Britain soon began (July 10–October 31, 1940), and it proved to be one of the turning points of World War II. British and German bomber fleets were ruthless, and civilians also suffered from their attacks. Bombers fought not only each other but also the transportation network and some of the major industrial cities. London was bombed regularly. To save their capital, the British came up with the idea of turning off all lights during the night so the enemy pilots wouldn't be able to see the city and target it. The German cities weren't so lucky, and some of them were destroyed. Dresden, for example, was razed to the ground for being a major industrial and communication center. But this city was even more than that. It was a military strongpoint, a city designated to be a defense against a possible Soviet invasion. The Royal Air Force and the United States Army ruthlessly bombed the city for what it represented. However, most of the casualties, which numbered between 18,000 and 25,000, were women and children. For this reason, the bombing of Dresden is one of the most controversial Alliance actions of World War II.

Germany was never able to defeat the Royal Air Force, and by the early summer of 1941, Hitler abandoned his plans to conquer Britain. Instead, he turned against his former ally, Stalin. The relationship between two dictators had cooled off a year earlier when both Hitler and Stalin laid claim to the oil fields of Ploesti, in modern Romania. While the Germans warred against Britain, the Soviets annexed the Baltic states and took Basarabia, which was previously under Romanian control. Russians continued to put pressure on Romania, which decided to side with Germany and join the secret plan of invading Russia. For Hitler, Russia wasn't the enemy just because it claimed the oil. It was a matter of racial supremacy, as well. Like Jews, Slavs were a lesser race in Hitler's eyes, and their territory needed to be populated with the superior Aryan race. By 1941, Germany had conquered Yugoslavia as well as Hungary and Greece, making them a part of the Axis Powers. Hitler had his troops stations in the Balkans, where they prepared for the invasion of the Union of Soviet Socialist Republics (USSR). He made a deal with neutral Sweden and Finland to allow safe passage for the troops coming from Norway. Everything was set, and on June 22, 1941, under the code name Operation Barbarossa, the invasion of Russia began.

Over three million German troops crossed the Russian border from three different points: Finland, Poland, and Romania. Repeating the blitzkrieg tactics they had used to occupied France,

Germany drove deep into the Russian territory. By December 21nd, the Red Army was almost defeated as Hitler's troops moved towards Moscow. Hitler's army had reached a position only fifteen miles outside the USSR capital when the bitter Russian winter halted their advance. Badly equipped, German troops froze in the field, dying of hunger and frost while the Red Army regrouped for a counterattack. Accustomed to harsh conditions, the Russian army had the advantage and managed to eventually drive the Germans out of the country. The Russian front was the bloodiest point of World War II. The atrocities committed in the Soviet Union are some of the harshest actions against humanity that history ever saw. Aside from killing off a million Russian Jews, Germans killed 3.3 million Red Army soldiers and an uncountable number of civilians. The methods used to deal with the Slavs varied from gassing to mass shootings and planned starvation. Hitler's goal was to confiscate food from people and redirect it to Germany while the Russian soldiers and civilians starved to death. The estimated Soviet death count during World War II is over twenty-six million, of which eleven million were soldiers. This number represents 95% of the war casualties between the three major Alliance forces: Britain, Russia, and the United States of America. The bloodiest battle of World War II, the Battle of Stalingrad (August 23, 1942–February 2, 1943) completely turned the tide of war. The losses Germany suffered during the five months of constant battle in front of this city were never again recouped. Even though Hitler redirected soldiers from the western front to the east, they were unable to achieve any more major victories on Russian soil. The eastern front was at a stalemate.

In the west, Germany still held sway over Europe. Japan forced the United States to join the war by bombing Pearl Harbor on December 7, 1941. The United States retaliated in the Battle of Midway (June 1942) by bombing the Japanese fleet, making it useless for the rest of the war. In October of 1942, the British and the Americans combined their forces to attack the Germans and

Italians stationed in North Africa. Their success marked a change in the course of the war, but the war was far from over—the nightmare has only just begun. When Anglo-American forces landed on Sicily in June of 1943, the German alliance with Italy crumbled. Italians were forced to retreat from war while the Allied forces marched on Rome. A year later, the Americans entered Rome and Italy and joined the Allies against Nazi Germany. After a few days, the invasion of Normandy, known as D-day, took place.

On Tuesday, June 6, 1944, the massive force of Allied soldiers landed on the beaches of Normandy, in northern France. Under the codename Operation Neptune, the Allied forces disembarked the overseas carriers while the air force offered them protection. From the beaches of Normandy, they advanced to break the German garrisons and establish the Allies' foothold in France. At this point, the liberation of France (and later the rest of Europe) began. Allied forces were fighting their way forward while under the constant attack of the Germans, who defended their position in northern France. It took several months for the British and American soldiers to conquer some of the strategic points along the Normandy coast, but the efforts to bring warfare to Europe's mainland were successful. Gradually, the German frontier was pushed back, and the Nazi soldiers were forced to go on the defensive. Both eastern and western fronts saw a major change. By 1944, Germany felt its shortage of men, and those who survived fought a losing battle. The beginning of 1945 saw the Red Army of the Soviet Union ready to invade the German territories from the east, while the rest of the Allied forces would push from the west. But Hitler wouldn't give up. He still thought he could turn the tides of the war, but his big final plan never saw the light of day. In February of 1945, the Russians were nearing Berlin, while the Americans and the British were just crossing the Rhine. On April 30, 1945, finally realizing that Germany was helpless, Adolf Hitler committed suicide with his wife, Eva Braun. Two days later,

Russians overran Berlin, and German forces everywhere started surrendering.

The official fall of Germany occurred on May 7, 1945. Admiral Karl Dönitz, who took control over Germany after Hitler, declared Germany's full surrender to the Supreme Commander of the Allied Expeditionary Force, General Dwight Eisenhower, who would later become the president of the United States. World War II—the result of one person's megalomania and Europe's unresolved problem after World War I—officially ended, leaving Europe in ruins. Germany was defeated and its people left in disgrace to further suffer foreign rule. The Soviets occupied eastern parts of Germany, and as if to punish the Germans for daring to invade mother Russia, they raped, pillaged, and murdered civilians. After the initial shock of losing the war, the people of Germany had to face the atrocities they had committed while under the spell of Hitler's propaganda. They had to confront the rest of the world, which blamed them for the deaths of millions of Jews and an uncountable number of soldiers and civilians.

The Holocaust

Map of Europe showing the location of all major concentration camps, massacres, and deportation routes
https://en.wikipedia.org/wiki/The_Holocaust#/media/File:Extermin ation_camps_in_occupied_Poland_(2007_borders).png

While the Germans fought the Red Army in the invasion of Russia, Hitler doubled his efforts to eradicate the Jews of Europe. He set up a special paramilitary organization known as the Einsatzgruppen to round up the Communists, the Gypsies, and the Jews for mass executions. These death squads of Einsatzgruppen were commanded by Heinrich Himmler and his Schutzstaffel, the Protection Squadron commonly known as the SS. The members of the SS were chosen for their racial purity and their devotion to Nazi ideology. They alone were responsible for the death of hundreds of thousands of people. But their methods were ineffective, and in January of 1942, the commanding SS officers gathered in Berlin to come up with the "Final Solution of the Jewish Question."

Himmler, who deeply believed in the Nazi ideology of racial purity, believed that the mass shootings were damaging the mental health of the SS soldiers. Besides that, they were inefficient when applied to large-scale mass extermination. Together with Hitler and another SS officer, Reinhard Heydrich, Himmler drafted concentration and work camps and planned their expansion with the addition of gas chambers in which people would be killed by poisonous gas. These camps were first raised in the occupied territories of Poland, and with time, in other parts of Europe as well. Some of the most well-known concentration camps are still in Poland, including Auschwitz and Treblinka, and they serve as standing monuments, reminders of the Holocaust and human brutality.

The Nazis were often aided by frightened local people or collaborators when they rounded up Jews for transport to the death camps. They used all the modern industrial infrastructure to help them realize their extermination plans. Aryan ideology was so important to Nazis that they diverted some of the resources needed for war to fuel the trains that took Jews to concentration camps. By the end of World War II, around six million Jews had died in the Holocaust. But they weren't the only ones. Germans imprisoned and executed political and religious dissidents, Soviet prisoners of war, the Gypsies, and all the people Nazis considered degenerate (racially impure, homosexuals, mentally and physically disabled, etc.).

When it was evident that Germany was losing the war, the mass extermination didn't stop. 1944 was the year most people were killed in Auschwitz—over 500,000. Jews from Hungary were sent there to be immediately killed. By mid-1944, Europe had lost two-thirds of its Jewish population to the Nazi regime. Facing the Soviet invasion from the east, the Germans quickly dismantled their death camps, leaving no evidence of what was going on in them. The surviving inmates were pushed on a death march to the camps in the west, in Germany or Austria. Sick, exhausted, and starved, many people were unable to finish their journey. If they fell behind, the Germans would immediately kill them. But in the west, the same destiny awaited them—the gas chamber and the cremation furnace. At the end of the war, when the Allied forces marched into German territories, they were horrified by the scenes they found in the camps. The unburied bodies of starved inmates numbered into the thousands in a single pile. The Red Cross took care of most of the Holocaust survivors, but many of them were past salvation. Some of them died due to malnutrition and the sicknesses they were exposed to in the camps even after the liberation.

Chapter 12 – Modern Germany

After World War II was over, the Allied powers gathered at the Potsdam Conference, which lasted from July 17th until August 2, 1945. The main goal was to decide what to do with Germany, which had surrendered unconditionally. The Allies divided Germany into four administrative territories to be governed by Britain, the United States, France, and the Soviet Union. The three western zones occupied by the British, French, and the Americans cooperated very closely, but the eastern zone under the Soviets strove for separatism. A dangerous rift between the east and the west was created, and even the former capital of Germany felt this division. Berlin was divided among the Allies, even though it was positioned deep within the Soviet zone. However, the western powers had free access to their part of the city to supply people with everything they might need.

While the western powers worked to stabilize the economy of post-war Germany, Russia concentrated on tightening its grip on Eastern Europe. When the Allies issued a common currency for the entirety of Germany to improve the conditions within the country, Russia responded with anger.

Post-War Germany

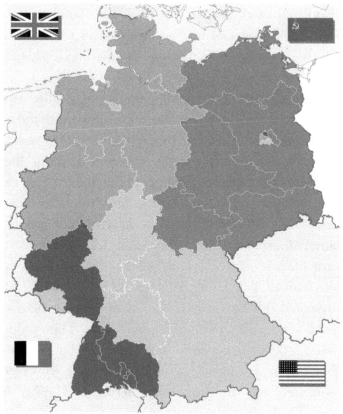

The occupation and division of Germany
https://en.wikipedia.org/wiki/Allied-
occupied_Germany#/media/File:Deutschland_Besatzungszonen_8
_Jun_1947_-_22_Apr_1949.svg

After the war, the German nation, as well as its country, was in ruins. Many Germans lost their homes in the ruthless bombing of major German cities at the end of the war. Millions of refugees of German ethnicities poured into the country once they lost their homes in the German-controlled territories of Czechoslovakia, Poland, the Baltic States, and other Balkan countries. They required homes, sustenance, and medical care. But they were not the only ones. More than a million ex-inmates from concentration camps had to be provided for by the Allies. Some were willing to leave Germany and settle in the United States or Britain, but many decided to stay and search for their lost family, homes, or possessions. The chaos of war brought hunger to Germany, and the nation was starving while the Allies worked tirelessly to rebuild the country.

Before they could start rebuilding Germany, the victorious Allies had to denazify the population. This started with the arrest of former Nazi officials and collaborators, but the effort was expanded to civilians, who were thoroughly questioned about their war activities. War crime tribunals were established to try war atrocities and other violations of human rights. Known as the Nuremberg Trials, they were conducted under the international laws of war to justly punish those who were responsible for Nazi leadership as well as for the war crimes. Adolf Hitler, Heinrich Himmler, and Goebbels had all killed themselves at the end of the war and obviously could not be tried. However, twenty-four Nazi officials were tried and convicted of different war crimes. Their punishment varied from a death sentence to imprisonment, but several of the high officials were found not guilty. Among those who received a death sentence was Reichsmarsall Hermann Göring, but he committed suicide the night before his execution.

During the Potsdam Conference, it was decided that Germany should pay war indemnities to the Allies worth $23 billion. However, since the country was in a post-war economic crisis, the Allies agreed that the payment could be made in industrial machinery and materials. Many factories were closed and dismantled, and Germany never fully paid the war reparation in money. But the Allies took Germany's scientists, intellectuals, and civilians and conscripted them into forced labor in France, Britain, the United States, Belgium, and in occupied Germany. But while western Allies worked on repairing Germany, the Soviet Union sought to make its eastern part into a Communist puppet state. They dismantled all of Eastern Germany's industries and sent them to Russia by railroad. The banks and remaining factories were nationalized, and soon the Soviets started confiscating agricultural land so it could be converted into communal production zones modeled after the Communist regime. German Communists were sent to the Soviet Union for training, and once they were back in their home country, they would be assigned administrative jobs. The first political parties to emerge in the east were the Soviet-sanctioned Communist Party and the Social Democratic Party. They were both up and running in 1945, but later that year, they merged to form a single party known as the Socialist Unity Party (SED).

Denazification efforts in eastern parts of Germany were extremely effective, as the Communists strived to create a Marxist-Leninist utopian state. Former Nazi officials were all executed, while the collaborators were sent to reeducation camps. After 1946, German youth were obliged to join the Free German Youth organization, in which they would be indoctrinated with Communist ideology. Women organized their Democratic Women's League to advocate equality and fight for women's rights in universities, workplaces, and government. The Soviet Union was rebuilding Germany in its image, but so were the rest of the Allies. In the west, a new democratic government was established with the purpose of building a capitalist enterprise in the occupied zones. The zone administered by the United States developed more quickly than any other. But the denazification wasn't as successful as in the east. Western Allies feared Communism would spread from the east and thus allowed some of the Nazi officials to remain in state administration. In West Germany, political parties also emerged, the first being the Christian Democratic Union (CDU). CDU was a conservative alliance of Catholics and Protestants who advocated for capitalism in Germany.

The western zones, which were administered by the United States, France, and Britain, unified under a single administration in the spring of 1949. But the Cold War was about to start, as the

West and East couldn't agree on the transfer of war reparations between the zones. Open conflict never broke, but the ideological struggle between the Soviet Union and its Communist allies and the United States and its western allies started. The rest of the 20th century would be dominated by this cold conflict fought with propaganda, espionage, and proxy wars in distant lands. It was British ex-Prime Minister Winston Churchill who came up with the term "the Iron Curtain" in 1946 to describe the dictatorship and Communist control which had descended upon Eastern Europe. Soon, the Iron Curtain became a reality as the east became separated from the democratic nations of the capitalist west.

By 1947, Europe was still feeling the effects of the war and struggled to revive its economy. The United States announced its plan (named the Marshall Plan) to give billions of dollars of aid to European countries to rebuild their economies and provide the United States with a market for its exports. Germany was one of the countries hit the hardest by the economic crisis, as its industry and railroad network was completely dismantled by the Allied forces. The people were malnourished and ill, their homes destroyed in the bombings during the last days of the war. The Soviet Union feared that its allied Communist states of Eastern Europe would desire the aid America was offering, so they forbade the states to take part in the Marshall Plan. But this only widened the gap between West and East. Once the US aid arrived in Western Europe in 1948, the economy was suddenly boosted. The result was not only the rejuvenation of the western European nations but also the creation of economic and military ties with the United States. Europe started integrating under one economic administration, and the first idea of the European Union was born during the Cold War. The areas of Germany administered by the Allies received more than one billion US dollars in aid, which only deepened the divide between western and eastern Germany. The fast development of western Germany angered the Soviets, and they retreated from the joint administration of Germany.

Provoked by the American Marshall Plan, the Soviets announced, in June 1948, that they would cut off all the railroads and roads leading from western to eastern parts of Germany. This meant that even those parts of Berlin which were under western administration would be cut off. The inhabitants of West Berlin were threatened with starvation, as the Allies wouldn't be able to supply them. The Soviets hoped that the western Allies would be forced to beg them to supply West Berlin, giving them de facto control over the entire city. Instead, they started the largest aerial relief operation, known as the Berlin Airlift. It lasted from June 1948 until May 1949, and the British, Americans, and French demonstrated not only their will and resolve to help Berlin but also their power and dominance over the Soviet Union. Around two million tons of supplies were delivered in what remains the biggest aerial relief operation in human history. Once the Soviets realized that the Allies had the resources and will to supply Berlin with necessities, they decided to lift the blockade. But the blockade itself wasn't about Germany. It represented the growing animosity between the East and the West, between Russia and the Allied forces.

Realizing the power of their alliance, the western powers continued to work together to create a new German state. They gathered representatives of all three western zones in Bonn on July 1, 1948, to draft a constitution for a united, federal state. Delegates from the German states created the constitution of West Germany, renaming it the Federal Republic of Germany (Bundesrepublik Deutschland, or BRD). The constitution guaranteed various civil rights, the establishment of a government, and a judiciary system. The new republic would have a president, a chancellor, and two legislatures bodies (the Bundestag and the Bundesrat) to govern the nation of West Germany. When the first Bundestag elections were held in August 1949, the CDU won a majority, with the Social Democratic Party (SDP) claiming only a handful of seats. Konrad Adenauer of the CDU was elected the first chancellor of

Bundesrepublik, while Theodor Heuss of the Free Democrats was elected president. He was an ardent liberal, and although his position within the government was largely ceremonial, he worked hard to repair Germany's reputation on the international level.

In the east, Russians were busy creating their own Communist puppet state in Germany. The German Democratic Republic (GDR) was founded on October 7, 1949, in the zone administered by the Soviet Union. The GDR constitution was different than the BRD's, calling for the formation of a single legislative body, the Volkskammer, which would elect the members of the Council of State, an executive body. The GDR was never recognized by West Germany and its western allies, but the division of Germany was already set in stone. The border between the Federal Republic of Germany and the German Democratic Republic was a front line of the Cold War fought in Europe.

The Two Germanies

The western Allies ended their occupation of Germany in 1949, leaving it in the capable hands of its new chancellor, Konrad Adenauer. The new leader was quick to earn the trust of his people and his western allies. He served five terms (from 1949 until 1963) and brought progress, stability, and continuity to Germany. Slowly, through effort, Germany was leaving the chaos left by World War II. In the east, the GDR was under the leadership of able and determined statesmen, Wilhelm Pieck, who had fled to Moscow when the Nazis took over Germany and soon became Stalin's trusted associate. Elected by the Volkslammer, Pieck became the first president of the GDR in 1949. Together with Otto Grotewohl, first prime minister of GDR, Pieck started building a new Communist state in Europe in the image of the Soviet Union. After the death of Wilhelm Pieck in 1960, power was transferred to the leader of the dominant Socialist Unity Party, Walter Ulbricht. He constructed the central economy of East Germany, intending to rebuild and industrialize his country.

In response to the Marshall Plan, the Soviets formed the Council of Mutual Economic Assistance (COMECON), an organization that would help them plan the central economies of their Communist puppet states. Under its direction, the GDR issued a five-year plan that ambitiously called for the nationalization of all industry and agricultural land. But to meet the five-year quota, the plan focused heavily on pressuring the workers and bureaucrats spreading discontent. In 1953, the government demanded an increase in the production quota, and the workers had no other choice but to take to the streets in protest. Strikes and mass demonstrations took over the cities as the people demanded changes. The government responded with violence, and backed by the Soviet tanks and army, the security forces of GDR quelled the demonstrations. Hundreds of German workers were killed before the end of the uprising. The remaining workers were forced back into the factories without even the promise of better conditions in the future. Even though the five-year-plan failed, Ulbricht's government issued another even more ambitious plan in 1956. The quotas were again increased dramatically, but this time through the modernization of industry and collectivization of agriculture. But the GDR was incapable of achieving the rapid economic recovery of West Germany. East Germany lagged heavily behind the West, but in the Soviet sphere of influence, it became the economic leader capable of exporting produced goods into the rest of Eastern Europe.

The 1950s proved to be much more gentle in Western Germany, where the economy recovered with astonishing speed thanks to capable leadership and the Marshall Plan. In Germany, this period is remembered as the "economic miracle," as the government managed to integrate the millions of war refugees into the capitalist ideology of the West. The government of West Germany let the economy follow the rules of the free market, with only nominal direction and regulation. However, the consequences of the war were still visible among the civilians of Germany, and to provide social security for its people, West Germany came up with an extensive social welfare system. During the 1950s, Germany transformed from a war-torn and devastated country to a leading economic power, not only in Europe but also in the world.

The economy wasn't the only aspect in which West Germany thrived. Its chancellor and president worked tirelessly to improve the reputation of Germany, destroyed in World War II. To continue forward, Germany had to make amends with the survivors of the Nazi regime, and the government in Bonn agreed to pay billions of dollars as reparation to Israel due to the suffering Germany inflicted on the Jews. But the French continued to distrust Germany. To repair its relationship with France, Germany announced that the Ruhr region would be administered jointly by France, Germany, Belgium, Luxembourg, the United States, and the Netherlands. Appeased, France accepted the cooperation and started the economic unity of the western European nations. The 1950s also brought Germany other benefits, such as permission to rearm itself and join the North Atlantic Treaty Organization (NATO). But the culmination of the West Germany government's efforts to elevate the country's diplomatic status came in 1952 with the Bonn-Paris conventions. On May 5, 1955, the three western Allies agreed to grant the Federal Republic of Germany full sovereignty. Although the occupation of Germany was officially over, the Allies retained the right to administer western parts of Berlin and oversee the possible reunification of Germany in the future.

The acceptance of the Federal Republic of Germany into NATO resulted in a Soviet response. The Warsaw Treaty Organization was formed, better known as the Warsaw Pact. Founded on May 14, 1955, the pact gathered Communist states Albania, Bulgaria, Czechoslovakia, Hungary, Poland, Romania, East Germany, and Russia into a military alliance. The hopes of a unified Germany died with the Warsaw Pact, but the Adenauer government didn't give up. In September of 1955, West Germany issued the Hallstein Doctrine, which was used to prevent the international recognition of the GDR. The doctrine warned that the Federal Republic of Germany would stop all diplomatic efforts with nations that recognize the sovereignty of East Germany. Ulbricht responded with his own doctrine, which called for the members of the Warsaw Pact to refuse recognition of West Germany until Adenauer recognized the GDR.

The Berlin Crisis and the Unification of Germany

The Berlin Wall
https://upload.wikimedia.org/wikipedia/commons/5/5d/Berlinerma uer.jpg

The divide between West and East Germany culminated in November 1958 when the new Soviet premier, Nikita Khrushchev, demanded that western Allies leave Berlin. He claimed Berlin wanted to become a free city, and he threatened that if the Allies didn't leave voluntarily, the Soviets would take the city in the name of the GDR. When NATO refused the Soviets' demands in December of the same year, the Berlin Crisis began. Unable to fulfill his threats, Khrushchev offered an alternative. He proposed a permanent division of German territories, with Berlin as a demilitarized zone. But NATO refused this proposal too, aware that the Soviet Union had nothing but empty threats. In the meantime, life in East Germany became unbearable due to the Communist regime, growing poverty, and lack of prosperity. The Germans started defecting from East Germany to West Germany in the hopes of a better life. By 1961, the number of defectors had risen above two million. To stop its people from escaping, the GDR began construction of the famous Berlin Wall— a barrier that separated the eastern part of the city from the western part for almost three decades. Although it no longer exists, the Berlin Wall remains a symbol of the oppressive nature of Communism. The wall didn't just divide the city: it also divided people. Families were torn apart as communication between the two parts of Berlin came to a halt. The GDR installed border police to guard the wall, and several hundreds of young people were killed trying to climb the wall and escape the regime, the ideology, and the political oppression.

But the wall was just a beginning. The GDR fortified the outskirts of the entirety of Berlin, including its western zone. The mayor of West Berlin, Willy Brandt, feared the city would be cut off from the rest of the world, and he called on the United States to help. For twenty-two months, Soviet and US soldiers stationed themselves on each side of the barrier, and the war was about to start. On June 23, 1963, US President John F. Kennedy came to Berlin and delivered his famous speech, "*Itch bin ein Berliner*" ("I am a Berliner"), promising support for West Berlin. This was enough to convince the Soviets that the United states was very serious in its intention to safeguard the western area of the city, and they gave up on their intention to send tanks over the border. Nevertheless, the unification of Germany was still very far away.

Although West Germany continued to prosper economically, the country reached its first crisis point. In 1968, radical student protests erupted as a response to campus unrest in the United States and France. The protests were organized against the United States' military efforts in Vietnam between 1965 and 1968. But the Vietnam War wasn't the only reason for discontent in West Germany. The young people started realizing that oppression continued in their home country through the restriction of the freedoms of the press and speech. The *Spiegel* Affair occurred earlier in 1963 when this German magazine dared to criticize the government. Adenauer ordered the police to raid the magazine's headquarters, and its publisher, Rudolf Augstein, was charged with treason for daring to publicly comment on Adenauer's security policies. The West German government was heavily criticized, and Adenauer was forced into retirement. The next chancellor elected was former Nazi official Kurt Georg Kiesinger. The youth of West Germany were astounded that their government would allow a former Nazi to enter politics again. The leftist student organizations started violent protests throughout the country, blaming defective German society for the government's hypocrisy. The students accused their government of having an authoritarian nature and of being unable to atone for its Nazi past. They also blamed it for having too much faith in the capitalist economic system, which was, in their eyes, a moral ruin. Students demanded democratic changes on all levels of the government. To quell the increasingly violent uprising, West Germany's government passed the German Emergency Acts by which the executive branch was empowered to operate without the approval of the legislative body. The Acts also restricted some of the constitutional rights of the citizens and approved the use of military force to restore order in the country. The Emergency Acts were very much like Article 48, which Hitler had used to elevate himself as the Nazi dictator.

The leftists started influencing the politics of West Germany during the late 1960s. Their growing popularity helped end the CDU's monopoly on political power in the government. In the Bundestag elections of 1969, the SDP ran a close second to the

CDU, but once the SDP entered a coalition with the Free Democratic Party (FDP), Socialist leader Willy Brandt (former mayor of West Berlin) became the new chancellor. He abandoned the politics of the Hallstein Doctrine and implemented the policy of Ostpolitik, seeking to work closely with the GDR and the allies of the Warsaw Pact to establish fruitful diplomatic relations.

Ostpolitik was a complete turnaround and a move away from the conservative politics of the Adenauer government. In the past, West Germany wouldn't even consider recognizing the GDR as a legitimate state, but now, in the early 1970s, Brandt sat at the same table with the GDR's minister-president. Although nothing much was achieved during the first meeting, the path to the establishment of formal relations was paved. Brandt also negotiated a treaty with the Soviets, the Moscow Treaty, by which the signing partners were to avoid military conflict and respect the existing European borders. The diplomatic efforts of the West German chancellor succeeded when the Soviets agreed to guarantee free access from West Germany to West Berlin. Willy Brandt received a Nobel Peace Prize in 1971 due to his work in establishing diplomatic relations between the two Germanies. But this was not the end of his success. In 1972, the Federal Republic of Germany and its eastern counterpart, the German Democratic Republic, signed the Basic Treaty by which they recognized each other's sovereignty. They also guaranteed to maintain peace between themselves, beginning an era of successful dialogs, diplomatic visits, trading relations, and cultural exchange.

But Brandt's political opposition, the members of the CDU and FDP, accused his Ostpolitik of being traitorous. The chancellor himself was accused of collaborating with the GDR, and on April 24, 1972, the government authorized a vote of no confidence to remove Brandt from the office. But the opposition failed by only two votes. The chancellor's reputation was further eroded by the tragedy which occurred during the Olympic Games of 1972. A Palestinian terrorist organization known as the Black September raided the Olympic Village in Munich where the athletes were housed, taking Israeli contestants and their coaches as hostages. They demanded the release of more than 200 Palestinian militants who were imprisoned in Israel and also demanded incarcerated leaders of the Red Army Faction be released from West Germany's prison. Two months later, in the new elections, Brandt and his party managed to secure a victory. Serving as a chancellor once more, he continued his diplomatic mission to connect West and East, and he extended a peaceful hand towards the nations of the Warsaw Pact, creating diplomatic relations with Hungary, Czechoslovakia, and Bulgaria. In 1973, Both Germanies joined the United Nations. But another crisis hit West Germany when oil prices skyrocketed due to the unrest in the Middle East. The "miracle economy" of the West showed exactly how fragile it was during a crisis, and more than one million West Germans lost their jobs by 1975. That number doubled by the 1980s. But Brandt was completely discredited in 1974 when one of his close associates turned out to be a spy, working for the secret police of the GDR. There was no recovery for the chancellor's reputation, and he had to resign. His replacement was another member of the SDP, Helmut Schmidt.

Even though Schmidt proved his capability in dealing with a terrorist attack in 1977 known as the German Autumn, his reputation suffered greatly due to the economic crisis in the mid-1980s. After the massacre during the Olympic Games, Schmidt organized a special anti-terrorism unit known as the GSG 9. He used them to save the hostages of the hijacked Lufthansa airplane in 1977 when another terrorist crisis occurred. Again, the Palestinian terrorists demanded the release of Red Army leaders, but the GSG 9 assault team stormed the plane on October 8, 1977, rescuing the hostages and killing or arresting the terrorists. But the economy of West Germany continued its downfall, and the working class was on the brink of an uprising due to unemployment when the CDU opposition called for a no-confidence vote. This time they succeeded, and Schmidt had to abandon his position as chancellor of West Germany. His replacement was CDU member Helmut Kohl.

Kohl's politics were completely different from his SDP predecessors. Instead of continuing the diplomatic relations with the East, he turned to Germany's western allies. First, he allowed NATO's nuclear warheads to be stored on German soil, and then he worked on tightening relations with France. In 1984, he met with the French president in a ceremony that was staged as a reconciliation for the bloodshed between the two nations during both World Wars. This ceremony, held in Verdun, is considered the foundation of future European integration. But during his second mandate, which started in 1987, Kohl reversed his policy again and started building relations with the Eastern Bloc. He invited the East German leader, Erich Honecker, to visit West Germany—the first eastern official to do so. All of Eastern Europe's Communist regime was under enormous pressure as its citizens pressed for democratic reforms. Individuals appeared who were able to expose the corruption of the Communists, pressuring the government to negotiate. One such incident occurred in Gdansk, Poland, where a non-governmental trade union rose from the shipyards. The idea that organizations were not controlled by the government quickly spread to the Eastern Bloc and, in 1984, reached the GDR. By that time, East Germany was facing a serious economic crisis.

In the GDR, the Communist regime failed to provide for its people. The idea of production quotas proved to be impossible to carry the economy of the whole country, and the first to suffer this failure was the working class. The living conditions in East Germany were falling rapidly. Supply shortages imposed hunger on people, and some of the survivors still testify to the inability to buy basic ingredients to sustain a family. But it wasn't only the economics of the GDR that bothered its people. The government oppressed its people, and it did so through espionage and strict control. The government had a file on everyone, and everyone's phones were tapped—even the public phones on the streets. Practicing religion was frowned upon, and those who went to church were forbidden from receiving higher education, as they were considered politically inappropriate—even children. People's mail was read by the government, and it would often not be sent because it was considered dangerous information leakage. Many East Germans had brothers, sisters, mothers, and fathers in the West, and they couldn't even communicate with them. All of this was too much for people, and during the 1980s, many of them sought asylum in foreign countries. On January 15, 1986, angry protests occurred in the GDR, with the people demanded changes. But Erich Honecker pronounced the protests illegal, and many of its participants were arrested and sentenced to prison. When, in 1985, Mikhail Gorbachev became the general secretary of the Communist Party of the Soviet Union and started reforms, the whole Eastern Bloc began to falter.

In 1988, Gorbachev announced that the Soviet Union was abandoning the Brezhnev Doctrine implemented twenty years earlier, by which it had guaranteed military intervention to preserve Communism in the members of the Warsaw Pact. This meant that each country was now free to pursue the political direction it wanted. The people in the Eastern Bloc organized a demonstration demanding change. One after another, the Communist regimes of Eastern Europe fell. In August of 1989, Hungary opened its borders with Austria, and the Germans from the Eastern Bloc took the opportunity to run to the West. But the government of East Germany responded by suppressing the demonstrations, drawing worldwide criticism. Feeling the support of the world, the people continued their efforts to fight for freedom. The situation was out of the government's control, and finally, on October 18th, the German people ousted Honecker. On November 4th, Berlin was a city of massive demonstrations that succeeded in persuading the government to back down another step: it officially proclaimed freedom of movement for East Germans. Over the next few days, an incredible crowd gathered along the Berlin Wall, and the border police had no other choice but to open the crossing.

Once on the other side of the wall, Eastern Germans were welcomed by a cheering crowd of westerners and their long-lost friends and family members. Scenes of the reunions behind the wall were quickly broadcast all over the world by various news agencies, and the whole world celebrated. The wall, once a symbol of separation and oppression, now meant nothing. The Communist government of the GDR fell, and the free elections were about to be held for the first time. But Helmut Kohl saw the opportunity to unite the two Germanies. At the end of November, he reached out to Eastern Germans with a ten-point plan offering them generous economic aid as well as cultural and social exchange. His plan was the foundation on which the future German Federation would be built. The next year new democratic parties arose in East Germany, including New Forum, Democratic Awakening, and Democracy Now. These parties were essential to securing fair democratic elections in the future, and East Germany was finally moving towards complete democracy.

In 1990, Kohl traveled to the Soviet Union to meet Gorbachev and discuss the reunification of Germany. Once the German chancellor promised that united Germany would not be any threat to the Soviet Union, the Russian premier announced that he would not stand in the way of reunification. But Kohl also had to secure the acceptance of the reunification from the western powers. Europe was still insecure about Germany's past and fears of another major crisis, such as world war, had to be dealt with. The German chancellor proved capable of securing the approval of the western Allies (the United States, Britain, and France), and on May 18, 1990, the two Germanies signed an agreement to join their economies. Not long after, on August 31, 1990, the Unification Treaty was signed, and East and West Germany were officially united into a single nation. The new country fell under the federal constitution, and Berlin was chosen as its capital. It was decided that the new German nation would remain a member state of the UN, NATO, and the European Economic Community (EEC). The powers that administered Germany after World War II—Britain, the United States, France, and the Soviet Union—signed a Treaty of the Final Settlement on September 12, 1990, removing the remaining restrictions of Germany's sovereignty in place since World War II. The new Germany was born, and it would again take its rightful place on the stage of the world's politics.

The only thing remaining to remind the people of the deep divide caused by the consequences of World War II was the Berlin Wall. Although it was filled with holes made by a bulldozer as the people opened the way to their western cousins, parts of it remained standing until 1991. A symbol of division, oppression, and bitter German history, the Berlin Wall was a place where many famous people of the time gathered to deliver hope for a better future—from various politicians to American presidents and famous artists. Singers such as David Bowie and Bruce Springsteen had held concerts near the wall so they could be heard by the people of both sides (1987 and 1988, respectively). They sang songs of freedom and unity, inspiring people to fight for their rights. On New Year's Eve in 1989, David Hasselhoff held a concert suspended above the wall, celebrating the upcoming unity. Both West and East Berliners climbed the wall, celebrating the end of a dark era for Germany. The demolition of the wall started as soon as Germany was united and was completed almost a year later, in November 1991. Parts of it still stand as monuments, a warning to humanity not to repeat the mistakes of war and division. In some places where there is no more wall, a line is drawn to symbolize the oppressive past of one nation. Parts of the wall were even transported to various cities around the world to be displayed in museums, city squares, universities, government buildings, etc. Every continent in the world has at least one piece of the Berlin

Wall. This way, everyone can witness it and learn from Germany's darkest days.

Contemporary Germany

In 2019, Germany celebrated thirty years since the fall of the Berlin Wall, but the differences between the western and eastern parts of the country are still visible. Many cultural differences divided the people. But with each passing year, and with the birth of new generations, the cultural gap is becoming almost invisible. Still, the economic gap is impossible not to see. Even today, wages are 20% lower in the east than in the west. No major modern company wants to open its headquarters in the eastern parts of Federal Germany. When the unification started, in only several years most of East German's industrial sector was privatized. But it was a failed Communist dream and could not survive the economy of capitalism that ruled the rest of the country. Factories shut down, and millions of people lost their jobs, forced to move to the west to find new employment. The east was left abandoned, unable to progress and develop. German Federation continued to invest in its eastern states, and although in time the economy recovered, it still lags behind western Germany. Nevertheless, the German people managed to build a new Germany, one where it didn't matter if you were from the west or the east.

But building a new country didn't come without any controversies. The first one arose immediately after the reunification when the new capital had to be chosen. Westerners were reluctant to abandon their previous capital, Bonn. But finally, a year later, a vote was held, and the majority decided that the capital should be moved to Berlin, a city which was a historical legacy of both Germanies. Another crisis occurred with the integration of East Germany into the capitalist economy of the Federal Republic. The country had been bound by the same currency since the economic treaty signed before unification, but East Germany was unable to follow the example set by the industrial sector and production of its western brother. Enormous amounts of money had to be invested in modernizing industries, infrastructure, and communication systems of the eastern states, and at times it seemed as if the former GDR was a hole without a bottom that sucked money from the Federal Republic. Despite the huge investment in the former GDR, many easterners were resentful of western politicians taking positions within the government, education, and business. It seemed that all the best career positions were occupied by westerners who were educated in a completely different system. The people of former East Germany were unable to grasp capitalist ideals and suffered the loss of social security benefits guaranteed by the Communists. The unification of Germany failed to live up to their expectations. But the government didn't want to give up. In 1992, it came up with the Solidarity Pact, which included tax hikes used to help with the rejuvenation of East Germany.

Instead of concentrating only on its internal problems, the Federal Republic of Germany proved capable of developing further international diplomacy. In fact, since the reunification, Germany was the leading force behind European integration. The plan was to work with its neighbors to construct strong economic and political ties. In November of 1993, Germany signed the Maastricht Treaty, forming the European Union (EU). In 1951, France and Germany had signed the Treaty of Paris, founding the European Coal and Steel Community. This grew into the European Economic Community (EEC) in 1957 when Belgium, the Netherlands, Luxembourg, and Italy joined France and West Germany. But in 1993, the European family grew even more, with Denmark, Ireland, Greece, Spain, the United Kingdom, and Portugal joining the economic and political partnership of the European Union (EU). The unification of Europe had expanded beyond simple economic deals, and member states now enjoy coordinated European diplomacy, justice, immigration policy, and defense.

As the differences between West and East Germany began to dissipate, the first German chancellor born in the GDR came to power: in 2005, Angela Merkel won the popular vote. Besides having been raised in the East, she also became Germany's first female chancellor. Angela studied physics and earned a doctorate in chemistry at the Academy of Sciences in Berlin, but while only a student in 1989, she became interested in the political transformation of Eastern Europe, which also swept her own country. After the fall of the Berlin Wall, she joined the Democratic Awakening party, and after the unification of the country, she joined the cabinet of Helmuth Kohl. But she became a more prominent public figure with her new appointment in 1994 as the minister of environment and nuclear safety. In 1998, when Kohl was ousted, Merkel became secretary-general of the CDU. Under her direction, this political party was rejuvenated and, in 2000, became the head of the party. Nevertheless, when the elections in 2002 came, Merkel wasn't chosen as the opposition to chancellor Schröder, even though she was already very popular with the people. As a vocal critic of Schröder's politics, she did manage to place herself as the opposition candidate in 2005, winning to become the new chancellor of Germany. At the dawn of the 21st century, Merkel proved a capable leader of a nation that proudly emerged from its dark past. She worked on improving diplomatic relations with the United States and continued Germany's role in the EU, the UN, and NATO. In fact, she was proclaimed *de facto* leader of the European Union and the longest-serving head of a government within the EU. *Forbes* Magazine named her the most powerful woman in the world fourteen consecutive times and the second-most powerful person in the world, just behind Russia's President Vladimir Putin. With Angela Merkel, the politics of Germany became an integral part of the politics of the EU. She served as the president of the European Council and used this position to start reform within the European Union. The 2007 Lisbon Treaty serves as the constitution of the EU, strengthening its political and economic coherence. For her role in the Lisbon Treaty, Angela Merkel was given the

Charlemagne Prize in 2008, which has been awarded by the German city of Aachen since 1950. The award is given to individuals who, through their performance, have brought about Europe's unity. Since then, Merkel has received numerous prizes all over the world. From the United States to India, she is recognized as a "leader of the free world." Remembering her life behind the Berlin Wall of post-war Germany, Merkel fights to destroy the walls, figurative and literal, which continue to divide people across the world. In her own country of Germany, Merkel was given the nickname "Mutti," a German word children lovingly use to call their mothers.

Conclusion

Germany succeeded in shaking off the weight of its turbulent past, and today, it is a federal parliamentary republic. Germany is a multicultural country, as it welcomes many migrants from the Mediterranean, Eastern Europe, and the rest of the world. In 2015, a new migration crisis hit the continent as millions of refugees poured in from the Near East. Germany proudly opened its doors, inviting many of them to find permanent new homes within its federal republic. Germany even changed its laws to make it easier for foreigners to gain citizenship. The new leaders of Germany see strength in diversity, even though that same diversity is not without its controversies.

Germany has placed itself among the leading nations of the world and is a confident and brave member of NATO, Group of Eight (G8), and the EU. It continues to grow economically and is at the top of the list of the richest nations in the world. But its main importance lies in its diplomatic efforts, as Germany has taken the key position in European affairs and built strong relationships with various countries across the world. The new Germany embraced liberal democracy after centuries of constant conflict and autocratic rule. Even though Germany went through years of oppression of racial minorities and the division of its nation, today it is one of the most liberal and democratic countries in Europe.

The German people reevaluated what it means to be German, and through a different kind of unity—one based on a shared set of civic values—it came to accept other ethnicities under its wing. To be German today means much more than to speak the Germanic language or have racially pure blond hair and blue eyes. Being German is about freedom, tearing down walls and cages that separate and enslave whole nations, and respecting the rights of all human beings. Through thousands of years-long history filled with tragedies, triumphs, bloodshed, and shame, the Germanic peoples have gathered experiences and have used them to create the modern-day state of Germany.

Here's another book by Captivating History that you might like

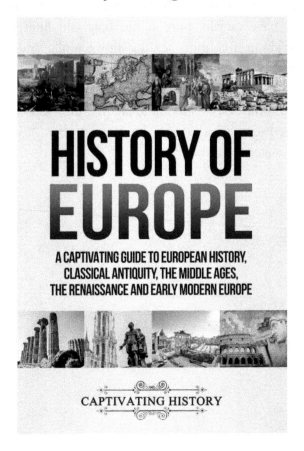

Free Bonus from Captivating History (Available for a Limited time)

Hi History Lovers!

Now you have a chance to join our exclusive history list so you can get your first history ebook for free as well as discounts and a potential to get more history books for free! Simply visit the link below to join.

Captivatinghistory.com/ebook

Also, make sure to follow us on Facebook, Twitter and Youtube by searching for Captivating History.

References

Acton, John Emerich Edward Dalberg Acton, Ward, A. W., Prothero, G. W., & Leathes, S. M. (1969). *The Cambridge modern history, volume 4, the Thirty Years War.* Cambridge: Cambridge University Press.

Blackbourn, D. (1998). *The long nineteenth century: A history of Germany, 1780-1918.* New York: Oxford University Press.

Boog, H., Krebs, G., & Vogel, D. (2015). *Germany and the Second World War.* Oxford: Oxford University Press.

Brecht, M. (1985). *Martin Luther.* Minneapolis: Fortress Press.

Carlyle, T. (1969). *History of Friedrich II of Prussia called Frederick the Great.* Chicago: Univ. of Chicago Press.

Collinson, P. (2004). *The Reformation: A history.* New York: Modern Library.

Cunliffe, B. W. (2003). *The Celts.* Oxford: Oxford University Press.

Curtis, B. (2013). *The Habsburgs: The history of a dynasty.* London: Bloomsbury Academic.

Fichtenau, H., & Munz, P. (2000). *The Carolingian empire.* Toronto: University of Toronto Press in association with the Mediaeval Academy of America.

Fisher, T. (2001). *The Napoleonic wars: The rise of the Emperor 1805-1807.* Oxford: Osprey.

Hart, D. (2014). *Calvinism A History.* Cumberland: Yale University Press.

Haverkamp, A. (1992). *Medieval Germany: 1056-1273.* Oxford: Oxford University Press.

Herwig, H. H. (2014). *The First World War: Germany and Austria-Hungary, 1914-1918.* Bloomsbury USA Academic.

Holborn, H. (1982). *A history of modern Germany.* Princeton, NJ: Princeton University Press.

Leyser, K. (1982). *Medieval Germany 900-1250.* London: Hambledon Press.

Regino, Adalbert, & MacLean, S. (2009). *History and politics in late Carolingian and Ottonian Europe: The chronicle of Regino of Prüm and Adalbert of Magdeburg.* Manchester: Manchester University Press.

Stearns, P. N. (1974). *1848: The revolutionary tide in Europe.* New York: Norton.

Unterreiner, K., & McGowran, M. H. (2011). *The Habsburgs: A portrait of a European dynasty.* Vienna: Pichler.

Warner, P. (2008). *World War One: A chronological narrative.* Barnsley: Pen & Sword Military.

Whaley, J. (2013). *Germany and the Holy Roman Empire.* Oxford: Oxford University Press.

Wilson, P. H. (2017). *The holy Roman empire: A thousand years of Europes history.* London: Penguin Books.

Wolfram, H. (1997). *The Roman Empire and its Germanic peoples.* Berkeley, CA: University of California Press.

BABYLON BERLIN. Directed by Henk Handloegten, Achim Von Borries, and Tykwer Tom. Berlin: Netflix, 2017.

Browning, Christopher R. ORDINARY MEN. New York: HarperCollins, 2013.

CAPTIVATING HISTORY, THE TREATY OF VERSAILLES: A CAPTIVATING GUIDE TO THE PEACE TREATY THAT ENDED WORLD WAR 1 AND ITS

IMPACT ON GERMANY AND THE RISE OF ADOLF HITLER. Captivating History, 2020. Available on Amazon.com.

Crankshaw, Edward. BISMARCK. London: A&C Black, 2011.

Dear, Ian, I. C. Dear, and M. R. Foot. OXFORD COMPANION TO WORLD WAR II. Oxford: OUP Oxford, 2001.

Deighton, Len. WINTER. London: Penguin Classics, 2020.

Evans, Richard J. THE COMING OF THE THIRD REICH. London: Penguin, 2005.

Evans, Richard J. THE THIRD REICH AT WAR: HOW THE NAZIS LED GERMANY FROM CONQUEST TO DISASTER. London: Penguin UK, 2012.

Evans, Richard J. THE THIRD REICH IN POWER. London: Penguin, 2006.

THE FIRST WORLD WAR. Directed by Hew Strachan. n.d. Hamilton Film, 2002. DVD.

Freedman, Russell. WE WILL NOT BE SILENT: THE WHITE ROSE STUDENT RESISTANCE MOVEMENT THAT DEFIED ADOLF HITLER. Boston: Houghton Mifflin Harcourt, 2016.

Gaskill, Matthew. THE GERMAN ARMY AND STORMTROOPERS OF WORLD WAR ONE: TACTICS OF TERROR. Nashville: Amazon, 2014.

Goldhagen, Daniel J. HITLER'S WILLING EXECUTIONERS: ORDINARY GERMANS AND THE HOLOCAUST. New York: Vintage, 2007.

Haffner, Sebastian. DEFYING HITLER. Plunkett Lake Press, 2019.

THE GREY ZONE. Directed by Tim B. Nelson. 2001. Film.

"HOME." WALL MUSEUM - MAUERMUSEUM - MUSEUM HAUS AM CHECKPOINT CHARLIE - STARTSEITE. ACCESSED MAY 5, 2021. HTTPS://WWW.MAUERMUSEUM.DE/EN/START/.

HOLT, A., & HOTTUM, R. (DIRECTORS). (1991). HEIL HITLER! THE CONFESSIONS OF A HITLER YOUTH [FILM].

HEIMAT (PART I). Directed by Edgar Reitz. 1984. Berlin. Film.

Hilberg, Raul. THE DESTRUCTION OF THE EUROPEAN JEWS. Google Print Common Library, 2003.

Holmes, Richard, Hew Strachan, Chris Bellamy, Hugh Bicheno, and Professor of the History of War and Fellow Director Oxford Program on the Changing Character of War Hew Strachan. THE OXFORD COMPANION TO MILITARY HISTORY. New York: Oxford University Press, USA, 2001.

"How Many Refugees Came to the United States from 1933-1945? - Americans and the Holocaust - United States Holocaust Memorial Museum." Online Exhibitions — United States Holocaust Memorial Museum. Accessed May 4, 2021. https://exhibitions.ushmm.org/americans-and-the-holocaust/how-many-refugees-came-to-the-united-states-from-1933-1945

"Introduction to 19th-Century Socialism." Common Errors in English Usage and More. Washington State University. Last modified October 12, 2016. https://brians.wsu.edu/2016/10/12/introduction-to-19th-century-socialism/.

Isherwood, Christopher. THE BERLIN STORIES. New York: New Directions Publishing, 2008.

Johnson, Eric A. NAZI TERROR. New York: Basic Books (AZ), 1999.

Junger, Ernst. STORM OF STEEL. (PENGUIN CLASSICS DELUXE EDITION). London: Penguin, 2016.

Kershaw, Ian. HITLER: A BIOGRAPHY. New York: W. W. Norton & Company, 2008.

Lowe, Keith. SAVAGE CONTINENT: EUROPE IN THE AFTERMATH OF WORLD WAR II. New York: St. Martin's Press, 2012.

MacMillan, Margaret. PARIS 1919: SIX MONTHS THAT CHANGED THE WORLD. New York: Random House, 2007.

MacMillan, Margaret. THE WAR THAT ENDED PEACE: THE ROAD TO 1914. New York: Random House, 2013.

Musolff, Andreas. "Wilhelm II's 'Hun Speech' and Its Alleged Resemiotization during World War I." Welcome to UEA Digital Repository - UEA Digital Repository. Accessed March 27, 2021. https://ueaeprints.uea.ac.uk/id/eprint/65777/1/Accepted_manuscript.pdf.

Neitzel, Sonke, and Harald Welzer. SOLDATEN - ON FIGHTING, KILLING AND DYING: THE SECRET SECOND WORLD WAR TAPES OF GERMAN POWS. New York: Simon & Schuster, 2012.

Nelson, Anne. RED ORCHESTRA: THE STORY OF THE BERLIN UNDERGROUND AND THE CIRCLE OF FRIENDS WHO RESISTED HITLER. New York: Random House, 2009.

Noakes, Jeremy, and Geoffrey Pridham. DOCUMENTS ON NAZISM, 1919-1945. New York: Viking, 1975.

Rhodes, Richard. MASTERS OF DEATH: THE SS-EINSATZGRUPPEN AND THE INVENTION OF THE HOLOCAUST. New York: Vintage, 2007.

Röhl, John C. KAISER WILHELM II: A CONCISE LIFE. Cambridge: Cambridge University Press, 2014.

"The Royal Navy in WW1." Naval Encyclopedia. Last modified June 18, 2020. https://www.naval-encyclopedia.com/ww1/royal-navy-1914.

Sandford, John. ENCYCLOPEDIA OF CONTEMPORARY GERMAN CULTURE. London: Routledge, 2013.

Sarotte, Mary E. 1989: THE STRUGGLE TO CREATE POST-COLD WAR EUROPE - UPDATED EDITION. Princeton: Princeton University Press, 2014.

Shirer, William L. THE RISE AND FALL OF THE THIRD REICH: A HISTORY OF NAZI GERMANY. 1980 edition.

"Treblinka: Revealing the Hidden Graves of the Holocaust." BBC News. Last modified January 23, 2012. https://www.bbc.com/news/magazine-16657363.

Weitz, Eric D. WEIMAR GERMANY: PROMISE AND TRAGEDY, WEIMAR CENTENNIAL EDITION. Princeton: Princeton University Press, 2018.

Wetzel, David. A DUEL OF GIANTS: BISMARCK, NAPOLEON III, AND THE ORIGINS OF THE FRANCO-PRUSSIAN WAR. Madison: University of Wisconsin Press, 2003.